Max Décharné was a member of the band Gallon Drunk, and has been with The Flaming Stars since 1994. An authority on the 1950s and 1960s counterculture, he is the author of *Vulgar Tongues: An Alternative History of British Slang*, as well as *A Rocket in My Pocket* and *Hardboiled Hollywood*. He lives in London.

Praise for *Teddy Boys*

'In his genial and entertaining *Teddy Boys*, rock journalist Max Décharné takes a calm look at the phenomenon and strips away the myths that coloured it' *Telegraph*

'A persuasively detailed chronicle of an entire country ... an engrossing read, meticulously researched' *Record Collector*

'[An] enormously enjoyable history of the Teddy boys ... plenty of historians have mentioned them in passing, but none has ever investigated them with Décharné's enthusiasm and attention to detail' Dominic Sandbrook, 'Book of the Week', *Sunday Times*

'*Teddy Boys* is excellent on the social conditions within which the style evolved ... Décharné's book is a loving reclamation of an important youth type – now seen as reactionaries, but who were ground breakers, in their early phase at least' Jon Savage, *New Statesman*

'Taking in everything from the birth of rock 'n' roll to the Notting Hill riots, [*Teddy Boys*] takes us back to an era when working-class teenagers first began to assert themselves in the UK ... Décharné's cultural history offers a fresh take on one of the most maligned youth cultures in twentieth-century British history' *Herald*

'Enjoyable ... diligently researched ... a powerful, almost poignant, story' *Englesberg Ideas*

'Expert research, insider knowledge and a love for the subject all make for a thumping good read' *Classic Rock*

'[A] rise-and-fall chronicle of the New Edwardians, from the early '50s cosh boys to the Notting Hill Riots of 1958 ... offers repeated riches in its lovingly curated assemblage of news articles and interviews that reveal how this working-class cultural revolution was reinterpreted, co-opted and demonised' *Mojo*

'Offering a lively and thoroughly researched investigation into the sharp fashions and tabloid moral panics of the time, it casts a refreshingly sympathetic look at this working-class chapter of British rebellion' *Sight & Sound*

'Décharné has delivered a superb study of an underexplored side of British youth culture' *Vive le Rock*

'When you look back at the various revolutionary British subcultures you wonder if there was a more exciting and influential, and dangerous and thrilling, time than that of the Teddy boys and the late fifties Rock 'n' Roll tours that sparked riots of mischief and pure unadulterated joy – we wish we'd been there ... it's terrific' Mark Ellen, *Word In Your Ear*

'A joyous celebration of the founding fathers of British youth culture, and a great slice of social and cultural history' Alwyn Turner

TEDDY BOYS

Post-War Britain and the First Youth Revolution

MAX DÉCHARNÉ

Profile Books

This paperback edition first published in 2025

First published in Great Britain in 2024 by
Profile Books Ltd
29 Cloth Fair
London
ECIA 7JQ
www.profilebooks.com

1 3 5 7 9 10 8 6 4 2

Typeset in Garamond by MacGuru Ltd
Printed and bound in Great Britain by
CPI Group (UK) Ltd, Croydon CRO 4YY

A CIP catalogue record for this book is available from the British Library.

ISBN 978 1 84668 979 6
eISBN 978 1 78283 037 5

For my mother Margaret
1938–2022

CONTENTS

INTRODUCTION

DON'T FEAR THE CREEPER

I grew up in Portsmouth, the dockyard city on the south coast of England. When I was a schoolboy in the 1960s and 1970s, Teddy boys were still a common sight, whether walking down the streets in full gear, or running the dodgem cars and sixpenny shooting galleries at the funfair on the seafront, the music blasting out in a time-warp world in which Del Shannon was always singing 'Runaway', and Eddie Cochran never got over the 'Summertime Blues'.

The Teds were an exotic breed. They were creatures from another planet – one that was dangerous and exciting and far removed from my grim daily grind of school, with its maths lessons, corporal punishment and wasted afternoons playing sport on swamp-like pitches as the freezing wind blew in from the English Channel. They were flash, and by the early 1970s already had an air clinging to them of a lost decade when things were different: a time before three-day weeks, electricity cuts and flared trousers. Teddy boys were older than me, and tougher, many of them first-generation originals who were by this point in their late twenties or early thirties, but had stuck with the style that defined them, and with the music – early rock'n'roll.

By the time I was at secondary school, successive waves of youth cultures had followed the Teds and were now mashing up against each other, sometimes with violent consequences. You

Teddy boy fashions advertised in the *New Musical Express* by a Portsmouth retailer, 1974

could often judge someone's musical allegiance by the clothes they wore, long before you spoke to them.

In the case of the early skinheads, it was generally considered best to keep your distance. Their chosen look was stripped-down, sharply functional and custom-built for anything which might transpire. You kept your head down, and crossed the road rather than pass them on the pavement.

Other teenagers of the day favoured the residual hippie look, or climbed aboard the glam-rock bandwagon which had just started rolling. I vividly remember sitting on the top deck of a bus in around 1973 when up the stairs came two girls who had splashed out a serious amount of pocket money to get their hair dyed Dayglo orange and styled to resemble David Bowie's cut on the cover of *Aladdin Sane*. They looked absolutely superb, and although they affected a deadpan expression of unconcern, they had clearly set out to make an impact in a grey world where looking different could lead to trouble. Shouted insults from strangers in the street were often the least of your worries, and if you stood out even slightly from the norm, there was very often someone – and probably a few of their mates – waiting around the next corner looking for any excuse to punch you. Clothing was a serious business, and could have consequences.

None of this would have been news to the Teddy boys. With their Edwardian drape jackets, velvet collars, elaborate waistcoats and drainpipe trousers, they were not only one of the most recognisable working-class youth movements, they had also been the first. Trailblazers for a long line of fashion-conscious teenagers who were accused of dragging the country into the gutter, they were the council-house inheritors of a dandy tradition stretching back to the eighteenth century, minus the money and the indulgent parents. To many, they were layabouts, thugs and criminals. In 1953, the year they were initially given a name and provoked national newspaper headlines,[1] they had been the first in the firing line – a newly identified target for everyone to throw stones at. Long before the beatniks, mods, hippies, skinheads, glam rockers, metalheads or punk rockers, the Teds had run the gauntlet of public opinion. The sequence of events was similar in most cases: dressing up in front of the bedroom mirror, brushing aside parental mockery or barbed threats, then walking out of the front door to take their chances as a self-invented moving sideshow in a world which seemed to prefer conformity and muted colours. It wasn't a matter of life and death, but it could feel like it.

Blitz-era children raised among the bomb-sites of post-war London, the original Teds subverted the British tailoring industry's attempts to sell a revival of Edwardian styles to the wealthy. Instead, they stole them back from the upper orders in a two-fingered salute to a society that offered working-class teenagers little more than prolonged rationing, a repetitive job of manual labour after leaving school at fifteen and an overpowering sense that whoever else had the advantages in life, it wasn't supposed to be them.

The press had a field day with these young people, especially after they had acquired the name 'Teddy boy' in 1953 – from Ted, short for Edward, meaning someone who wore Edwardian-style clothing. Anti-social behaviour, burglaries, car thefts, grievous bodily harm, race riots and sometimes murder – all this was laid at their door, and 'Ted' became a multi-purpose shorthand for someone below a certain age who was causing trouble, or was considered likely to do so. More than sixty years after the event, when I contacted a gentleman who as a teenager had appeared in a very well-known 1950s Teddy boy photograph, he politely declined to be interviewed for this book, saying 'it was all a long time ago'; another who had appeared in a similar picture turned me down specifically because of the mistaken assumptions people might still make about him today.

It was hardly a surprise that one of the late-fifties wave of novels featuring this new phenomenon was entitled *The Whipping Boys.*[2]

I Am One Hell of a Guy

'I hope you're not going to grow up to be a Teddy boy?'

Shop assistants are not supposed to make personal remarks to customers, but there I was, fourteen years old, in a sports shop in Havant, being forced to account for the item I was trying to purchase. This was 1974, and the shop was mostly a place to buy football boots, tracksuits and a selection of things that wouldn't have interested me much, but there by the till they had something different – a wire stand from which hung a selection of bootlace ties. I can't remember what the tie cost, but I still have it, with its stainless steel cow's skull at the centre. The lady behind the counter seemed convinced that wearing this particular object would set me firmly on the path to a lifetime of crime. Mumbling something incoherent, I handed over the money and made my escape, clutching this supposedly dangerous fashion accessory.

As it happened, Ted styles had been making something of a public comeback in the early seventies. Indeed, Ringo Starr was in 1973 shooting scenes at my local funfair on Clarence Pier while playing a Teddy boy for the film *That'll Be the Day*.[3] Meanwhile in London, Malcolm McLaren and Vivienne Westwood had been selling drapes, creepers and other essentials to the cognoscenti for the last couple of years from their shop Let It Rock at the unfashionable end of the King's Road. It also seemed for a while as if there was at least one glam-rock band each week on *Top of the Pops* in full retro velvet-collared regalia – not just outright revivalists like Showaddywaddy, but groups such as Mud, and the finest of them all, Wizzard. The latter managed to combine long hair and face paint with authentic Ted gear and superb fifties-influenced music, as if turbo-charged with Phil Spector's Wall of Sound, just as Roxy Music managed to incorporate a great deal of pre-1960 references into their songs and visuals, while somehow still appearing to have come from several decades into the future. All these groups were beacons of hope in a wasteland of mass-market flared trousers and five-inch-wide lapels; living with the consequences of standing out from the crowd was not always easy.

Thirty years after I bought my subversive bootlace tie, John Peel recalled a similar instance during his 1950s schooldays in which the mere ownership of an item of clothing associated with Teds was considered equally shocking. 'I'm a nice middle-class boy,' he told me, 'but I had a pair of drainpipe trousers in the cupboard that I bought in Liverpool, and I never dared wear them. But just the knowledge that they were there was enough to make me feel, "I am one hell of a guy."'[4]

John wasn't the only teenager in Liverpool risking parental disapproval over his clothing. Local boy Ronald Wycherley – soon to become Billy Fury – took to hiding his Ted clothes in the outside lavatory in the family backyard to avoid detection, as he recalled in a 1970s television interview:

> Well, I had a lot of trouble in the beginning, wearing tight trousers and long jackets, velvet collars, because of my dear father. So what I used to do was go out in my baggy trousers. I used to dash up the entry, climb over the wall, into the toilet, change into my tight trousers etc and I was sort of out on the town for the night.[5]

The situation was the same across the Irish Sea, where Teddy boy fashions had spread from London as early as 1954, in part because of the regular flow of young men going over to Britain to work for a few months at a time and bringing the new clothing home with them. Ted Carroll, who went on to co-found the record labels Chiswick and Ace, was one such Dublin teenager when the first wave of rock'n'roll started to make an impression on this side of the Atlantic. He told me this:

Before Teddy boys came along there was just, *people.* For men, there was no such thing as fashion, and there was very little fashion for women as well, and teenagers. When you graduated from short trousers you started dressing like your father, with either a suit or a jacket and trousers with about twenty-two, twenty-four-inch bottoms – you know, bags – and there was no style at all, there was nothing.

And then Teddy boys came along and because they were so different – I mean, they kind of grew out of the spiv thing in England, and there were sort of overtones of the zoot suit thing in America, but it was peculiarly their own thing, as you could see, but they stood out like a sore thumb. They had this kind of rebel vibe about them, they were different, and they were asserting themselves, and there was always an undertow of violence, although most of them weren't violent, but things could kick off from time to time. And a lot of it was to do with the fact that ordinary people were scared of them. They thought they'd get done up.[6]

Regardless of any tendency towards anti-social behaviour, at times it seemed as if just the clothing was enough to stir up anger in some people, such as the outraged writer of a letter to the

Newcastle Evening Chronicle in 1958, who insisted that the only way to 'wipe out this disgraceful class' was a thorough whipping.

> No young man of culture and refinement would allow himself to be associated with the name Teddy Boy. They go about dressed like 'undertakers'. Bits of black rags tight round their skinny legs, which are supposed to be trousers and black sacks hanging from the shoulders, half-way down the legs, which are classed as jackets. They make one sick to see them pull out a piece of dirty comb to do their hair up in the streets. Even their hair is dirty-looking, in general keeping with their appearance. They certainly look a dirty unkempt and brainless lot who seem incapable of any ambition towards a successful life. The 'Trap' is waiting for them to run into sooner or later – Prison![7]

I'm reminded of taking driving lessons in Portsmouth in 1977. When my forty-something instructor spotted a couple of inoffensive-looking teenage punks out of the window, he remarked to me in disgust, 'Jesus Christ, imagine the likes of them growing up and having kids.' I was dressed in the gear I wore to school so looked vaguely presentable; it didn't seem the right moment to tell him that I'd seen X-Ray Spex play at the Oddfellows Hall,[8] not to mention a double bill of Wayne County's Electric Chairs and Alternative TV at Clarence Pier Ballroom.[9] At the latter gig, one of the punk audience arrived wearing a grey Teddy boy drape with black velvet collar and cuffs which he threw on stage halfway through Wayne's set, and the singer immediately put it on and wore it for the rest of the performance. It was a good-natured gig, with no hint of the scary glass-throwing violence I encountered the following week at the same venue watching Sham 69.[10] A few months later, the

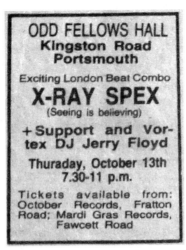

'Oh Bondage, Up Pompey', *Portsmouth Evening News*, 1977

Electric Chairs released a single called 'Eddie & Sheena' – the star-crossed tale of teenage love between a Teddy boy and a punk girl. In reality, when I emerged from the X-Ray Spex gig with the rest of the sparse audience, we were met by hostile groups of local Teds seemingly eager to engage in the King's Road sport they had been reading about in the tabloid press: punk-bashing.

I never quite understood why the Teds I ran into in the mid-1970s were so hostile to the younger punks, given that both groups had in their day been victimised by the media and the older generation on account of their taste in clothes and music. Even at that age, I didn't expect much tolerance from straight society, but the spectacle of one supposed outsider group taking offence at another simply because they didn't fit in seemed short-sighted and unnecessary to me. On New Year's Eve 1977, I caught a train to London to see the Ramones, Generation X and the Rezillos playing at the Rainbow in Finsbury Park.[11] Eleven months later, I caught another train to London to see Jerry Lee Lewis supported by Duane Eddy at the same venue,[12] and four weeks later I saw the Clash back in Portsmouth.[13] To me it was all rock'n'roll music, and those remain some of the finest gigs I've seen. I had short hair in an era when the default style for men was still overwhelmingly shoulder-length. I had a black leather jacket, I had drainpipe jeans, I had some brothel creepers, and I'd cut up old shirts and written slogans on them; I felt a huge sense of freedom in making my own clothing choices after years of school uniforms and chain-store ready-mades.

Teddy boy and Teddy girl outfits were a startling sight when they first appeared in the early 1950s, as were punk styles twenty years later, but when viewed today, the reactions they provoked from wider society seem overblown and absurdly disproportionate.

As the decades have passed, a Teddy boy caricature has replaced the more complex reality, alongside the mistaken impression that they emerged in response to the first wave of US rock music. For some in the UK, the use of Bill Haley's 'Rock Around the Clock' over the title credits of the 1955 film *Blackboard Jungle*[14] may well have been their first taste of the new music, and the following year British newspapers eagerly published articles about seat-slashings and 'riots' at showings of Haley's own film, *Rock Around the Clock*: 'A youth danced on the roof of a parked car,' the *Manchester Guardian* reported, while 'another performed a "snake dance" in a dazed, hypnotised fashion'.[15] Yet the streets, dance halls and coffee bars of the East End and South London had been frequented by teenagers in Edwardian clothing for at least two years prior to this.

Rock'n'roll might have been adopted wholesale by the Teds, but these supposedly sinister young men in drape jackets were the subject of hysterical media coverage long before this music made an impact in Britain. Once the two became linked in the public imagination, it was surely just a matter of time before dazed, hypnotised snake dancing would sweep aside everything in its path.

What follows is an attempt at clarifying things a little, accompanied of course by a selection of primal rock music and the bracing aroma of hair pomade floating on the breeze.

1

DRAPE EXPECTATIONS

Crêpe-Soled Shoes an Inch Thick

It started under the radar. In the early 1950s, increasing numbers of teenagers from the poorer districts of London began wearing a sharp-looking approximation of the styles of long-vanished Edwardian Britain. Long, fingertip-length drape jackets with velvet collars, narrow drainpipe trousers, thin ties and fancy waistcoats were the order of the day – a distinctly more flamboyant mode of dress than the baggier, nondescript fashions of the time. If you were wealthy, you could dress eccentrically or extravagantly, but everyone else was supposed to know their place and not draw attention to themselves. Yet although the general public may have seen this impulse among the Teds as a new development, the urge to branch out into something much more showy and provocative had actually been a recurring feature of working-class London life for many years.

In 1946, the writer Frank Norman escaped a loveless childhood spent in spartan residential homes for orphans, in which religion and corporal punishment held equal sway. He gained his freedom as a sixteen-year-old, sent out into the post-war world by his former guardians wearing 'an ill-fitting suit, shoes, two shirts, two sets of underclothes, socks, working boots and overalls'. As he later wrote, it was hardly the kind of clothing in which to make an impression on the northern fringes of London:

Dressed far from elegantly in my discharge suit, I prome-
naded up and down Waltham Cross High Street in search
of life and excitement. How very disappointing life can
be at times: it was the dullest place on earth. I was very
envious of the sartorial splendour of the local boys' clothes.
Draped suits were just coming into fashion worn with
white cutaway collars, loudly coloured ties and crêpe-soled
shoes an inch thick – known as 'creepers'. They had all the
girls, I did not get so much as a look-in. I vowed that one
day I would acquire such an *ensemble* and devastate the
world.[1]

This was the proto-Teddy boy look, but it would not have
been called that at the time. The most likely words which might
have been applied were *wide boy*, *spiv*, or *flash boy*.

To be *wide* was late-Victorian slang meaning well-informed
or shrewd. In Arthur Morrison's 1896 novel of the Shoreditch
slums, *A Child of the Jago*, the lawless residents of the area, whose
first commandment is 'thou shalt not nark', proudly boast that
they are 'as wide as Broad Street'. They also share an admiration
for sharp clothes, although all but the most successful thieves in
the area could not afford them:

They and their friends resorted to a shop in Meakin Street,
kept by an 'ikey' [Jewish, also meaning clever] tailor, there
to buy the original out-and-out downy benjamins [coats],
or the celebrated bang-up kicksies [trousers], cut saucy,
with artful buttons and a double fakement [theatrical slang
for a decoration or accessory] down the sides.[2]

Here was a true forerunner of the Teddy boy impulse for working-class flash clothes, more than half a century before its time.

A later novel which helped establish the term *wide* in the public consciousness was Robert Westerby's *Wide Boys Never Work* (1937), the story of Jim, a tough youth from out of town who falls in with a gang of racetrack criminals from London that wear sharp clothes 'with a Charing Cross Road cut'. This was the street where dance band musicians and petty mobsters could buy the kind of styles usually seen in Hollywood films or the pages of jazz papers like *Down Beat* and *Melody Maker*. Jim moves to the Smoke, where he hangs around Soho with some 'proper flash boys' who drive Buicks, gets into razor fights, and winds up at parties where people wear blue suede shoes (two decades before Carl Perkins made them world famous). Anyone looking for a happy ending would have retired disappointed, and Westerby – who later wrote film scripts for Disney – does a fine job of conjuring up the low-life scrabble for existence in the capital during the last years before war broke out:

> Over in Bethnal Green and Stepney cockroaches and bugs seep out through the damp plaster. In small rooms the children sleep, their paper-white faces too old for their bodies. And who cares about that, anyway? That's not your business. It's that fellow's over there – or isn't it? . . .
>
> In the back rooms off Lisle Street ageing tarts who are past it wish the hell they could just go to bed and sleep and sleep and sleep . . .
>
> Down in Fleet Street, the Presses roar. Ten million sheets of schmooge, pouring from the machines like vomit.
>
> Houses, buildings, straggling suburbs, new-brick factories. Miles after miles of them. Narrow, twisting alleys in the City – nightmares to turn old Wren over in his sleep. Tall, wide dignity near the Parks . . .
>
> Wotcher, London! How's the girl?[3]

The Razor Boys of the Horse and Dog Tracks

The term 'wide' could apply to both sexes, and was recorded in a female context in another classic Soho novel of the time, *Night and the City* by Gerald Kersh (1938), in which streetwalker Zoë is taunted by the police for not knowing that her boyfriend was deceiving her: "'Love is blind,' said the first detective. "Oh well, Zoë, and I thought you were wide. Why, didn't you know Harry's been carrying on with some tart from Phil Nosseross's club?"'[4]

Another London crime story, *Wide Girl* by Michael Hervey, was published in 1945 with the words 'Cheap 1 Shilling Edition' proudly displayed on the cover. That shilling bought you thirty barely coherent pages by the prolific author of other delights such as *No Crime Like the Present*, *Toughs Afloat*, *Murder Thy Neighbour* and *Dames Spell Trouble*. Hervey had already written a story called *Wide Boy*, and in this new one, the business of being a 'wide girl' seems to have largely involved taking the shortest route to various kinds of degradation:

> Her temperament was such that she couldn't bear restric-tions – of any sort. Those of us who are, shall we say, more amenable in that respect, can never hope to understand the working and behaviour of such free souls. To us they will always remain queer, shocking, even depraved. Whilst we to them appear dull, unexciting, stodgy and clod-like. They waltz in the clouds whilst we slog in the mire – and who is to say that their mode of existence is wrong and ours is right? Of such people worlds are made. Yes, and Hell too . . .[5]

Unsurprisingly, the wide girl in question ends up at Picca-dilly Circus, selling herself on the street.

'She couldn't bear restrictions – of any sort.' *Wide Girl*, 1945

If wide boys and girls had a somewhat cavalier attitude to the laws of the land – an accusation later often aimed at the Teds – then spivs were a similar breed. This type of character, first identified in the late 1920s, is defined in the *Oxford English Dictionary* as 'a man who lives by his wits and has no regular employment; one engaging in petty black-market dealings and frequently characterized by flashy dress.' They were often associated with racetrack gambling, but in 1937 the word gained more publicity when John Worby wrote a book of memoirs misleadingly entitled *The Other Half – The Autobiography of a Spiv*.[6] The title of the US edition offered a truer indication of the work – largely an account of his travels as a rough sleeper – with the word 'spiv' dropped in favour of the phrase, *The Autobiography of a Tramp*. Indeed, in Britain his book was reviewed in *The Spectator* under the pointed headline, 'Love Among the Lice'.[7] Hardly a flashy dresser.

The following year, Walter Greenwood's novel *Only Mugs Work: A Soho Melodrama*[8] was introduced by its publisher with the words 'Gangsters in London! "Ponces", "Spivs", smash-and-grab men, the razor boys of the horse and dog tracks', which suggests that they believed that enough of their readers would be able to understand the word 'spiv'. These days, the term might conjure up an image of Private Walker in the 1970s TV series *Dad's Army*, the smoothly dressed wartime chancer adept at side-stepping all manner of food and clothing shortages. Yet while this helped reinforce the impression that the Blitz years were in some way the classic spiv era, a search of newspaper archives shows that the word essentially disappeared between 1939 and 1945 – except when recording the exploits of a popular racehorse named Spiv, which ran regularly at that time.

It may be that in the heavily censored wartime newspapers the term was suppressed on official instructions as being counter-productive to the national interest. Whatever the case, within months of the cessation of hostilities, it swiftly reappeared in many written sources, as well as on radio. In October 1945, for example, the BBC broadcast a show about conmen called *It's Your Money They're After*; the *Birmingham Evening Despatch* wrote that it showed how 'the comparatively harmless fairground "spiv" and the suave high-power confidence trickster are cast from the same mould'.[9] Six months later, Hartlepool journalist Constance Noville informed her readers that she had uncovered the existence of a female equivalent:

EX-SERVICE GIRLS THINK OFFICE WORK TOO TAME

I have been learning about girl 'Spivs' from Dr J. Macalister Brew, educational secretary of the National Association of Girls' Clubs. Definition of a Spiv: a wise guy, who knows all the answers, who wears flashy clothes and lives off his wits. His feminine counterpart is the 'Good-time Annie'. She always has the latest film-star hair-do; wears a head scarf draped low at the back; uses heavy cosmetics on her legs, and chooses fancy shoes.[10]

The word 'spiv' was also thrown around in a jocular fashion in the House of Commons in August 1947, during a debate around extending the emergency powers available to the government under the Supplies and Services Act of 1945. Attorney General Hartley Shawcross complained to Quintin Hogg MP that the proposed amendment 'would make it necessary to have a debate in Parliament before an individual direction was given to an individual "spiv" that he was to engage in work useful to the community'. This prompted various members to ask, 'What is a "spiv?"', to which Hogg immediately replied, 'a Minister without portfolio'.[11] In a similar way, 1950s MPs would use the Teds as a handy stereotype when criticising their political opponents, such as the occasion when Barbara Castle accused Harold Macmillan's Conservative government of introducing 'Teddy Boy economics'.[12]

His Clothing Out-Stares the Mid-Day Sun

On the music hall stage, comedians from humble backgrounds had been appearing in lavishly draped, outlandishly patterned and spivish suits since the 1930s. The theatre critic Ivor Brown offered the following description of Max Miller's performance at the London Palladium in 1943: 'He is full of meat and mettlesome. His clothing out-stares the mid-day sun.'[13] Three years later, when reviewing the variety show *Piccadilly Hayride* at the Prince of Wales Theatre, Brown wrote the following about Sid Field, another music hall giant: 'Give me Field, whose pastoral name so richly belies his genius for showing us the essence of nark and spiv, the flash and sparkle of a town lit up.'[14]

Another working-class type who dressed extravagantly was the illegal boxing arena betting tout, identified by Ralph L. Finn in a December 1945 article for *The People* entitled 'Flash Boy':

He is not a Spiv. The Spivs originated in trying to imitate him. But where he is flash, they are cheap. He is the Flash-Boy: they are the Spivs. His clothes are beautifully made, either by some perfect craftsman of an East End tailor sitting crossed-legged in his back room, or even by Savile Row. But they are too beautiful. You can appreciate their quality and style and cut and choice of material a hundred yards away.[15]

The idea was gaining ground that you didn't need to have been born wealthy to cause a stir with your choice of clothing, and that you should not care whether it offended society's conceptions of good taste or appropriate behaviour. Similarly, in America during the early 1940s, jazz figures such as Cab Calloway popularised extravagantly draped zoot suits, which also became heavily associated with Latino youth movements in Los Angeles.

As Britain slowly gained some respite from wartime restrictions on clothing materials, especially after cloth rationing finally ended in March 1949, sartorial self-expression became more possible, yet money was often scarce. Cultural life had taken a battering during the war, and continued to do so during peacetime austerity. As the historian Robert Hewison pointed out, 'In the depths of the winter fuel crisis of 1947 the Ministry of Fuel and Power decided that the entire periodical press was not an essential industry, and for a fortnight no magazines of any kind, from *Punch* to pornography, were published. For good measure the BBC's Third Programme [forerunner of BBC Radio 3] was taken off the air.[16]

A Blessing in Disguise

Many of those Londoners of the 1930s and early 1940s who the press termed 'spivs' and 'wide boys' would have gone on to have children themselves, raising them in a city that had been hit hard by German bombing. Indeed, the post-war landscape of many inner London districts in which the future Teddy boys and Teddy girls grew up was marked by significant areas of complete devastation. As the writer John Pearson later put it, 'during the massed raids on the docks, whole districts died. In Bethnal Green alone, ten thousand dwellings were destroyed; the heart of the East End became a wilderness.'[17]

Walter Musto lived in South-West London, worked in Millbank, and kept a diary throughout the war. His entry for 17 April 1941 describes the stricken landscape he witnessed during his morning commute:

> Last night London had its fiercest blitz of the war. With transport badly disorganised, by train I could travel no nearer the office than Clapham Junction and thence by tram only so far as Wandsworth Road station. For the rest the two-mile walk in bright spring sunshine would have been enjoyable but for the havoc caused by enemy bombing, which everywhere was a gruesome reminder of the horrors of war in this bitter struggle for mastery. For almost two miles a continuous line of hosepipes, fire brigades and ambulances, the scores of tired firemen attested to the intensity of the attack and its effects. So spent were the firemen, I found some asleep in doorways and corners amidst the ruins of burnt-out buildings.[18]

Once peace finally came, however, significant areas of the city still lay in ruins. Here is how architectural writer Harold P. Clunn described the fate of a typical East End district in his 1947 survey of the capital, *London Marches On*:

> Most of Shoreditch High Street was destroyed in the early air raids of September, 1940, and the buildings which still remain are all at the northern end. On the east side the huge dry goods store of Messrs Jeremiah Rotherham & Co., Ltd, which stood next to the former London Music Hall, was completely demolished and so also were most of the buildings on the opposite side of the High Street. Bethnal Green Road has shared the same fate and

whole roads of buildings at the western end have been destroyed.[19]

It may sound as if Clunn was writing a lament for the old city, but this hardly seems to have been his intention. In fact, like many other cultural commentators at the time, he adopted the view that most of the surviving old buildings should also be torn down and replaced wholesale by 'modern' flats – preferably high-rise – and he comes dangerously close to cheering on the Luftwaffe for their pioneering efforts in overhead town planning:

> Although the destruction of many of our ancient and beautiful churches, hospitals and other historical buildings by enemy action is a loss which every Londoner cannot but deeply deplore, on the other hand the disappearance of large areas of mean property, totally unworthy of this great and proud imperial city, will ultimately prove a blessing in disguise.'[20]

This was hardly a minority opinion, at least among those in charge, who were often writing from their homes in affluent districts like Hampstead or Chelsea, rather than any of the areas they were keen should be razed to the ground. Many of those in positions of influence in post-war Britain seemed to have loathed the buildings constructed by previous generations, whether the classic terraced houses of the working people or the large-scale dwellings of the rich.

It is odd to read such things from the vantage point of the twenty-first century, where surviving houses of that era have mostly long since been restored and now command high prices. British novels of the 1950s also routinely referred to 'hideous' or 'absurd' Victorian and Edwardian architecture. In the sixties, this led to an overwhelming urge to 'modernise' those buildings that were not pulled down – ripping out original fireplaces and stained-glass decoration or covering panelled doors with hardboard. In London districts such as Islington or Notting Hill, one ironic result of this was that the building trade who made money removing all of those fireplaces then made a killing by putting them all back once such 'original features' had become desirable again twenty years later. We can only guess what the Teds of the 1950s who grew up in such houses when they were working-class dwellings might have made of this.

The Up-Ended Packet of Fags

For thirty years following the war, an entire generation of British planners and architects were seemingly in thrall to the modernist doctrines of architects like Le Corbusier, who in his own career variously sought the patronage of Stalin, Mussolini and collaborationist Vichy France, and breathlessly wrote to his mother in October 1940 that 'Hitler can crown his life with a great work: the planned layout of Europe.'[21] Large sections of historic Berlin were also destroyed in the latter stages of the war, as Ian Fleming noted when visiting the city at the end of the 1950s. 'The seventy million cubic metres of rubble in Berlin are gradually being made into mountains,' he wrote. 'The total operation is known as "Hitler's Collected Works".' Viewing one of Le Corbusier's new developments there, 'vaunted as the "new face" of Berlin', Fleming was less than impressed:

> This 'new face' is the 'new face' we are all coming to know – the 'up-ended-packet-of-fags' design for the maximum number of people to live in the minimum amount of space.

This system treats the human being as a six-foot cube of flesh and breathing-space and fits him with exquisite economy into steel and concrete cells. He is allotted about three times the size of his cube as his 'bed-sitter', once his cube for his bathroom and once for his kitchen. So that he won't hate this cellular existence too much, he is well warmed and lighted, and he is provided with a chute in the wall through which he can dispose of the muck of his life – cartons, newspapers, love-letters and gin bottles – the last chaotic remains of his architecturally undesirable 'non-cube' life. These untidy bits of him are consumed by some great iron stomach in the basement.[22]

When the British cheerleaders for high-rise developments were eyeing up the post-war landscape, they didn't have to look far to find rubble-strewn bomb-sites in post-war London, Portsmouth, Coventry, Hull and Liverpool. For architects and builders these sites represented a business opportunity, but for ordinary people, they had simply been home.

The writer Sally Worboyes was born in 1945 in working-class Stepney, and recalled the war-torn London landscape of her childhood in her 2006 autobiography, *East End Girl*:

Times were hard for us back-street children. We were under-nourished and at risk from illness and malnutrition as it was, never mind the fact that we ran wild during those early post-war years living in bomb-damaged areas – especially in and around Stepney and Bethnal Green. Even when I was a tiny child, just a toddler, I played on the streets in broken houses. It was a depressed and confused time when scrawny girls wore faded frocks and spindly boys lived in patched trousers, old jerseys and hand-me-down boots.[23]

Whichever architect, town-planner or politician was charged with re-shaping it, this was the world from which the Teddy boy generation emerged. They grew up in a society where peace had arrived but rationing continued; housing was scarce but jobs were increasingly easy to come by, not least because the population was depleted by wartime casualties. The whole-sale slaughter of a generation of working-class males led to a situation which favoured the jobseeker and not the employer – in contrast to the desperate pre-war years of the Depression. As a result, businesses had to be more careful about how they treated their staff, who might resign on a Friday knowing they could easily walk into a similar job with a different company on Monday morning.

In this, and countless other ways, the rules had changed. And with many of the old pre-war assumptions looking increasingly unreliable, a nostalgia for earlier days began to take hold in late-1940s Britain.

Is It the Muff-Like Draping?

Teddy boys did not arrive out of a clear blue sky. Theirs was a far more gradual evolution, most of which happened under the radar.

The post-war revival of Edwardian styles began as the artificial creation of exclusive fashion houses, aimed specifically at the few people rich enough to be able to ignore rationing restrictions. Nostalgia for the era was clearly in the air. Indeed, as early as January 1946, little more than three months after the war's end, a group of left-leaning but well-heeled painters called the Artists' International Association threw a lavish Edwardian Ball at the Royal Watercolour Society's Galleries in Conduit Street, Mayfair, with specially commissioned portraits on the walls and décor by Bernard Sarron, later a distinguished art director in the film industry.[24]

At this point, clothing coupons were strictly controlled, so for most people such upmarket fancy dress occasions – or indeed any kind of fashion extravagance – was out of the question; in the event of a wedding, ordinary families would pool their ration books to enable the bride to obtain sufficient material for a dress. Across the Channel in France, sales of cloth were not restricted, so when designs from the Paris catwalk shows of 1947 imitated the lavish women's gowns of 1910 no such difficulties arose. UK newspapers were soon informing their female readers that Edwardian hairstyles, dresses and jackets were back in fashion.

'An Echo of Edwardian Elegance', gushed one headline.[25] 'Is it the muff-like draping, or the giant chenille spot on her veil?' Doubtless these were the sort of questions obsessing millions of young women as they struggled to bring up their families in the bombed-out wreckage of the big cities, in a year when the new Labour government's President of the Board of Trade warned parliament of 'an extreme shortage of clothing'.[26] For many this was true, but Sir Stafford Cripps presumably did not deliver this speech wearing a fig leaf to a group of MPs dressed in rags. Cripps was the main politician associated with post-war austerity measures, yet according to his entry in the *Dictionary of National Biography*, he had enjoyed the huge income in 1939 of £30,000 per annum.[27]

Edwardian Ease and Elegance

Despite the constraints of many of their readers, the press determinedly encouraged the tendency towards all things Edwardian. For instance, in March 1946 the *Sunderland Daily Echo and Shipping Gazette* gave notice of the latest womenswear trends in an instalment of its regular bulletin from the capital, 'Our London Letter':

> In the first display of modern fashions since 1939 shown in a London West End store this week Edwardian styles stood out. There were suits cut to a point behind, blouses and skirts for evening wear, coats with all the fullness at the back and, most Edwardian of all, an ivory voile housecoat known in its day as a negligee.[28]

The message was repeated throughout that year in newspapers across the country, with headlines such as 'Edwardian Again',[29] while one journalist noted that 'waists are small, but basques are full, being pleated, trimmed with braid in the Edwardian manner'.[30]

British fashion, from centuries-old habit, looked across the Channel to the French capital for inspiration. A May 1946 photo feature in *The Sketch* stated that 'night and day signs of the revival of Edwardian ease and elegance are strikingly evident in the Paris collections,'[31] citing Pierre Balmain as a prime example. Their article was entitled 'Re-Enter the Gibson Girl', a reference to the idealised images of women drawn by American illustrator Charles Dana Gibson between 1890 and 1914. For some reason, however, when Christian Dior launched his first collection in February 1947, it was hailed by *Harper's Bazaar* magazine as the 'New Look' – an odd choice of label, given how heavily it was in debt to the shapes and styles of forty years before.

Indeed, in John Paul's 1952 espionage novel *Murder by Appointment* – set in the recently liberated Europe of 1946 – an agent visiting Paris offers the following description when his female partner returns from a shopping trip with a new outfit more redolent of the era of hansom cabs than jet fighters:

She wears a turquoise-blue satin cocktail frock with a big bustle and a tight-fitting bodice. The tight sleeves reach just under the elbow. Her blonde hair is thrown back loosely over the exquisitely embroidered lace collar . . .

'How do you like Balmain's latest creation?' she asks.[32]

In April 1946, the illustrated magazine *Britannia and Eve* highlighted this trend. A series of pictures accurately captioned 'Fashion History Repeats Itself'[33] showed tailored women's suits with narrow waists and velvet collars, and then in a February article they called for a rejection of wartime designs:

Madame, You're Missing Something – You have the excitement of your hard-won freedom, your emancipation – for what it's worth – the honour of your blitz record and the fun of the battle blouses that went with it. Your grandmother had none of these things, but she had glamour, the gracious, delicious allurement of her clothes.[34]

Standing in the Fish Queue

Not everyone was enamoured of the latest trend. Here, for example, is a US ex-serviceman from New Jersey who wrote to *Life* magazine in 1947 protesting about their recent fashion pictorial, 'Gibson Girl Clothes':

What a mess! What has become of the millions of Miss Americas who for centuries have tried to captivate the male? To think of the years I spent in the Pacific, dreaming of the day I'd return to a barracks bag tied in the middle. So long, brother! I'm going back to New Guinea where a fella can see what he's getting![35]

The extravagant use of cloth in these designs was expressly criticised by the British magazine *Picture Post* in a lengthy article entitled 'Paris Forgets This Is 1947':

> Straight from the indolent and wealthy years before the 1914 war come this year's much-discussed Paris fashions. They are launched upon a world which has not the material to copy them – and whose women have neither the money to buy, the leisure to enjoy, nor in some designs even the strength to support, these masses of elaborate material.[36]

As well as noting the difficulty of obtaining cloth in Britain, Marjorie Backett pointed out that the sheer impracticality of many designs showed that they were aimed at the idle rich rather than anyone who actually had to work: 'try lifting a bale of tweed – and imagine voluntarily adding to the fatigue of standing in the fish queue by having twenty yards of it hanging from one's waist.'[37]

There were other dissenting voices too, with one fashion commentator pointing out that 'the use of egret plumes in Edwardian days resulted in the almost total extinction of the egret in Lower Egypt';[38] by 1948, a columnist north of the border was optimistically claiming that Scottish women were rejecting the new styles:

> Already there are signs that the revolt is on. Not so long ago the women used to conform slavishly to the dictates of fashion, but this year the 'New Look' has been subjected to the scornful regard of the majority of women, who regard longer skirts, bustles and furbelows as the outmoded trappings of Edwardian times. This is an encouraging sign.[39]

Nevertheless, women's clothing in the late 1940s largely gave way to a sea of Edwardian-influenced fashions; for a while it appeared that almost every wedding reported in a regional or national newspaper featured the bride and bridesmaids decked out as if it was 1910, with hairstyles to match. At a society wedding in Knightsbridge in 1948, the bride wore 'a picture frock of white satin, following contemporary ideas of an Edwardian fashion,'[40] while at another less-expensive occasion in Nottingham the bridesmaids were dressed in a winning combination of 'cherry moss crêpe, in Edwardian style, with skunk muffs.'[41] Even the royal family came under the influence: when the future queen visited Paris in May 1948, it was reported that 'for dinner at the British Embassy last night Princess Elizabeth was wearing a new dress of lime green cut in Edwardian style, with a round neckline and folds at the shoulders.'[42]

Indeed, the Edwardian trend even persisted when the purpose of an occasion was to wear as few clothes as possible. One of the less risqué promotional shots given out by the capital's most famous burlesque club was captioned, 'vivacious "starlet", Pat Hamilton, wears this Edwardian ensemble in "Revudeville", the Windmill Theatre (London) show.'[43]

In these and many other ways, the stage was gradually being set. When the Ted and Teddy girl styles began appearing in the early part of the following decade, the only people who should have been surprised were those who had not been paying attention.

2

JUST LIKE EDDIE

All the Rage in London, Sir

After lobbying the female population of the UK to adopt the styles of their grandparents for several years, fashion designers, clothing manufacturers and the press then turned their attention to the other 50 per cent of the adult population. 'Sooner or later it had to come,' wrote one commentator in May 1948 with a hint of unease. 'Men had to get a "new look" too.'[1] However, exactly what form this would take was anybody's guess: 'If men were to follow the women thus far into the remoter days of fashion, soon they might be in bottle-green tights and breeches to match bustles and trailing hems.'

Such clothing was mercifully thin on the ground in late-1940s London. However, just as Alec Guinness was being dressed in a wide variety of Edwardian costumes for his multiple roles in the Ealing comedy masterpiece *Kind Hearts and Coronets* (released June 1949), designers were finally waking up to the sales potential of the pre-First World War look.

A tentative revival began in the south of England, but some up north – such as the writer Keith Colling – found the prospect grim:

> When I went to my tailor to order a new sports coat and slacks, it was with more than a little surprise that I gazed at

the style booklet which he offered. For to my lay mind, the glassy faced young men with Olympian figures pictured in the book were dressed in a fashion almost resembling that of a late uncle photographed in the early 1900s. The tailor noticed my expression. 'New style, Sir,' he commented. I asked him if he thought the trouser bottoms were a little too narrow. 'All the rage in London, Sir,' said the tailor. 'Some gentlemen are ordering their trousers to be made only seventeen inches wide, and they are discarding the turn-up.'[2]

Such were the perils of being marginally ahead of your time in the fashion world. It recalls the story told by Spike Milligan in the first volume of his war memoirs, *Adolf Hitler: My Part in His Downfall* (1971), about the time when he showed up to play trumpet with his regular London dance band wearing a draped dinner jacket considerably longer in the body than usual. Necessity, rather than fashion, had prompted his decision. Worried that he was suffering from a hernia, he had hastily improvised a truss, which in turn created a disturbing outline in his trousers:

> Mother came to the rescue; she sewed on an additional length of dyed black curtain which covered the bulge but brought the jacket half way down my thighs. Embarrassed, I explained it away by saying, 'This is the latest style from America. Cab Calloway wears one.'
> 'He must be a cunt,' said the drummer.[3]

Had he known it, Spike was actually eight or nine years ahead of the game. Alison Settle, investigating London menswear trends for *The Observer* in May 1949, reported that 'the Tailor and Cutter Academy invited me to inspect the work of their apprentices making men's suits ("Very Edwardian they are now," said my guide, "quite an inch longer in the coat").[4'] The *Manchester Guardian* followed up on this story several days later, implying that it would only suit wealthy clubmen of a wide girth, who could somehow subvert the restrictions of food rationing:

> Modern trends in tailoring, on the authority of 'The Tailor and Cutter', indicate narrow trousers, 'skirted' jackets with long lapels and single buttoning. This outline, approximating to that current in 1909, seems to present a frontal view roughly like a lozenge, and a return to the 'heavy swell' of Edwardian days. Certain physical attributes are necessary to carry off this style with aplomb. An Edwardian outline requires Edwardian menus, and our waistlines are not what they used to be.[5]

The removal of woven cloth from the list of items that were rationed in January 1949 freed many to think about the increased options in menswear. One shop on the Strand saw a fourfold increase in sales of ready-made suits on the first day after the new legislation came into effect,[6] yet at the top end of the market, where a Savile Row suit retailed for between £32 and £35, little change in demand was observed. If those prices sound low to modern ears, a copy of the *Daily Mirror* at that time was one penny – and there were 240 pennies to the pound.

On 15 February 1949 the *Mirror* included an article by Pete Willis outlining Savile Row's keenness to push what he variously termed their 'back-to-1914 movement', including 'close fitting jackets, 2 in. longer in the skirt' and 'narrower trousers, only 19 in. wide in the leg'. Yet again, the sense of both men's and women's fashions being entirely imposed from above comes through strongly, especially when he describes the activities of the 'Council of Fashion for Men, the West End tailors who dictate the trends in men's clothes. They decide what the West End, fashion-plate, club men will wear – *and this means that probably next year you will wear it too*.'[7]

Gentlemen, We Are Going Edwardian

By the dawn of the 1950s, there were growing signs that the pre-1914 trend was taking hold. Indeed, some gentlemen of a slightly older vintage had never stopped dressing in the Edwardian style of their youth, but everyone else was hardly supposed to have a mind of their own when it came to such matters. As J. H. Wallis of the Marriage Guidance Council put it at a 1962 conference at Nottingham University, 'Twenty years ago men wore not clothes so much as a uniform – the morning coat for the affluent and the corduroy trousers for the working man.'[8] If the so-called lower orders stepped out of line and put on something that called attention to themselves, they were generally looked on as suspect. Eccentricity of dress was all very well among the gentry, but the poor were supposed to blend in.

In the spring of 1950, the *Daily Herald* ran an article alerting their readers to the new trend in male attire, with the unspoken assumption that a certain level of disposable income was required:

> Are you fed up, as I am, with reading about what M. Christian Dior decrees shall happen to women's fashions? You are? Good. Let's have a bit about men's fashions. Gentlemen, we are going Edwardian. Yesterday I met John Taylor, the editor of *Tailor and Cutter*, by tradition the arbiter of what the English dandy should wear. His grey suit had

lapels to the waistcoat, turn-up cuffs to the sleeves, narrow trousers, and a single slit up the tail of the jacket. Several of London's leading tailors who were at the meeting confirmed that men's clothes are reverting to the styles Grandpa wore.[9]

A few weeks later the *Manchester Guardian* joined the debate, complaining that wealthy men were letting the side down:

How drab, how conventional we are all getting! Each year private view day at the Royal Academy, once both a parade of fashion and revolt against formality, becomes more and more ordinary: no striped trousers, only a few corduroys; half a dozen beards but not a notable moustache. Connoisseurs, business men, gentlemen of leisure (there are still a few), artists, and critics all wear the same subfusc lounge suit and no man's face betrays his work or his interests.[10]

This lament concluded, 'one begins to hope that the "Tailor and Cutter" is right and that men are soon to return to Edwardian styles'. In fact, *Tailor and Cutter* had been predicting this trend for at least a year by that stage, and on 27 April duly awarded their annual 'Dandy' trophy for the suit of the year to an Edwardian-style outfit by 'an eminent firm in Albemarle Street'.[11] A short Pathé newsreel about the winning entry shows that it featured a fingertip-length jacket and turn-back cuffs, but no velvet collar; although the trousers were narrower than customary, they would still have been judged too wide by the Ted fraternity later that decade. Nevertheless, such styles were eventually adopted by the kind of people who were more likely to hang around the local dance hall or coffee bar than drift languidly about at a private view at the Royal Academy wishing they had a 'notable moustache'.

Gay Knitted Waistcoats Run Up By the Little Woman

In the spring of 1951, Harrods advertised a cut-away women's Edwardian-style jacket with a narrow waist and velvet collar very similar to those adopted two years later by Teddy girls, but these retailed for the substantial sum of 29 guineas (£30.45).[12] To put that price into context, Air France at that time were running return flights to Paris for £10,[13] while a seafront hotel in Cornwall was advertising rooms in *The Times* starting at 30 shillings (£1.50) per night.[14]

For another bracing sample of a fashion item aimed at the wealthier end of society, here is the introduction to a picture feature in the magazine *Tatler & Bystander*, showing a variety of gentlemen posing in the height of men's bespoke tailoring:

> Since the war there has been a steady, gradual change in men's fashions. After duffel coats and handle-bar moustaches, Edwardian elegance is now the goal. Some people may achieve this effect by still wearing the suits they bought in 1910, some with the aid of gay knitted waistcoats run up by the Little Woman, but few will compete with the resplendent Edwardiana displayed on the opposite page by Messrs. Frank Bower and Bunny Roger.[15]

Although Bower is pictured wearing what the magazine termed an 'embroidered fancy waistcoat', for the most part he resembles nothing so much as a middle-aged prosperous city businessman of the time, complete with bowler hat. There is little in his clothing to suggest any resemblance to a Teddy boy.

Bunny Roger, on the other hand, was an altogether more singular gentleman.

Neil Munroe 'Bunny' Roger was born into a wealthy family in 1911 – one year earlier and he would have qualified as a genuine Edwardian. He set up in business as a West End couturier in 1937, designing women's gowns for the luxury market. Clothing had fascinated him since he was a small child, although, as Clive Fisher wrote in his entertaining and sympathetic obituary, 'What [his parents] can have been thinking when they gave their six-year-old middle son a fairy's costume of filmy skirts and butterfly wings, with the promise of a wand to further his caperings, it is hard to imagine.'[16] With the outbreak of war, after initially driving ambulances, he joined the Rifle Brigade, and went on to display conspicuous bravery. A newspaper report of 1951 somewhat grandly attributed the entire post-war revival in Edwardian men's fashion to Bunny's influence, saying that he 'had been wearing drainpipe trousers since 1943',[17] a year when he would mainly have been wearing battledress. Drainpipes or not, he too combined the Edwardian look in *Tatler*'s article with a bowler hat – an item which failed to make the transition when the revival moved downmarket from the gentlemen's clubs of the West End.

Black Suede Shoes

A leader column in *The Times* addressing Savile Row's enthusiasm for Edwardian styles pointed out that although women might know a great many of the technical terms used by the fashion industry, men remained largely ignorant of such things, despite the fact that the use of bespoke tailors was much more widespread in those days:

Men are being taught at the moment that this is the season of the backward-glancing Mid-Century look. Their jackets are to be lengthened, their trousers narrowed and their cuffs turned back. Not to look Edwardian is not to look up to date. So far the receptive listener is in the picture. He may not want his trousers narrower or tighter than they already are, but he understands what is expected of him. Then he is told that the 'drape', a product of his age, has been retained for comfort . . . Nobody likes to admit that he has not the slightest idea that his suit has a drape.[18]

Drape cuts in men's clothing had been a Savile Row fashion innovation of the 1930s, creating an effect in which the jacket hangs from broad shoulders down to a more trim waist, of which the 1940s zoot suit could be seen as an exaggerated development. The drape had gained a hold on both sides of the Atlantic during the 1940s, and in a 1950 edition of mass-market newspaper *Reveille*, the link between such things and all manner of jazz-inspired depravity was clearly implied in their statement that school authorities were attempting to rescue students from a life of sin by banning the '"drape" clothes and long haircuts affected by the boppers': 'American teen-age boys and girls who are fans of be-bop music have found a secret way of telling each other about immoral acts they have committed . . . It is claimed that there is an Inner Circle of boppism – and members of it wear a triangular badge with symbols denoting immoral acts.'[19]

It was also assumed that readers of post-war American hardboiled crime fiction would be familiar with the existence of drapes, judging by the following piece of deadpan narration from one of the finest examples of the genre. In *Halo in Blood* by Howard Browne (1946), the laconic detective hero Paul Pine brings out his dinner jacket for an important date, last used on an evening when he wound up in a hotel room 'with a north-ern exposure and a southern blonde': 'I wondered about taking along a gun, decided it would spoil the coat's faultless drape and locked it away in a drawer. If Miss Sandmark made improper advances I could always appeal to her better nature.'[20]

According to a 1950 article in *The Economist*,[21] a suit from a Savile Row tailor at this time cost between 35 and 40 guineas (£36.75 and £42) – a significant increase from their immediate pre-war rate. As prices rose, another change had occurred; the newspaper now estimated that 'something over one-third of the total product of the first class London tailor is exported – far more than before the war.' One local resident who was still in the market for such custom-made apparel was Princess Eliza-beth's husband, the Duke of Edinburgh, who ordered a pair of two-piece suits at 40 guineas each (£42) prior to a royal tour of Canada. However, he had little time for the pre-First World War revival, as the *Daily Mirror* explained: 'One new fashion, "The Edwardian Look" – narrow trousers and high lapels – was dismissed by the Duke as "just uncomfortable".' Even so, Teds might have approved of his habitual choice of footwear: 'The Duke seldom wears anything with his lounge suits but £10 hand-made suede shoes with thick sponge rubber soles.'[22] Top-of-the-range creepers, in other words.

The article concluded with some rather extravagant claims as to Prince Philip's alleged influence as a fashion icon: 'Savile-row agrees that 6,000,000 men in Canada and 67,000,000 in the USA will eagerly watch everything the Duke wears.'[23] Presum-ably Savile Row managed to call in at the local branch of the Colonial Baking Company in Jackson, Tennessee, to canvas the opinion of one of the firm's pan-greasers – the nineteen-year-old son of a poor sharecropping family who'd been writing songs on his cheap guitar. Lounge suits costing 40 guineas would have been way out of Carl Perkins's price range, but four years later he wrote a song about suede shoes which sold millions of copies worldwide, both in his original version and one by someone who in 1951 was still a sixteen-year-old usher at the Loew's State cinema in Memphis, Elvis Presley. If anyone from Savile Row had asked him about the Duke of Edinburgh's supposed influence as a role model, he would probably have told them that if he could ever afford a bespoke suit, it would be one of the wilder models he had seen in the window of Bernard Lansky's clothing shop on Beale Street.

Dated in a Doublet?

The Edwardian high-fashion revival was enjoying its last years of tranquillity, before narrow trousers, velvet collars, and drape jackets would become inextricably linked with a different clientele altogether. For now, it was just another trend. With the arrival of the new monarch, some in the press began writing about a 'new Elizabethan age', at which point various designers decided that modern men should begin dressing up as if they were in the early seventeenth century. Unsurprisingly, the general public had other ideas, but not before bemused Londoners in Oxford Street and Regent's Park were treated to the sight of three male models – two in Elizabethan costume and another in an Edwardian suit, by way of a contrast – striking poses for the benefit of eager journalists from *Picture Post*[24] and the cameras of Pathé Pictorial, whose jovial commentator Bob Danvers-Walker drawled:

> Hold tight, girls, look what this year's brought out in Regent's Park; the new Elizabethan look. The beau in the bowler shows that an Edwardian hangover has its good

Savile Row's Edwardian clothing revival demonstrated by
a model for Pathé Pictorial and *Picture Post*, 1952

points too, especially if the figure's not cut out for doublet
and hose. Natty, hey? The cuffs might help to cushion the
shock for a modern male who dares to lay down the law,
but girls don't be misled by his swagger coat and drainpipe
trousers, it's my guess he's nothing more than a stooge for

the Sir Walter Raleigh touch. Wouldn't you rather be dated in a doublet?[25]

Significantly, Danvers-Walker also gave the distinct impression that 1910 was last year's thing. However, in a final sequence showing the three men walking down a nondescript London street past a cockney flower-seller, he imagined the latter's mocking response to any suggestion that the working man might be wearing doublet and plus-fours any time soon.

As suggested in this newsreel, the bowler hat continued to be seen as a vital ingredient of the Savile Row Edwardian revival. It was certainly an authentic item of the pre-1914 era, often sported by Edward VII himself. *Picture Post* also implied that this typical item of a city gent's wardrobe was an essential part of the new Edwardian look:

Apart from the duffle-coat – the semi-official hair shirt of the new poor – no noticeably new men's fashions had appeared in London since the war until the revival of Edwardian stove-pipe trousers, curly-brimmed bowlers and high-buttoned coats which, the trade predict, may even outnumber the present orthodox styles in Guards-dominated circles before next year's Coronation.[26]

The description leaves no doubt as to their assumption that this fashion was aimed at people who had attended the 'right' schools and universities, accustomed to discussing tailoring options over dinner at their club. For an insight into the social attitudes of the wealthy, we might consider a 1951 article by Beryl Seaton in *The Spectator*; in 'Class in the Kitchen' the author drew various conclusions from her observations of that alien race, the working class:

This house is excellently placed for a social study. As in so many London districts, where slums and select neighbourhoods jostle each other in a manner incomprehensible to the outsider, we live on a frontier. Occupying the end house in the last road of one postal district, we use the shops, the cinemas, the buses, trains and taverns of the other – or could. On the one hand are the tall houses, with their big rooms, big windows, big gardens, of the upper middle classes; on the other, the little Victorian rows of town cottages for the workers. I might shop with my charwoman, stand behind her in the fish queue, sit next to her at our local cinema; the odd thing is that I never do . . . [The charwoman and her husband] know and love television stars I have not even heard of. They *never* listen to the Third Programme . . . In all our association together we have never exchanged a single thought as equals or even contemporaries. We are of a different species, as un-like as, say, a mare and a cow.[27]

It is hardly surprising that commentators from backgrounds such as this found the Teds and Teddy girls who emerged several years later to be an equally alien phenomenon.

In Protest Against the Edwardian Clingers

As for the Edwardian style itself, it looked sharp – considerably sharper, in fact, on a fifteen-year-old Teddy boy from Tottenham or the Elephant and Castle than on a middle-aged City gent of expanding girth – not least because the Teds dropped bowler hats unceremoniously into the dustbin of history as surplus to requirements. In an era when men routinely wore hats, going bare-headed was a statement in itself, but with Teds, the hairstyle – carefully greased, sculpted and combed – was an integral part of the show. By the standards of the time, in which an army-approved short back and sides still held sway, these teenagers had offensively long hair. This was fine by them, and they discovered a feeling enjoyed by every successive youth movement: the pleasure of provoking that magical reaction from parents and the adult world in general, 'You're not going out looking like *that*?'

Nevertheless, the British press continued to promote the upper-class version of the Edwardian clothing revival. Couturier Bunny Roger was once again pictured – this time in the *Daily Mirror*[28] – alongside a caption noting his drainpipe trousers and comparing him to an Edwardian dandy, while the Queen's favoured dressmaker, Hardy Amies, was profiled by the *Daily Mirror*, who reported that he too followed the drainpipe fashion.[29]

A prominent overseas visitor to London in the spring of 1953 was Prince Akihito of Japan, who arrived in town with 157 pieces of luggage. Yet no matter how many items of clothing he had brought with him, Akihito landed with the firm intention of acquiring more, and had placed an advance order from Japan with a West End tailor, who told the press that 'the prince will get absolutely the latest Savile-row suits of Edwardian style'.[30]

Still, not everyone from the upper social circles was convinced. One well-heeled Cambridge university student – a grandson of the Earl of Mar – was reported to be wearing bell-bottom trousers 'in protest against the Edwardian clingers'.[31] Two decades later he would have found himself at the height of the flared-trouser craze, but apparently his attempt to publicise what he termed 'Cambridge wides' failed to catch on with the general public. While Prince Akihito was in London buying Edwardian suits, the public was treated to some fashion advice from the *Daily Mirror* columnist Douglas Howell. A quiz entitled 'Know Your Girl!'[32] was designed as a tongue-in-cheek guide for men hoping to find the ideal marriage partner:

IF SHE LIKES YOU IN	THIS IS MY ADVICE
Drape suits	Pray she will grow out of it
Duffle coats	If you like tinned food, marry her
Your best blue	Dull but safe
Edwardian suits	Not the marrying kind
Ties she chose herself	You'll never guess she's a nagger until you marry her
Bowler hats	You'll marry her Mother, too
Your oldest clothes	She's the one for you

All very informative, but what if you favour an Edwardian drape, twinned with a bowler hat and a tie chosen by your girlfriend?

3

I'M NOT A JUVENILE DELINQUENT

Bad Characters in the Streets

In the years following the Second World War, all manner of feature films, crime novels, newspaper articles and radio and television pundits lined up to complain that an unprecedented epidemic of young hooligans was on the loose, waiting on a street corner near you, ready to pounce. Many members of the public seemed to agree, including the reader who wrote to the *Portsmouth Evening News* in 1950, saying, 'The adage, "Spare the rod and spoil the child" is as true today as of yore, so away with your modern methods of teaching. You have given it a trial and look what you turn out – cosh boys, thugs and illiterates with no respect for man or beast.'[1]

Consider these newspaper headlines from around England:

JUVENILE DELINQUENTS

REPORT OF THE COMMITTEE FOR INVESTIGATING THE CAUSES OF THE ALARMING INCREASE OF JUVENILE DELINQUENCY IN THE METROPOLIS

TRUE CAUSES OF THE INCREASE OF CRIMES AMONG THE YOUTH OF THE COUNTRY

The first of these reports quoted a member of the River Police at Wapping, who spoke of 'a great number of boys, between the ages of ten and fifteen years, many of whom prowl about in gangs' who were said to be responsible for 'numerous robberies'.[2] The next article listed individual case studies gathered by a committee investigating London youth crime, including that of a seventeen-year-old identified by the name S.T. who had turned to crime after losing his job as an errand boy two years earlier: 'He first became initiated into vice by forming an acquaintance with bad characters in the streets, and gambling with them. They soon led him into criminal practices.'[3] The final article claimed that 'productive industry has for several years been on the decline in this country . . . Clerks are not wanted – apprentices are not wanted – and the professions are overstocked with candidates . . . Hence the increase of juvenile delinquency.'[4] The writer of this piece laid the blame on the malign effects of the recent war.

'Ah, the youth of today,' parents might have said. Yet these were, in fact, headlines from Regency and late-Georgian England, and the conflict being blamed for the rise in youth crime was not the battle against Hitler, but one started by another megalomaniac who also invaded most of Europe – Napoleon Bonaparte.

Gimme Gimme Shock Treatment

The Teds would have the term *juvenile delinquent* thrown at them repeatedly. It was almost as if it had been coined for them, yet its earliest recorded uses occur in the years following the Battle of Waterloo, when it quickly became a favourite of politicians, commentators and moralists alike. Fowell Buxton, MP for Weymouth, told the House of Commons in 1821 that 'there were in London from 8,000 to 10,000 juvenile delinquents, living by theft,'[5] and this situation was regularly claimed to be deteriorating as each new generation appeared.

In 1839, the *Boston Herald* in Lincolnshire approvingly noted the actions of a local doctor who had inflicted a 'novel punishment on a juvenile delinquent', having been 'sorely annoyed by the tintinabulary and rat-tat-tat propensities of certain practitioners of the ring-and-run-away manoeuvre'.[6] Being of a scientific mind, he built a mechanism which would deliver a sufficiently powerful electric shock to anyone ringing his doorbell that it would knock them to the ground. Imagine the legal prosecution which would be brought against anyone copying this initiative today.

Half a century later, the Chief Constable of Dundee commented on the case of two 'juvenile delinquents' who had been fined for daring to play football in the streets on a Sunday. Finding the sentence too lenient, he announced that 'preparations were being made for flogging boys guilty of this offence',[7] although it is unclear whether he was intending to have the pleasure of inflicting the punishment himself. The game had been growing in popularity during the latter half of the nineteenth century – especially since the formation of the Football Association at a Covent Garden pub called the Freemason's Arms in 1863 – but if it was leading the youth of the 1890s astray, the next generation allegedly had their morals corrupted by a newer form of entertainment: moving pictures.

At Preston in 1914, Justice of the Peace J. W. Hoole told a public meeting that 'juvenile delinquency was greatly on the increase', and that he was 'very pained to see young girls lounging about the street at unseemly hours'.[8] He warned of the dangers of picture palaces, and claimed that there were 'girls of eleven to fourteen years of age who bartered their honour for admittance to places of amusement' (precisely how he came by this information was not revealed). Nevertheless, the idea had staying power: in 1931 the Tunbridge Wells branch of the National Council of Women solemnly declared that the problem of juvenile delinquency was growing because of immorality in motion pictures;[9] four years later delegates at the North of England Education Conference in Lancashire were offered the startling revelation that there had been an 'increase of juvenile delinquency'.[10] Meanwhile in Hull, local judge Sir Reginald Mitchell Banks, KC, detected in the modern world signs of 'a sort of anarchy, intellectual, religious and moral'.[11]

In 1939, yet another representative of the legal profession weighed in with a doomsday prediction, published in the *Daily Herald* under the headline, 'The Younger Generation – By A Judge', which was at least based upon direct observation: '"What's happening to the younger generation?" Mr W. Blake Odgers, Southampton's Recorder, asked a jury yesterday. "Unless something is done," he said, "it will grow up nasty little sneak-thieves."' Mr Odgers had found that ten out of twenty-one prisoners to be tried by him were under twenty-one years of age.[12]

In fact, there were some 1939 school-leavers who would grow up swiftly over the coming two or three years instead to be infantrymen, nurses, Spitfire pilots, munitions workers, commandos, submariners or code-breakers, and many would never live to see twenty-one.

Yet a society which had been claiming an ever-increasing incidence of juvenile delinquency for more than a century was hardly liable to change its pessimistic views about the next generation once the Second World War was finally over. Show them a teenager, and some would see a hooligan.

An Unlucky Stroke So As to Kill Him

In 1945, Pelican Books published a thoughtful book by A. E. Jones entitled *Juvenile Delinquency and the Law*, which summarised the situation immediately prior to the rise of the Teddy boy. Jones, who had twenty years' experience as a magistrates' clerk, noted that a particular eighteenth-century law remained on the statute books, compared to which electric shock treatments and flogging seem positively restrained:

> In 1706 it was judicially held that 'If a parent or master be provoked to a degree of passion by some miscarriage of the child or servant, and the parent or master shall proceed to correct the child or servant with a moderate weapon, and shall by chance give him an unlucky stroke so as to kill him, that is but a misdemeanour.' This ruling was enshrined in the text-books and still theoretically expresses the law on the subject.[13]

In practice, anyone in mid-twentieth-century Britain killing their children when 'provoked to a degree of passion' would have been charged with murder or manslaughter, but it was still common for parents to administer corporal punishment in the home, as it remained in state schools until 1986 (and continued in English public schools for more than a decade afterwards). For any minor falling foul of the courts at the time of Jones's study and sent to an approved school, the prospect of being beaten by the staff was an ever-present threat, with boys running the greater risk of more degrading procedures than girls:

> Only the headmaster or principal teacher is authorised to use the prescribed cane or tawse [leather strap]. The maximum dose for boys under 15 is six strokes on the

posterior or three on each hand; the over fifteens may get eight strokes (or twelve exceptionally), but only their posterior, and not their hands, can be made to suffer. Girls under fifteen may be given up to three strokes of the cane on each hand, but they are not liable to corporal punishment once they have reached fifteen.[14]

Jones itemised the types of crime committed by teenagers that could land them in such an institution just before the Second World War, in a table showing the numbers convicted in each category. These varied quite widely, although the vast majority of cases involved stealing: housebreaking, shoplifting, theft from employers, from vehicles, vending machines and gas meters – indeed pretty much anything that wasn't nailed down. Further down the list were offences like 'joy-riding', truancy from school and 'sexual misconduct in relation to females'. Fraud, forgery and arson registered in just a handful of instances, there was one conviction for cruelty to animals, and one child appeared on the list for the supposed crime of 'attempting to commit suicide'.[15] In the 1950s, the teenage Teddy boys and Teddy girls who fell foul of the law would be charged with similar crimes at juvenile courts across the country; this process was familiar to anyone who had worked in the justice system over the years, despite the consistent assertions from the media and politicians that this new generation was somehow more lawless than those which had come before.

Young Folk Are Liars

These figures reflected the state of things just before the Second World War changed the moral landscape of the nation. Juvenile delinquency had been highlighted as an ever-growing problem for more than 120 years by this point, but the Teddy boys and Teddy girls of the 1950s, many of whom were born during the war, would be decried in the popular press and in political circles as if every previous generation of teenagers had been model citizens.

Consider the patrician attitude towards working-class youth expressed in November 1946 by Rosamond Fisher, wife of the Archbishop of Canterbury, when addressing a body in London called the Public Morality Council. Her husband, Geoffrey Fisher, went on to preside at the Queen's coronation and is perhaps best remembered as the man who weighed into the nuclear debate in 1958 by saying 'the very worst the bomb can do is to sweep a vast number of people from this world into the next into which they must all go anyway.'[16] Judging from her speech, reported in the *Daily Herald* under the headline 'Young Folk Are Liars Says Archbishop's Wife', Rosamond seems to have had an equal ability to blithely dismiss large sections of the population:

> They have a gross disregard for truth and an extraordinary disregard for fidelity to vows and contracts ... Our people have no faith. Our children have not grown up with the kind of solid security afforded by the late Victorian and early Edwardian times, but with the background of two disintegrating world wars ... We hear with grave misgivings of the figures of illegitimacy, juvenile delinquency and young girls being married who are already pregnant.[17]

These sentiments may have won a sympathetic hearing at the time, but the young in Victorian England grew up in a society that only outlawed the barbaric and often fatal practice of sending the children of the poor up chimneys as cleaners at the late date of 1875.

Caning, Flogging and Manhandled Policemen

So great was the media's fascination with tales of young criminals in the aftermath of the war that it was mocked in a fictional news item in the satirical magazine *Blighty*: 'At East London Juvenile Court it was said of a 14-year-old boy that he has escaped from remand homes and approved schools thirty-four times. Up to the present he has not agreed with any publisher to write a book about his life.'[18]

When young people fell foul of the law for less serious offences, they were often simply referred to as a *hooligan*, a word meaning troublemaker that dated back to the late nineteenth century.

Journalist Clarence Rook published a book in 1899 called *The Hooligan Nights*, which claimed to be the true story of an eighteen-year-old criminal named Alf, from Elephant and Castle – a future Teddy boy stronghold – who had a simple life philosophy: '"Look 'ere," he said, "if you see a fing you want, you just go and take it wivout any 'anging abart. If you 'ang abart you draw suspicion, and you get lagged for loiterin' wiv intent to commit a felony or some dam nonsense like that. Go for it, strite."'[19]

In an echo of later territorial disputes between the Teds, Alf's gang meet for an organised battle with a rival outfit from north of the river:

> He explained that there was a bit of a street-fight in pros-
> pect. The Drury Lane boys were coming across the bridge,
> and had engaged to meet the boys from Lambeth Walk at
> a coffee-stall on the other side. Then one of the Lambeth
> boys would make to one of the Drury Lane boys a remark
> which cannot be printed, but never fails to send the
> monkey of a Drury Lane boy a considerable way up the

pole. Whereafter the Drury Lane boys would fall upon the Lambeth boys, and the Lambeth boys would give them what for.[20]

A fair number of people who were called hooligans would by the mid-1950s simply have been called Teddy boys. For example, in 1949, the *Daily Herald* used the word hooliganism in reporting what they described as 'a series of "Men Without Pity" attacks'.[21] As to what might be the solution, the usual remedy of corporal punishment was suggested, but in this case those recommending it were not the adult population, but teenagers themselves:

MORE CANING WILL CURE IT SAYS YOUTH

A group of London boys and girls have told the LCC [London County Council] that more caning is the answer to hooliganism. They are members of the Crossway Young People's Institute, Southwark, SE, whose leader, Mr A. Paice, said yesterday, 'We believe the best person to administer the caning is not the schoolmaster or mistress, but the head of the household. But we also favour more corporal punishment in schools and reintroduction of flogging for some criminal offences.'[22]

While it might seem unlikely that a group of young people were calling for teachers to wield the lash, the reason for such apparent fearlessness was revealed in the article's final line: 'None of the members, aged 15 and upwards, is still at school'.[23]

Another news item, also from January 1949, dealt with the kind of recurring trouble at London dance halls that five years later would certainly have been laid at the Teds' door, but that particular species had yet to be identified:

Hooliganism at Saturday-night dances has forced Padding-ton to draw up a code of conduct for its teen-age dancers. Hirers of the Paddington and Porchester halls, says the Baths Committee, should be asked to: employ 'bouncers' capable of dealing with disorderly persons; ban jitter-bugging, pass-out tickets and the lowering of lights; keep the gallery closed. Ald. H. Hobsbaum, the committee's vice-chairman, said last night: 'Once when the hall was invaded by young hooligans, a policeman was manhandled. . . Some of the girls have been badly treated when the lights have been dimmed or when the spotlight was switched on and other lights put out. We have had several reports about beer being thrown down from the gallery. Several girls have had their dresses ruined.'[24]

None of these accounts mention the styles of clothing worn by the young people concerned, but most teenagers of that year would have looked very similar to each other. Indeed, measured against such relative conformity, the London correspondent of the *Dundee Courier* felt it worth noting the following in a January 1949 column headed 'Odd Glimpses': 'Youth in Savile Row wearing a lurid green tie with bright yellow daisies on it – and a collar to match.'[25] Clearly, the moral fibre of the nation was close to breaking point.

Terrific Force and Ugly Effect

As the 1950s dawned, according to the popular press, the nation was apparently under siege from a newly identified working-class hooligan: the cosh boy. In a pattern that would be repeated with each successive generation, as soon as a new public menace had been identified by the media, sightings of them multiplied in towns and cities across the country.

Qualifications for this special category were deceptively simple; there was no dress code, and no rule book. As far as the press, the police or magistrates were concerned, if you were a boy – or even a man in your twenties or thirties – and carried a cosh either for self-protection or with malicious intent, then you were a fully paid-up member of the new breed. In fact, you didn't always even need a real one, as the *Daily Mirror* were keen to point out:

> Any cosh boy who is arrested in London these days, and found to have a handkerchief and a shillingsworth of coppers in his pocket, is in for trouble. Because these blighters have found that a bobsworth of coppers knotted in a handkerchief makes a cosh that can be swung with terrific force and ugly effect.[26]

Of course, all manner of everyday objects can be turned into makeshift weapons – including a tightly rolled newspaper – and coins were an easy option. However, by that logic, any member of the House of Commons could have been arrested on the grounds that they had the same objects in their own pockets – but at least this newspaper article would have spread the word to any aspiring hooligan who was so far unaware of the do-it-yourself cosh procedure.

Coshes themselves were nothing new. Weighted saps designed for beating an opponent over the head, they made their first appearance under that name in a memoir by Frank Henderson entitled *Six Years in the Prisons of England* (1869), a book awash with thieves' slang and ready-made explanations for the uninitiated:

> O! that's a very common racket. He meant a 'flash-tail', or

prostitute who goes about the streets at nights trying to pick up 'toffs'. When she manages to do this her accomplice the coshman (a man who carries a 'cosh' or life preserver) comes up, when she has signed to him that she has got the 'toff's' watch and chain, and quarrels with him for meddling with his wife. Whilst the quarrel is going on the moll walks away with the booty.[27]

A generation later, in Arthur Morrison's novel of the Shoreditch slums, *A Child of the Jago* (1896), arming yourself with a cosh was virtually obligatory among the residents of one of the most deprived areas in London:

Cosh-carrying was near to being the major industry of the Jago. The cosh was a foot length of iron rod, with a knob at one end, and a hook (or a ring) at the other. The craftsman, carrying it in his coat sleeve, waited about a dark staircase till his wife (married or not) brought in a well drunken stranger: when, with a sudden blow behind the head, the stranger was happily coshed, and whatever was found on him as he lay insensible was the profit of the transaction.[28]

Although some less villainous members of the public carried them simply for protection, a man or youth found with such an item about his person was generally considered by the police to be up to no good, but prior to the year 1950, anyone wielding one would not have been called a cosh boy, because that specific term was not yet in general use. The 1948 crime novel *They Never Looked Inside* – one of many written by the lawyer Michael Gilbert – features a teenage thug skilled in the use of this custom-made implement:

It was a beautiful little weapon, fashioned of closely woven net around a hard flexible core made with infinite care out of hundreds of scraps of tinfoil and silver paper. It had a thong to go round the wrist and a grip of smooth leather.[29]

Zoot Suit Cosh Boys

Cosh attacks were a regular part of the post-war landscape. Such weapons were used in the brutal assault on the stationmaster of St Rollox Station in Glasgow, in which three young men escaped with the considerable sum of £1,100.[30] In the same year, during a house-breaking attempt in Wallington, Surrey, one of the criminals said to a victim, 'Sit down on that chair, lady, and keep quiet, else we'll cosh you one.'[31] The term 'cosh boy' itself seems to have passed into widespread use in 1950, following a week-long series of articles under that name in the *Daily Herald*. Within a week or two of the series, it seemed as if the nation was suddenly knee-deep in cosh boys. The articles were trailed on the front page of the newspaper on 31 March 1950:

> One of the *Herald*'s best writers, Victor Thompson, was told to investigate the life of a typical 'cosh boy' – to inquire into his upbringing, his early criminal exploits, and all the steps which led him to a heavy prison sentence. Thompson has visited the haunts of young gangsters; talked to probation officers, and detectives; found the answers to the question, 'What turns an ordinary lad into a thug?'[32]

The series ran in five parts between 3 April and 8 April; by 18 April, the *Lincolnshire Echo* – fearful that crime and gangster movies were encouraging young people to break the law – was asking Gainsborough Studios film star Jean Kent, 'Do

"Toughies" Make or Reform the Cosh Boys?' Despite the headline, she unsurprisingly concluded that they did not, saying, 'films are often unjustifiably blamed as a bad influence, whereas they frequently do a tremendous amount of good'.[33] A week later, a headline in the *Sheffield Telegraph* combined the new term with an echo of wartime gang styles: 'Zoot Suit Cosh Boys Find Pace Too Hot'.[34] Meanwhile, in Chelsea, a victim attacked by a cosh memorably described their attacker as 'a man of the spiv errand-boy type – a rat with dark, haunting eyes'.[35]

In truth, the term was already in the air that spring, as parliament debated then finally rejected the reintroduction of the flogging and birching of offenders. The *Sunday Pictorial* published their own examination of the cosh menace on 19 March, under the front-page headline 'A BOY THUG TALKS'. Billed as 'the frankest revelation yet published about the brutal thuggery which flourishes in London and other big cities', it consisted of a substantial interview subtitled 'A "Cosh Kid" Confesses', in which a seventeen-year-old used much the same justifications for carrying a weapon as those put forward by some Londoners of a similar age today. 'It gives me a hoarse laugh to read how some people can't understand why a kid should carry a razor or a cosh in London. They just don't know the facts of life.' The reason, he claimed, was 'sheer self-defence':[36]

> Although I had run away once from the approved school [a residential home for young offenders], I was allowed occasional home leave like the others, and me and a chap called Duke, wearing our Sunday greys, went to a café he knew in the Mile End Road, London. He said he had friends there. They were all older than us, about twenty or twenty-two, and very smart in their birds-eye suits and long draped jackets ... They asked us to join in a gang battle which was

going to take place in Victoria Park, East London, against the Elephant and Castle boys and the Brickies. Some of them had bicycle chains which they were sharpening on a grindstone. Held by a handle taken from a lavatory or something similar, these bike chains with each link sharpened, make a very nasty weapon. Other blokes had coshes – bits of rubber hose filled with lead – or razors and brass knuckle-dusters.[37]

Several of these characteristics would feature in many descriptions of Teddy boys, both in real life and fiction: the long draped jackets, a fondness for improvised weapons, and the rivalry between East End and South London gangs, with mass fights in agreed locations.

That Dreadful Instrument

A leader column in the *Leicester Daily Mercury* in April 1950 called on the Home Secretary to take action to deal with 'the growing numbers of cosh-boys and other young hooligans, who are now resorting to attacks on girls and women'.[38] In the same week, a magistrate in Hull told a young offender in the dock that they were 'heading to be a cosh boy'.[39] This might sound like classic folk-devil hysteria, but the statistics tend to support the idea that urban streets were less safe than in previous decades.

Figures presented on 23 March by Viscount Simon during a House of Lords debate on urban violent crime suggested that the situation had worsened since before the Second World War, but if the conflict had been a major contributing factor, it was unclear why the equivalent statistics for such crimes had shown a drop after the First World War. Overall, the number of such offences had multiplied very significantly since 1914. In that year,

Simon explained, 'the number of robberies with violence known to the police of the whole country was 178', yet by 1948 – the most recent year for which figures were available – the national figure was 1,101. Other types of crime, for instance burglary, followed a similar upward trend. There had been 1,612 in 1914:

> But what is the number of burglaries known to the police in a single year now? The number is 4,174. When you come to other classes, such as housebreaking or shopbreaking, it is still worse. Therefore the public are perfectly right, even though they may not know these statistics, in feeling that there has been a most prodigious increase in the class of crime which we are considering . . . It is no consolation, of course, for the man or woman who has been stunned by what is called a 'cosh' and robbed, to be told: 'We shall endeavour to increase the number and improve the quality of boys' clubs.'[40]

The spectre of the cosh was adopted as a fashionable issue by many public figures, and remained one for several years, until it was conveniently replaced by the next moral panic: the Teddy boy. Despite their seeming ubiquity, mentions of cosh boys dwindled to a trickle after 1953 – both in the media and in parliament – before dying out completely.

The terms spiv, hooligan, cosh boy, Teddy boy were convenient shorthand for commentators, politicians and satirists, but cosh boys, by their very nature, were carrying and often using dangerous and potentially lethal weapons. The name Teddy boy was used to denote a huge range of types and behaviour – from schoolboys who liked the cut of the clothes, to hardened, tooled-up wide boys who were no strangers to violence and lawbreaking that had also adopted the new fashion. For the moment, though, there were plays to be written, films to be made, and newspapers to be sold.

Birch the Brute!

There were plenty of suggestions of what should be done about the perceived upsurge of bad behaviour among teenagers, like the one from Mr D. H. Stott, who had worked at a reform school for four years, and wrote to the *Daily Mirror* claiming that 'a new national sport of gravel pit climbing is the answer to the cosh boy'.[41] Why had no one thought of this before?

Alternative proposals for channelling youthful energy included involving them in boxing matches as a regulated and healthy diversion from street fighting and criminal activities. The *Daily Mirror* were happy to publicise a success story of this kind with an article in February 1950 under an insipidly cheery headline that might have come from a parish magazine:

AND A JOLLY GOOD TIME IS HAD BY ALL

There's a lot of fighting going on just now inside the London Federation of Boys' Clubs, but nobody is at all unhappy about it. For it's all confined to the boxing ring. A big tournament is in progress, and by the time the finals at the Royal Albert Hall are reached on February 27 about 200 separate bouts will have been decided.[42]

With the benefit of hindsight, the following sentence sounds a different note, especially taken in conjunction with the accompanying photograph of a serious-faced eighteen-year-old landing a punch on his opponent: 'Here R. Kray slings a hay-making right in his battle with J. H. Prime'.[43] From the picture it appears to be Ronnie, but equally might be Reggie; with identical twins it is hard to be sure. Either way, within five years they conclusively proved to the East End and the police that they no longer needed to rely on the London Federation of Boys' Clubs to provide outlets for their violent impulses.

Some people at the time were less impressed by the idea of sports-based cures for delinquency, and favoured instead a return to the hands-on approach of the good old days. The *Western Daily Press* printed a letter in March 1950 entitled 'Birch the Brute!' from a reader signing herself 'A Woman Realist', for whom only the sternest measures would suffice: 'When caught these criminals should at least be birched – and a taste of their own cosh also would be beneficial! They should be sentenced to not less than five years hard labour for a first offence, and birched at intervals while serving sentence.'[44]

Many people in other cities appear to have shared this view. When the journalist Eric Bradshaw from the *Nottingham Journal* conducted a survey in the streets of his city, he found that 'at present there would be ten votes in favour of corporal punishment to every one in opposition'. He also noticed that the women he spoke to were more in favour of it than the men; fifty-eight-year-old Mrs Lillian Jebbett said, 'The thugs and hooligans are frightened of a good hiding. They should be flogged good and hard. I'd like to do it myself.'[45]

Still, through it all, at least one victim of a cosh burglar seems to have kept his sense of humour. Roland Aubrey Field returned to his flat in St John's Wood to find that burglars had made off with furs, silverware and clothing worth around £1,000 – far more than a manual worker would earn in a year. He and his friends had been to a live recording of the popular BBC radio comedy series *Take It from Here*, and, as Mr Field remarked laconically of his loss, 'We were seeing "Take It from

Here" while the thieves were taking it from here.' Despite this, he had at least gained a souvenir: 'We found a beautifully made cosh made of heavy wood, mounted with lead and bound in pigskin, with a pigskin handle, which the thieves had dropped.'[46]

Luring Young People into Pagan Ways

Having hit a nerve with his series of articles about cosh boys for the *Daily Herald* in April 1950, Victor Thompson embarked upon a further investigative series for the paper a month later. Titled 'The Rising Generation', it attempted to give a balanced picture of the nation's youth. Appearing every day during the final week of May, it was trailed on their front page as follows: 'In Britain there are nearly 5,000,000 boys and girls between the ages of 13 and 18. What problems do these teen-agers face? What are their values and ambitions and beliefs?'[47]

Of particular interest was an article titled 'Bop Boy', which gave an impression of a typical music-loving teenage boy called Jimmie. These were the immediate pre-rock'n'roll days in Britain, and Thompson seemed unclear as to what kind of sounds appealed to the type of teenager under discussion:

> Twenty-five years ago it was jazz and the Charleston. Now it is bop and jive which are said to be luring young people into pagan ways. I have asked experts to give me definitions of bop music and jive dancing. All they can say is that the first is a highly technical form of jazz developed by coloured musicians, and the second a form of dancing in which rhythmic impulses are freely indulged.[48]

Thompson describes the clothes worn by teenagers of both

sexes at a large dance hall, and in each case the inspiration, like the music, has come from across the Atlantic:

> Some of the girls wear 'Sloppy Joe's' (loose-fitting sweaters – an American idea) and some of the lads wear flowery shirts outside their trousers (another American idea). Most of the dancers, however, are in tidy street-clothes. Jimmie wears a suit of rather bright brown. His shoes gleam, and so does his hair.[49]

Jimmie went to dances in order to meet girls, but as he explained to the journalist, he kept to himself most of the evening, because if you spent all your time with just one partner, then being the boy 'you have to buy her coffee'. Not only that, he concluded, 'you probably have to pay her bus fare home unless she lives near. And you're probably mug enough to date her up for the next time and pay her admission.'[50]

Perhaps the most valuable part of this article is the insight it gives into the financial world of such a teenager, who at seventeen has been working for two years but still lives at home and is awaiting the call-up for National Service. He earns £4. 15s. a week in a bicycle shop doing repairs and renovations. Out of that, he gives his parents 35 shillings for his keep, and puts away another £1 towards clothes and holidays. Ten shillings a week goes on cigarettes, another ten shillings on dancing, and three shillings and sixpence for visits to the cinema. This kind of pattern would have been reasonably typical of many Teds a year or so later.

Lord of the Teeming City Streets

The play *Cosh Boy* opened at the Embassy Theatre on 17 April 1951, with James Kenney in the title role.[51] As with the plot of

James Dean's landmark film *Rebel Without A Cause* (1955) – whose UK poster tagline was 'The Bad Boy from a Good Family' – the twist was that Kenney's character Roy Walsh, variously described in the press as a 'vicious delinquent'[52] and 'a seventeen-year-old horror',[53] came from a respectable background.

'Born of a war-widowed mother into a world shorn of ideals,' *The Stage*'s journalist began a breathlessly positive first-night review, 'lord of the teeming city streets at 17, king of the pintable saloon, pursuer of adolescent girls, gambler, robber with violence and the brains of the local gang... For him and his like the law, robbed of birch and "cat", has no terrors.'[54] The play had a successful run, and came to the attention of the British film industry, who were always keen to adapt works that had gained some publicity or notoriety. Romulus Films acquired the rights to *Cosh Boy*,[55] and hired thirty-two-year-old Lewis Gilbert as director, who would later make the key 1960s films *Alfie* (1966) and *You Only Live Twice* (1967). Shot at Riverside Studios in Hammersmith, the film's budget was decidedly modest, but the technical crew and production team were first-rate; many of them would soon be involved with the worldwide success of the Hammer film studio twenty-five miles further down the Thames at Bray.[56] There was even a twenty-four-year-old focus puller – uncredited onscreen – by the name of Nicolas Roeg, with a hugely distinguished directing career ahead of him.

For the title role, the producers of the film looked no further than James Kenney, the star of the stage play. However, for the part of his glamorous teenage girlfriend they chose Joan Collins, who had been making a name for herself during the previous year. Indeed, in early 1953 she was the proud recipient of three separate awards: 'Forces No. 1 Pin-up; Best Bad Girl in British Films; and Miss Press Clippings, 1952.'[57] The *Daily Herald* felt that she was 'lush and insisting,'[58] while the *Daily Mirror* called her a 'saucy and sexy lass'.[59] How could the cinema-going public resist?

The film of *Cosh Boy* is a valuable record of how a teenage youth gang was represented on screen immediately before the label 'Teddy boy' took hold. None of them are shown in Edwardian clothes; their trousers are not narrow, but the jackets are relatively long, as is the hair, which is also well-greased. James Kenney's character, Roy, obsessively pulls out a comb and runs it back through his blond locks in a manner reminiscent of Jerry Lee Lewis half a decade later. When Kenney dresses up to try to impress Joan Collins, he wears a black shirt and narrow tie – as opposed to the much wider 'kipper' version favoured by 1940s spivs – and his new suit creates a stir when he meets the rest of the gang in a local pub:

> Gang member: 'Blimey, get a load of the whistle and flute.'
> Roy: 'Like the drape? Latest cut.'
> Gang member: 'Very nice. When do you go for the next fitting?'
> [laughter]

Here we have clothes-conscious working-class teenagers who hang out on bomb-sites, jive to what sounds like insipid jazz at the youth club dances, and cosh old ladies in the streets for whatever loose change might be in their handbags.

All things considered, the film was a well-acted, enjoyable B-movie which hardly set out to portray its central character as anything other than an ungrateful wretch who betrays or abuses virtually everyone around him, as the film critic Andrew Weir noted in one of the few even-handed reviews published at the time:

It is an indication of the sound acting ability of young James Kenney, who plays the title role in 'Cosh Boy' (Ritz), that he makes us impatient for the moment when he receives the thrashing he richly deserves. By that time, he has directed assaults on two aged women, robbed his own grandmother, left his girl (Joan Collins) in the lurch and broken his foolishly fond mother's heart.[60]

A Lecherous Young Coxcomb

Nevertheless, the intention of the picture did little to stop the chorus of complaints which greeted *Cosh Boy*'s release. The *Daily Herald,* which had helped to whip up the cosh boy frenzy in the first place, called the picture 'shallow and violent'.[61] The *Manchester Guardian* dismissed it in just a few lines, saying that it 'slurs over the essential nastiness of its subject and reduces it to cheap sensationalism and equally cheap and inappropriate humour.'[62] Meanwhile, *The Observer*'s regular critic, C. A. Lejeune, found it 'sketchily written and undistinguished', not to mention 'peculiarly distasteful', summarising the plot as 'a record of the activities, and eventual arrest, of a lecherous young coxcomb with little education and fewer principles and guts.'[63]

Shortly after its London opening, the Watch Committee of the borough council in Hull, responsible for matters of policing, banned *Cosh Boy* from being shown in their city,[64] presumably on the grounds that it would spark copycat violence among the young and impressionable; over the next few months many other local authorities followed suit, including Birmingham,[65] Coventry,[66] Hove,[67] Nottingham,[68] and the whole of Warwickshire[69] and East Suffolk.[70] This was an overreaction to a crime story that was no more shocking than many gangster pictures shown in British cinemas that year. However, this episode of censorship was trivial compared to the sustained hysteria that would seize the municipal moral guardians across the country in 1956 who imposed blanket bans on the Bill Haley film, *Rock Around the Clock*.

4

COMMON ASSAULT

A Group of Chaps at the Bandstand

It all started with a suit. A Teddy boy suit. Not a vague approximation, but the real thing.

During the following half-century, the simple act of walking past a group of teenagers while wearing unusual clothing styles and being insulted or physically attacked on the strength of it became a regular, if tiresome, rite of passage. This was usually nothing more than a few catcalls; childish banter, low-level bullying, nothing serious.

Ronald Coleman was a fifteen-year-old boy who had recently left school, where he had got into trouble for carrying and using a sharpened paperknife with a home-made sheath. His name alone would delight the press: Hollywood star Ronald Colman was a regular leading man in films of the time.

In the summer of 1952, while still at school, Ronald had appeared in front of magistrates along with six others charged with being among a gang of twenty youths on Clapham Common 'who persistently pushed and abused people who got in their way'. Now, on the evening of 2 July 1953, Coleman took exception to the remarks of some other youths on the common, setting in motion a rapid chain of events that left seventeen-year-old John Beckley dead of multiple stab wounds, and Matthew Chandler, eighteen, injured.[1]

Clapham Common murder victim John Beckley, 1953

Like many other teenagers that summer evening, Coleman had gone to Clapham Common to watch the dancing at the open-air bandstand and meet friends. He was wearing what was later described in court as 'an Edwardian suit'. Near the bandstand he met a girl he knew, Eileen Brannon, and together they walked a short distance to the Temperance Fountain at the top northern corner of the grassland, 150 yards west of Clapham Common Underground Station. Here they encountered four other teenagers sitting on the benches nearby, as one of those four later testified at the Old Bailey: 'Matthew Frederick Chandler (18), a bank clerk, of Long Lane, Bermondsey, said in evidence that he went to Clapham Common with [John] Beckley, John Ryan, and Brian Carter. They were sitting on two seats with their feet resting on the seats opposite. People could not have walked between them.'[2]

There had perhaps been some low-level provocation in forcing passers-by to detour around them rather than walk through, but nothing serious. The prosecutor Maxwell Turner then went into some detail with Chandler about exactly what happened:

Turner: 'Did [Coleman] speak to you?'
Chandler: 'Yes. He asked to come through. Ryan asked him to walk round. No one else said anything. He left us and walked towards a group of other chaps at the bandstand.'
Turner: 'What did you do?'
Chandler: 'We got up and started to move away towards a drinking fountain.'[3]

The lads evidently felt that Coleman had taken this previous exchange as an invitation to a fight, and had gone back to the bandstand to round up other members of his gang. However,

Eileen Brannon gave a different version of events, testifying that the youths on the benches had said something far more provocative to Coleman, mocking his Edwardian clothing, swearing at him and calling him, as the papers coyly reported it, 'a flash .....'[4]

Things escalated fast. According to Chandler's account, he and his three friends were attacked from behind at the fountain, after which they ran away in the face of superior numbers. He and Beckley succeeded in reaching a 137 bus which had pulled in at the stop on Clapham Common North Side, in front of a Georgian building called the Hostel of God. They jumped onto the open platform at the rear of the vehicle, but three of those following them managed to do the same and pulled them back onto the pavement. Chandler estimated that a further three then joined in the attack, with two of them concentrating on him, and the rest on John Beckley. When the scuffle was over, Beckley was fatally wounded, yet still managed to find his way about seventy yards east along the pavement, only to collapse in front of a 1930s mansion block. He was taken to Bolingbroke Hospital, but died soon afterwards.

King of the Common

That Ronald Coleman's choice of clothing provided the catalyst for these attacks was explicitly spelled out at the trial in the kind of detail more generally reserved for the fashion pages, as the *Daily Herald* explained:

> It was what was described as an 'Edwardian' suit that led to the death of Beckley and to Coleman's appearance on a murder charge ... The suit consisted of tight, peg-top trousers and a closely-fitting jacket with a high neckline buttoned right to the top. Coleman was wearing it on the

night of June 2 [*sic* – it was actually July]. And it was after he thought someone had passed an insulting remark about it that the fight broke out in which Beckley received 12 stab wounds.[5]

Six people were arrested and charged, and even though the person eventually convicted of murder for the offence was twenty-year-old Michael Davies, the press spent most of that summer focusing on Coleman, the alleged leader of the gang. A lengthy *Daily Mirror* feature article of 23 September had the headline 'COLEMAN WAS "KING OF THE COMMON" TO 40 THUGS'. In the event, though, the supposed ringleader and instigator of all the trouble was given just a short prison sentence:

> It seems much quieter on Clapham Common now since the night of the fights in which John Ernest Beckley was stabbed to death. But it is a deceptive calm for in the bombed buildings and streets surrounding the grassy common are sordid collections of weapons, cunningly concealed. They belong to a gang of thirty to forty young thugs of which Ronald Coleman was a leader ... a 'King of the Common' when he was not yet sixteen years old. The weapons are ready to be lifted by the pack and swung silently into action if 'the foreigners', rival gangs from the Elephant and Castle, Brixton and Peckham come looking for trouble. But Coleman will not be there if they do. He has gone to gaol for nine months. That was the sentence passed at the Old Bailey yesterday on the boy who left school only a year ago, the boy who, dressed in his Edwardian suit with drainpipe trousers, started a series of running fights which cost a life.[6]

It is not hard to see why the press latched onto the story, given the elements involved: a confrontation between rival members of distinctively attired teenage gangs, with no shortage of glamorous girlfriends testifying in court or packing the visitors' benches at the Central Criminal Court. Best of all, the defendants were known by a short and headline-friendly gang name, although it was not until the court case was well underway that it was made public on the front page of the *Daily Express*. Indeed, despite there being six gang members on trial, it was Coleman alone whose photo was chosen to accompany the front-page report, with a banner caption that called him 'The Problem Boy of England'.

RONNIE-THE-MASHER GETS 9 MONTHS – Leader of 'The Edwardians'

'Cleared of Murder', said the headline, and the paper highlighted his choice of clothing and hairstyle: 'He wore a grey well-pleated, well-waisted, half-belted Edwardian jacket with stovepipe trousers, and he arranged for a quiff of hair to fall forward. Then he went across Clapham Common (twenty-two acres in South-West London) as Ronnie-the-Masher – ready to challenge comment and spoiling for a fight.'[7]

Here for the first time the importance of the correct hairstyle was stressed – a quiff, rather than the brushed-back-and-plastered-down look which had prevailed for some decades. Completing the rebellious teenager picture, there was also a musical element, since the reason these teenagers had gathered on the common was either to go dancing at the bandstand, or stand around and watch. As for their gang name, the headline might have called them Edwardians, but as the reporter revealed, their female acquaintances had other ideas: 'Some of his followers – four of them were jailed with him yesterday – dressed like him. They became "The Edwardians" or – as their girl friends preferred it – the "Teddy Boys."[8]

Within months, that simple name was being applied more generally, and by the following year had become a catch-all term for a wide variety of boys – and a variety of wide boys.

How to Dress, How to Talk, How to Act

So there it was. A dress code, some hairstyle tips, and a name for the new movement – all in one package. Just in case the new term had not sunk in, the paper repeated it twice more on the inside pages as they ran through the history of this supposed youthful gang lord, and also linked his group with another activity for which they would acquire a persistent reputation: 'Creating trouble in cinemas was a favourite diversion for the Teddy Boys.'[9]

Coleman was reported to have stabbed a boy at school with a nail file, and on another occasion jabbed a cinema attendant in the face with the jagged edge of a broken piece of pottery. Vicious behaviour, but as a role model, he was hardly the Al Capone figure some of the papers tried to make him out to be. Even so, if you were a teenager that year, there was enough information in that issue of the *Express* alone to provide the inspiration for a new identity. Edwardian clothes did not make you any more or less likely to wind up on a murder charge, but the sense of belonging they conferred on young people who were looking for a way to distinguish themselves from straight society was undeniable.

As Iggy Pop said in a 1977 radio interview,[10] recalling his early 1960s lifestyle influences, 'There was a time when you could go see the Rolling Stones and learn something about how to dress, and how to talk, and how to act, and how to dance.' This, of course, was in the days when Mick Jagger and his fellow band members were still regarded by the establishment as something of a threat. Ray Coleman wrote an article in March 1963 called 'Would You Let Your Sister Go with a Rolling Stone?'[11] and Maureen Cleve in the *Evening Standard* raised the stakes two months later with another, headlined 'But Would You Let Your Daughter Marry One?'[12] However, by 1966 Charles Hamblett was wryly pointing out in *The Tatler* that 'people who a few months ago were asking "Would you let your daughter marry a Rolling Stone?" would now gladly forfeit a weekend of golf to have Mick Jagger at Penelope's coming-out dance'.[13] So swiftly are most youth revolutions accepted by society; by contrast, more than six decades after they first appeared, the Teds have yet to become the darlings of the old-school-tie brigade.

Later youth movements evolved more gradually: the mods slowly emerged from the loose grouping known as modernists as the fifties gave way to the sixties; skinheads had their roots in the mod movement; British punks arrived from a collision between the Detroit guitar attack of the Stooges, the hard-edged Canvey R&B of Dr Feelgood, the trash assault of the New York Dolls, CBGB bands like the Ramones and a solid chunk of UK glam rock, mixed in with the zipped-up spray-paint aesthetic of the Clash and the wildly overpriced bondage gear sold as a provocative art statement by McLaren and Westwood, which few teenagers could afford.

For the Teds, however, there was one flashpoint, one violent evening that projected them onto the front pages and set the pattern for most of the media coverage they have received ever since. Ironically, two of the greatest songwriters to emerge in the rock'n'roll era, Jerry Lieber and Mike Stoller, would write a rocking R&B vocal group tune in 1954 called 'Riot in Cell Block

#9', which describes a fictional prison riot on 'July 2, 1953', coin-cidentally the date of the Clapham Teddy boy murder.

Notorious Gangs of Hardened Thugs

In the blizzard of publicity which the case attracted in the media and in parliament – from the night of the killing up until the conviction and death sentence handed down to twenty-year-old Clapham labourer Michael John Davies on 22 October[14] – it is striking that during the first two months of reports no one mentioned Edwardian clothing or the gang name, 'Teddy boys'. Until that term appeared on the front page of the *Daily Express*,[15] this had largely been treated simply as a shocking murder in which the age of the participants was a matter for concern. As for the location, although a London park might sound tranquil, according to a lurid report published a fortnight after the murder in the popular Sunday newspaper *The People*, it was apparently a crime hotspot:

> Clapham Common lies in the heart of 'little Chicago'. It is a place where boy gangsters gather to recruit 'new blood' . . . Local opinion blames the long gang 'tradition' of the area. Four notorious gangs of hardened thugs ruled the roost in South London until a few years ago – the Brick Boys, the Walworth Road Team, the Brixton Mob and, above all, the Elephant Gang, who made the Elephant and Castle district the bane of the police.[16]

By way of illustration, an unremarkable photograph of some smartly dressed teenage girls standing under the trees in this alleged mobster location was made to appear sinister with the following caption: 'At Clapham Common's open-air dances young girls like these can see boy gangsters take the floor with their "molls." It is a sight that should be kept from these innocent eyes.'[17]

So there you have it – watching a group of teenagers dance at a bandstand can deprave and corrupt. By these standards, it is surprising that 90 per cent of the population did not wind up in prison by the age of twenty. Maybe they should have stayed in and watched television – although many poorer families would not have been able to afford the high cost of a set. What delights was the nation's only TV channel offering on the evening of the murder? There was coverage of the day's tennis from Wimbledon until 7 p.m., followed by an adaptation of a French play about Joan of Arc. Then came a half-hour panel game called *Down You Go!* and, at 9.45, *Portrait of a Rat-Catcher*, described as follows in that week's edition of the *Radio Times*: 'Every night Bill Dalton of Peckham catches rats in the basements of West End stores and hotels, as his father and grandfather did before him. In this programme he tells of the rat world he knows.'[18]

Small wonder some of a restless teenage audience opted instead for an evening of dancing and flirting in the park, despite the supposed threat to their moral wellbeing.

A Pretty State of Affairs

On the face of it, it might seem strange that an everyday teenage fight – which might just as easily have ended in a few punches rather than murder – received so much attention, especially at a time when it was sharing media attention with the psychopathic John Reginald Christie burying bodies in and around his house in Notting Hill, or the calculated brutality of the man who became known as the Towpath Murderer.

Yet before passing sentence of death on Michael Davies

for the Clapham Common murder, the judge suggested that teenage killings like this were very much out of the normal run of crime he would encounter. As the *Daily Mirror* put it:

> Before retiring, the jury had heard Mr Justice Hilbery reviewing the events of that night of music and dancing – and of death – on the common where thousands of South London couples love to stroll. The judge said that Davies and his companions after attacking young Beckley chased him and dragged him off a bus. Then they all closed around him, and in the fight that followed, he sank to the ground with nine wounds. 'That', exclaimed the judge, 'happened on Clapham Common in this year, 1953, after our young people have been put through public education. A pretty state of affairs it reveals![19]

Today, when stabbings in London have become a tragic commonplace, this story might have struggled to stay in the news more than a few days. In 2019, police figures indicated that '41 per cent of those being caught for knife crimes across London's boroughs are now aged between 15 and 19',[20] and on 24 April of the same year *The Independent* carried a news report that there had been seven different stabbings in the capital in seven hours.[21] On New Year's Eve in 2019, the *Daily Mail* noted that London's murder toll for that year was the highest in a decade:[22] 147 people had been killed, more than half of whom were stabbed. Even in the spring of 2021, when London was still under strict Covid lockdown measures, young people's frequent deaths at the hands of other youngsters with knives remained a regular enough occurrence; at the end of March a twenty-three-year-old was even stabbed to death in Croydon after a fight broke out at a vigil he was attending in tribute to another knife victim who had died several weeks earlier.[23] At the close of the year, the Metropolitan Police announced that 2021 was the worst ever for teenage homicides.[24]

Measured against these grim statistics, the London of 1953 seems a very different place. And what of a teenage stabbing near Clapham Common underground station, such as the one which gave the Teddy boys their name and occupied the news media for a good six months? By grim coincidence, another took place on 29 March 2019, when a forty-year-old man was stabbed to death roughly two hundred yards away from the site of the 1953 murder.[25] A nineteen-year-old and a twenty-one-year-old were eventually charged with murder. Whereas the 1953 Clapham killing occupied front pages for the better part of six months, in the capital today, fatal knifings are a weekly or even a daily occurrence, and the latest headlines replace the old with frightening speed.

The Edwardian Suits They Affected

The new year replaced the old, and as seems to be the way of things, there was a range of disturbing stories on the front page of the *Daily Herald* on 22 January 1954. 'The war goes on – how long?' asked the paper about a conflict in Vietnam that would drag on for another two decades. In America, President Eisenhower declared that the US should expand production of atomic weapons, while in Britain, the War Office announced that three British soldiers had been abducted and murdered in the Canal Zone in Egypt, with another two missing.

Despite these concerns, the paper's main headline that day brought joy to one London mother from Clapham. Mrs Maud Davies was pictured looking anxiously at the camera. Her twenty-one-year-old son Michael, awaiting execution on

2 February in Wandsworth Prison for the Clapham Common murder, had been granted a reprieve by the Home Secretary, Sir David Maxwell Fyfe:

> Michael Davies, first lieutenant of the 'Teddy Boys' gang (so called because of the Edwardian suits they affected) reached Wandsworth via two trials – the jury disagreed at the first – for the stabbing of 17-year-old John Beckley last year.[26]

In the six months since the killing, the local name of their gang had spread far and wide; in the coming year it would be established as a recognised term, both nationally and even internationally.

The Teddy boy look had spread across the nation by the time Davies received his reprieve. At the start of 1954, the regular dance-hall correspondent of the *Liverpool Echo* complained of 'the exaggerated Edwardian cult, which, in the closing months of the old year, brought dancing into disfavour with so many',[27] while in Edinburgh, a meeting of ballroom proprietors stated that 'all persons dressed in pipe-stem trousers, draped jackets and crêpe rubber soles should be refused admission to all dance-halls, as such garb usually distinguishes a trouble maker'.[28] This caution was sometimes justified, as in the case of a woman from Wandsworth who was punched and kicked on a train in February outside Bromley by a man wearing an Edwardian suit – although what role the thug's choice of clothing had to do with this vicious attack is difficult to say.[29] Nevertheless, these fashions had clearly spread a long way from their well-heeled West End origins.

Adolescent Gangsters

The association of this style of dress with anti-social and criminal behaviour was the last thing Savile Row and their wealthier clients needed, and some in the business began to cautiously back away from the trend they had previously been so keen to encourage. Marjorie Proops, reporting from the Paris fashion catwalks, noted that top designer Jacques Fath, while attempting to revive whalebone corsets for women, was still dressed in 'an Edwardian suit with drainpipe trousers',[30] but the orthodox London tailoring view as expressed in the fashion magazine *Men's Wear* was clearly one of resentment at the attention paid in newspaper reports of the Clapham Common murder trial to the clothing of the accused. They claimed that 'the garment bore small resemblance to those known to the trade by this name', and went on to blithely state that 'it is not likely to have an adverse effect on the influence that true Edwardian clothing has had on current trends, but it is likely to put an end to the exaggerated outfits ordered by some young men.'[31] Meanwhile Gordon Beckles, writing in the *Tatler & Bystander*, flatly denied any British influence whatever on Teddy boy clothes:

> One of the silliest synonyms encouraged by Fleet Street recently is 'Edwardian' when what is really meant is 'young thug'. What in the name of St Sartorius has the wearing of narrow trousers and long jackets by adolescent gangsters got to do with the era of King Edward VII?[32]

Evidently, all those pictures of Edward VII dressed in what can only be described as 'narrow trousers and long jackets' must have been cleverly faked. In any case, an article in the same magazine a few weeks earlier had suggested that this particular Savile Row fashion was already dying away:

THE EDWARDIAN TREND IS NOW A TRACE

The Edwardian revival has left its traces upon the narrower trousers and in a continuing affection for the collared waistcoat. Extremes of eccentricity are frowned upon with as much discretion as a good employee may permit himself.[33]

In other words, the rich could continue to be as eccentric as they pleased in matters of dress, but everyone else should beware of rocking the boat.

Where Have All the Cosh Boys Gone?

The Teds had arrived, but cosh boys were not quite yet on the endangered species list, as the play and film which they had inspired still toured the provinces. Indeed there were also sightings in other new theatrical offerings such as *The Maniac* by Jean Metaxas, currently delighting patrons in January 1954 at the Theatre Royal, Ashton-Under-Lyne. Its title was graphic enough, but the play had originally been entitled *Sex Crime*, and its unlikely plot was memorably summarised by a critic from *The Stage*:

[*The Maniac*] tells the story of an apparently high-principled Charing Cross-road bookseller who turns, overnight, into murderer, perjuror, and sex maniac. Albert Barnes, the philanthropic bookseller, suddenly wraps a cord round his unpleasant mother-in-law's neck and chokes the life out of her. Albert's cosh-boy brother-in-law, Jed Wills, walks in at that moment, and the bookseller pins the crime on him – thus killing two birds with one stone, for Albert already has eyes for Jed's girl-friend, Gloria. The plot thickens when

Ronnie, Albert's idiot son, takes a fancy to Gloria. The imbecile is eventually removed to Broadmoor accused of Gloria's murder, a crime actually committed by his father. Albert, presumably, finishes by taking over his offspring's cell in Broadmoor.[34]

Perhaps unsurprisingly, the reviewer concluded by offering his heartfelt sympathies to the cast for having to appear in such a play.

Meanwhile, in a foretaste of the reception which the film *Rock Around the Clock* would receive a couple of years later, a delegation of councillors, a probation officer and other local dignitaries in the Scottish town of Arbroath were invited by a cinema manager to a special showing of *Cosh Boy*. Rather than calling for a ban, they were of the opinion that it should be required viewing for all concerned parents, not to mention teenagers. 'The film is a good one,' said Provost J. K. Moir. 'It shows them the consequences which could so easily arise from what they think is "having a good time." It would probably do them more good than a talking to by a Magistrate. I have found that major crimes usually spring from small ones.'[35]

Despite this advice, the following month a mother told Scarborough magistrates that her son – one of two fourteen-year-olds charged with stealing four crates of empty mineral water bottles – had seen *Cosh Boy* and 'tried to live up to the part in the picture ever since'.[36] Her pleas fell on deaf ears and he was sent to a remand home. Such offences would likely have come as no surprise to Alan Dick, whose article surveying the lives of Britain's teenagers was published by the *Daily Herald* a week later, and for whom the silver screen was apparently some kind of gateway to depravity: 'A member of the Education Department of Birmingham University, a specialist in adolescent behaviour, was told by one girl: "Films teach you how to make love." By another: "I like to watch their technique." By a third: "They help me to learn the ways and means."[37]

And precisely what manner of nameless filth was luring people into cinemas that year? In 1954, the most successful film at the UK box office was the mainstream medical comedy, *Doctor in the House* – a film which even the archetypal guests at a vicarage tea-party would have struggled to find offensive – while the worldwide best-seller was *White Christmas*.

Glamorised by the Name of 'Edwardian' Or 'Teddy Boy'

In some instances, the newly identified Teddy boys were attracting attention for reasons far more serious than their choice of clothing. On 9 April 1954, towards the end of the evening's dancing at the Loretta Hall in Musselburgh, east of Edinburgh, a fight broke out among a group of young men which continued on the street after some were ejected by the management. A short while later eighteen-year-old Norry Henry was found on the pavement dying of stab wounds. The following day, John Robertson, aged seventeen, appeared in court charged with murder, dressed in the clothes he had worn the previous evening – 'drainpipe trousers, drape jacket, and a striped white nylon shirt without a tie'.[38] This came almost a year after the Clapham Common murder, but attracted considerably less media attention. Significantly, perhaps, the press did not use the phrase 'Teddy boy' in this case. However, two months later and 430 miles south, nineteen-year-old John Rowe was charged with attempted murder after stabbing ship's steward Peter Walsh twice in the chest and four times in the back with a commando knife while at a dance at the Royal Pier in Southampton. He appeared in the dock wearing 'a grey-coloured draped jacket with a dark blue velvet collar, and an open-neck white silk shirt'. The prosecuting counsel described him as 'the type which is today being glamorised by the name of "Edwardian" or "Teddy Boy"'. An article reporting this case was headlined unambiguously: '"TEDDY BOY" ON STABBING CHARGE'.[39]

In the short time between these two court cases, the name had reached a critical point in public awareness. Just as by the summer of 1977 few people in Britain were unaware that a new breed known as punk rockers had emerged, so it was with the Teds, and May 1954 stands out as the time when the phrase began to crop up repeatedly. Many people did not approve of them, but most knew who they were.

Their heads were fully above the parapet – and now it was open season.

5

WE ARE THE TEDS

Primitive Gang Life

It is hard to say exactly why the name 'Teddy boy' became ubiquitous around May 1954 – coincidentally the same month that the careers of both Elvis and Bill Haley went into overdrive – but this was the point at which the slow trickle of mentions which had occurred in the public sphere since the previous year suddenly became a flood, and the hitherto more common term 'Edwardian' rapidly gave ground. When the *Daily Mirror* used the phrase 'Teddy boys' on 11 May,[1] it was clear that their readership of all ages was presumed to be already conversant with it. Just to confirm that the bandwagon was well and truly rolling, a week or so later a new Max Bygraves comedy record entitled *Teddy Boy* began its journey into the Top Twenty, billed as 'a skit on the Edwardian gangs'.[2]

What had started as a purely London movement was now a well-established national phenomenon, to the extent that newspaper columnists, cartoonists and radio comedians used the Teds as convenient fodder for their daily trades. 'Who pays for those Teddy boy outfits?' demanded Lady Sheila Child. 'Do their parents produce the not-insignificant sums or has the Welfare State taken on yet another lighthearted commitment?'[3] If anyone among the young people that came into contact with the police or criminal justice system happened to be dressed in

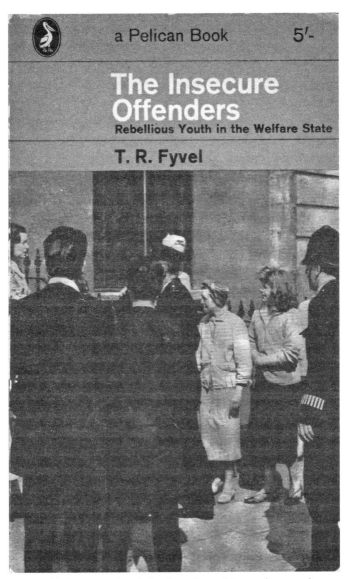

a Pelican Book   5/-

The Insecure Offenders
Rebellious Youth in the Welfare State

T. R. Fyvel

Teddy boys seen from behind in a Roger Mayne photograph
on the cover of T. R. Fyvel's 1961 survey of youth crime

that manner, their clothing tended to be singled out for attention as if it had been the sole motivating cause of their anti-social behaviour.

This accusation that Teds – and indeed teenagers in general – were being ungrateful in the face of enlightened social legislation and rising wages was quite often levelled at them by commentators of all hues and also by numerous members of the public in letters to newspapers. Indeed, the writer and journalist T. R. Fyvel, an old friend of George Orwell, published *The Insecure Offenders*, a study of juvenile crime, in 1961, just as the Teddy boy era was drawing to a close. Its subtitle, *Rebellious Youth in the Welfare State*, carried the implication that those growing up after the war were somehow a different breed from those that came before, benefitting from hitherto unknown advantages such as the National Health Service and free orange juice. The cover of the 1964 paperback edition of his book carried a photograph of a London street scene by Roger Mayne featuring several policemen in uniform, and two easily recognisable Teddy boys with 'DA' (standing for 'duck's arse') haircuts. Youth fashion had moved on considerably by that point, but Mayne's image reflected the book's contents, a great deal of which concerned what the author referred to as 'the Teddy boy problem'. He clearly seems to be using the name as a shorthand for the teenage population who fell foul of the law:

Even at the peak of the movement the number of Teddy boys in the Greater London area did not exceed a top figure of 30,000 (some observers thought it only half or a third of this figure), and most of these spent probably most of their time in boredom rather than activity. Nevertheless, the net result of their arrival was that lawlessness was going up. In spite of the change to Welfare State, Britain was more lawless in 1955 than in 1935, and above all among juveniles and young adults this lawlessness showed some definite new features.[4]

That's *all* youth crime between 1935 and 1955, even though Teds didn't exist for the first eighteen years of that timespan, and the terms of reference are so wide as to include literally anyone of the right age who threw a brick through a window, regardless of what they were wearing. By the same token, the percentage of the population who owned a motor car was significantly higher in 1955 than twenty years earlier, so perhaps the Teds were responsible for the increase in traffic congestion as well.

As for what might have encouraged them into such 'lawlessness', Fyvel laid some of the blame on the rise of the post-war consumer society, and on advertising for luring the working class into desiring things that they probably couldn't afford. Yet the 1920s had also been awash with advertising and desirable consumer goods, but they had largely been aimed at the more affluent sections of society, while minor members of the aristocracy regularly appeared in glossy magazine adverts extolling the benefit of soaps or cigarettes. Now, however, equally trivial 1950s examples were being held up as the sort of thing likely to send a working-class Teddy girl off the rails:

> Perhaps the worst fault of the current barrage of hedonist advertising and mass entertainment lies in the ambiguity of its message: is it true or not that use of a certain shampoo will lead a girl to romance and happiness? Youngsters exposed to this ambiguity do not necessarily commit more wrongs – but must find it harder to distinguish right and wrong.[5]

Added Cohesion

Shampoo may or may not have been the fast-track to a life of torrid romance, but this was nothing compared to the supposed evil influence attributed by some to the Edwardian clothing adopted by the young and impressionable, turning the wearer into a member of a new and more dangerous grouping, according to Fyvel:

> It was becoming clear that, within not more than two or three years, the primitive gang life of the 'submerged tenth' had under the impact of the Teddy-boy movement become more organized and sophisticated. The street corner was going out and superseded by the café as the centre of the new 'anti' groups. Secondly, the Teddy-boy fashions undoubtedly gave these groups an added cohesion. Some social workers saw this very early on as a new danger.[6]

So what exactly distinguished a Teddy boy suit from the clothing that everyone else was wearing? Ted Carroll, then a Dublin schoolboy, told me of the varieties he observed in that city in the mid-1950s:

> Well there were kind of two groups, if you like. There were the full-on Teds who wore properly made drape jackets and very narrow trousers, they wore suede shoes, and bootlace ties, and slim jim ties, and waistcoats were an important part of it, coloured like a maroon or a red or something like that. And then there were kind of lower-middle-class boys like me, who would have liked to have been Teddy boys but we were at school, so we didn't have the money, and it was too outrageous to go out and get a drape even if you could afford it. You'd have narrow trousers and slim

ties and maybe a coloured shirt and whatever you could do
in that direction. My friend Carl Killeen used to call them
'aspiring Teddy boys' [laughs], and that's what a lot of us
were, you know?[7]

Roger K. Burton, who set up the Contemporary Wardrobe
Collection in London in 1978 – an encyclopaedic resource of
original vintage street fashion, couture items and accessories –
kindly showed me a selection of rare examples of genuine 1950s
Teddy boy clothing in his archive and talked me through them:

> This is a New Edwardian one. It's pretty early. 'West End
> Clothiers, Leicester' – my home town. That's probably
> 1951, something like that. It's the beginning of that look.
> No flaps on the pockets, sloping pockets. It's just breaking
> the rules a little bit. I remember when we were doing the
> clothing for *Absolute Beginners*,[8] we interviewed an old Ted
> who was from Elephant and Castle. He used to talk about
> this little gang that used to roam around, and one of the
> guys – this was mid-fifties – used to wear a hunting pink
> jacket, and he actually had a hunting horn, and if there was
> a bit of trouble he'd blow on the horn.[9]

Next, Roger showed me an original black and white hounds-
tooth jacket from the late 1950s with a black velvet collar and
cuffs, velvet-edged pockets, and five buttons down the front:
'This is one of my favourites. Rosemans, who were an East End
tailor. If it was shorter, you'd think that was Italian. I quite like
that little feature as well, where they've picked out the leading
edge of the sleeve and just made it like a piping almost.'[10]

Teds were of course also readily identified by their trouser
style. Once rock'n'roll and the James Dean look – as seen in

Rebel Without a Cause (1956) – came along, English clothing companies began trying to come up with varieties of jeans – especially as US brands like Levi's were virtually unobtainable in the UK. However, according to Roger, their quality left a lot to be desired:

> This was a big Teddy boy thing, and we used to get tons of them back when we were dealing in old stock in the 1970s. These are ice blue jeans. There was a few companies that made them, and they were just like paper. They lasted about five minutes, about one wash, so consequently kids never used to wash them. You could either get ice blue, or you could get black with green stitching, with a big turn up, or the powder blue ones, sky blue. This is about 1955, '56. But what was great was the different colours that they used to come up with; bronze, you know, and there were like gold ones, and then of course the classic stripe that was emulating the City stripe. The other thing was, with the blue jeans, they couldn't get the dye right, and it was always this vile blue that they couldn't quite get right, it's got this pinky purple tinge to it.[11]

As for crêpe-soled suede shoes, Roger showed me a fore-runner of the classic creeper, brown suede with about an inch of sole with a slight heel, of a type that became popular in the late 1940s, and which Prince Philip was said to favour in the early years of the 1950s: 'He [Philip] was probably wearing what became known as The Playboy Shoe, they were so popular in those circles. You used to get them in leather as well. This particular shoe was made by various companies, and in the fifties leather and suede Playboys were incredibly popular.'[12]

The typical styles worn by working-class mid-1950s Teds

are visible in the wonderful photographs taken by Hugh Finnegan and his teenage friends in Portsmouth, many of which can be seen online. He paid fourteen guineas for his grey Ted suit, which was custom made in the city by Burton Montague in 1957, taking six weeks to complete.[13] Hugh's group of Teds took pictures of themselves out in the streets, in shelters on the seafront, enjoying the refreshments inside South Parade Pier, or at the local funfair. They also called in regularly to Jerome's Photography Studio on Commercial Road to pose for group portraits with cigarettes dangling from their lips, Jimmy Dean-style, sometimes jokingly clutching stray items like soft toys, cushions or footballs.

As for the Edwardian-influenced clothing they are wearing in these pictures, some jackets have velvet collars and cuffs, many do not, sometimes with multiple buttons but occasionally with just one, while a great many seem more like three-quarter-length coats. There are a fair few waistcoats, including a couple with what appear to be fake leopardskin trim at the pockets. Slim Jim ties are much in evidence, and there's the occasional bootlace tie, but others just wear an open-necked shirt. Shoes are a mixture of plain leather brogues, a few leather-topped creepers and the odd suede creeper. Socks, where visible, are usually garishly patterned in stripes or checks.

These were young people, easily identifiable by their choice of clothes, enjoying their teenage years before National Service conscription, marriage and other signs of adulthood took over. Each of them would have had to deal with the reputation that such outfits conferred upon the wearer in fifties Britain.

480 Teddy Boys Arrested in Six Months

In the House of Commons on 6 May 1954, Home Secretary Sir

David Maxwell Fyfe was asked 'what action he proposed to take to stamp out the hooliganism practised by young persons who in various parts of the country had banded themselves together into what were known as "Edwardian gangs" and who, by reason of their brutality, were becoming a menace to law-abiding citizens.' He replied that he was aware of the situation in London, and that 'the Commissioner of Police for the Metropolis assures me that the police are on the alert to suppress any tendency to hooliganism on the part of these youths'. He did however offer some precise figures about London youth offences in general: 'In the six months ended 31st March last, 24 persons under 21 years of age, and operating in groups of three or more, were arrested in the Metropolitan Police district for indictable offences involving violence against the person, and 456 youths were arrested for other offences involving rowdyism.'[14]

Despite the fact that this referred to the total figure for *all* youth crime during that period, the *Newcastle Evening Chronicle* managed to translate this into the sensationalist headline '480 Teddy Boys Arrested in Six Months';[15] the term was already a lazy shorthand that could be applied to any young troublemaker, regardless of their clothing.

By contrast, a surprisingly enlightened article appeared in the *Norwood News* the following day, based on talks with cinema operators in Balham and Tooting, South London. It was optimistically entitled '"Edwardian Toughs" Are Now Good Little Boys', with one manager flatly declaring, 'we've cleared this area of "Edwardian" toughs'. The anonymous author of the piece also struck a positive note, arguing that 'velvet collars and stove-pipe trousers are just another fashion', before examining the possible links between troublemakers and clothing styles:

It so happens that most criminals who come before the

courts are youngsters. And like most new fashions, the 'Edwardian' look attracts young people. It becomes palpably untrue to say that those who wear these unusual clothes are automatically those who would cosh old women and threaten taxi drivers by night. The 'Edwardian' fashion began in Savile-row. Guardees and men-about-town were the first to take it up. Does the fashion become tainted because suburbia liked it, too?[16]

Failure to Apply the Slipper

Adults were gradually becoming aware of the concept of the 'teenager' as a separate section of society – with their own attitudes, preferences, meeting places and styles of dress. By contrast, their parents could look back at their own teenage years and reflect that this had mostly involved an early transition at the age of fourteen into the world of adult work. This bore little resemblance to the choices available to many of their own children, and it is understandable if some of the older generation felt a mixture of resentment and incomprehension at what they observed.

Everyone, it seemed, had an opinion. One hundred miles north-west of the scene of the Clapham Common murder, a discussion panel run by a rural Women's Institute group near Rugby considered what they called 'the "Teddy Boys" question' and predictably decided that 'the failure to apply the slipper at the right time and on the right occasion was most probably the cause of the new vogue.'[17]

In London, it was widely reported that a Methodist vicar from Wandsworth had founded a club for teenagers after holding meetings with local gang members. As an article in the *Sunday People* stated, 'the "Teddy Boys" have told him that if they had such a club they could prove they know how to behave themselves, even if they like to wear Edwardian clothes. He said last night: "I think the lads will have to have a badge which they would only get in return for a promise of non-violence."[18] This seems unlikely to have swayed the more criminally minded, or even the casual offenders, such as the group of Edwardian-dressed youths who were fined twenty shillings each at a West London court in Hendon for the grave offence of having 'swung on the supports of shop window blinds in Kingsbury-road, annoying passers-by who had to step out of the way to avoid being struck'. They were duly warned by the magistrate C. B. Baggs that if they were not careful 'they would become what is known as "Teddy Boys"'.[19]

A more serious case came up in Birmingham the following day involving nine members of two local teenage gangs, the Brummagem Boys and the Northfield Mob, who were charged with having been part of a larger group that had fought each other in the street using improvised weapons including steel chairs, advertising boards and milk bottles. Some of them appeared in the dock wearing what were described as '"Slim Jim" ties [the narrow style favoured by Teds] and drape jackets'.[20]

A more sizeable group of around two hundred young people – half of them in Edwardian clothing – boarded a Slough to Reading train that same week, which the press inevitably dubbed the 'Teddy Boy Special'. By chance, a reporter from the *Daily Herald* happened to be on the same journey, and in writing up his experience made a valiant attempt to imply that this had been something akin to the last days of Sodom and Gomorrah. Yet his breathless statement that 'I saw drunks and petting sessions in darkened compartments all along the 50-minute journey'[21] could equally have applied to many teenage excursions of the time, regardless of dress code. If such behaviour was a problem, then it is probably just as well the journalist was not observing the actions of the average British cinema audience once the lights went down.

Warped Ninnies with an Exhibitionist Twist

Of course, having identified the new folk devil, the media had much to gain by flogging this particular horse. Whether such reports were exaggerated or not, few people in the public eye seem to have been able to restrain themselves from offering an opinion on the Teddy boy phenomenon. Tom Fallon, former Chief Superintendent of the Metropolitan Police, described them as 'spineless young hoodlums and warped ninnies with an exhibitionist twist',[22] but Dr John Spencer, addressing a conference at Swansea University, had a more sympathetic view, allowing that 'they spend a great deal more on clothes than the average man, and to me their dress does not seem to be a bad thing.'[23] Meanwhile, psychiatrist Dr Peter Scott from the children's department of the London County Council declared at the same conference that 'the "Teddy Boy" seemed to be well developed physically but had in his make-up effeminacy which prompted 7s 6d haircuts'[24] – implying that men of that era were supposed to consult a sliding price scale at the barber's lest their sexuality be called into question. Furthermore, Dr Scott stated that Teds often had tattoos, 'not of the "I Love Betty" variety but of ugly things like spiders'.[25] This observation was supported by the child psychiatrist Dr George Cross, who said he had encountered one teenager with the phrase 'I Must Have Guts' tattooed on his chest.

It was not just psychiatrists who had encountered the new breed: magistrates were also seeing a fair amount of traffic, at least according to Liverpool Justice of the Peace Councillor

S. Curtis, who wrote that 'unfortunately many of the young (toughs or hooligans) who appear before the juvenile and adult courts favour this style of dress and a long-suffering public is tired of seeing them slouching about the centre of the city with apparently no object in life, except looking for trouble, which they usually manage to find.'[26]

Come Over Here and I Will Beat Your Head In

Once the new youth movement was established, it soon became clear that there were Teddy girls as well as Teddy boys, who customised the look to suit themselves. If you stand out from the crowd, you inevitably run the risk of attracting sarcastic comments in the street; the Clapham Common murder had been sparked by precisely this kind of trivial provocation. An early report of violence involving Teddy girls appeared as the lead story on the front page of the *Portsmouth Evening News* on 23 June 1954:

15-YEAR-OLD 'TEDDY GIRL' IN SOUTHSEA BRAWL

Described as a 'Teddy Girl', a 15-year-old was said at Portsmouth Juvenile Court to have been involved in a Southsea brawl and to have told the police afterwards that 'it looked big' to carry a knife.[27]

A prosecution witness, herself sixteen, testified in court that she and her friend had seen two girls passing by on the seafront:

They wore an exaggerated form of dress, as worn by Teddy Girls. Because they were particularly conspicuous, I looked at them and the accused called out 'what are you looking at?' I said I was looking at her and she said 'Come over here and I will beat your head in.'[28]

A fight developed, during which the witness's seventeen-year-old female friend stepped in to help and was attacked with a knife: 'I slapped her in the face in self-defence. The other girl started fighting me and we both fell to the ground. I received several cuts on my face and head and several on my hand from the knife.'[29]

If someone is looking for a fight, they generally have little trouble finding one, and local papers across the country have always enjoyed reporting the results; had the new fashion not provided the excuse, another trivial provocation might have served equally well. But in 1954 Teddy girls were something new, so the front pages beckoned.

The idea that every teenage Teddy girl was a knife-carrying problem for the judiciary is absurd, but the criminal activities of a few who wore the clothing of a youth tribe were usually what attracted media attention. For many other adherents of such movements, the fashion, the music or the sense of belonging was the beginning and the end of the attraction. But that does not sell many papers.

Attempting to counteract these negative images, a parent signing herself 'Edwardian's mother' was moved to write to the *Liverpool Echo* asking that teenagers be judged on their actions rather than their appearance, claiming that 'these so-called "Edwardians or Teddy Boys" are not all "thugs or chain carriers"'. She said that her own son followed the style along with his friends, but went on to ask, 'does no one see any difference in "high spirits" and "hooliganism"? The hooligan draws attention to himself: the quieter Edwardian (who I am sure is in the majority) does not.'[30]

Nevertheless, the result of all this coverage was that by the summer of 1954, the message was coming through loud and clear: if you saw one of these strangely dressed youths coming down the road towards you, it was probably a good idea to cross the road.

Better Luck When the Fashions Change Again

Such was the association between the clothes and criminality that when David, a seventeen-year-old Ted from Acton, was fined in July for various minor anti-social acts, the court took him up on a promise he had made to a social worker that he would sell his Edwardian outfit as a measure of his determination to go straight. His father asserted that the teenager had never previously been in trouble until he bought this clothing, but David was said to be regretting his vow to dispose of his narrow trousers and velvet-collared jacket with turned-back cuffs. 'It's a wonderful suit. I wish I'd never promised,' he said, adding that neither other teenagers nor local pawn shops would take it off his hands. 'The police are always catching lads in Edwardian clothes. Now no one wants to buy this kind of suit. The lads are all scared.'[31]

Later youth styles also came freighted with sometimes outlandish assumptions: anyone wearing hippie clothes in 1967 was supposedly a drug addict practising 'free love'; those in punk clothes in 1977 were written off as glue-sniffing morons who mugged old ladies; in the eighties long hair and a biker jacket covered in heavy metal patches were a sure sign that you would soon embark on a killing spree having received Satanic messages from an LP played backwards. It said so in the newspapers, how could it not be true?

An early attempt to test whether this prejudice was justified was made by Terry Farman, an eighteen-year-old plumber from

Middlesbrough who bet his workmates in 1954 that adopting the Edwardian look would not transform him into an anti-social thug. Accordingly, he went to a tailor and ordered his own distinctly colourful version of a Teddy boy suit: 'a red corduroy jacket with velvet patch pockets, powder blue drainpipe trousers, red corduroy shoes with twin buckles, white socks, two-tone brown and green shirt with a black shoelace tie'.[32] The £15 he paid may not sound a great deal by modern standards, but a tin of baked beans that year cost eight pence and a pint of milk was seven pence, so Farman's wager was hardly cheap, even before he had paid for the matching Ted haircut. His family and friends were not impressed with his outfit, and when his story was publicised, neither was a self-described Ted from Manchester who wrote to the *Daily Mirror* to argue that 'a real Teddy boy' ought to be wearing 'a charcoal-grey Edwardian suit; black leather-soled shoes with rounded toes; white shirt with "Billy Eckstine" collar; light grey waistcoat'. He signed off his letter with the comment, 'better luck when the fashions change again, Mr Farman'.[33]

The Purposeless Slouch of the Corner Boy

The working-class adaptation of the Edwardian look had polarised opinion from the start. A newspaper correspondent from Belfast who was seemingly offended just by the sight of London Teds was one of many who set the tone for an attitude that would become familiar:

> Not until I visited the town of Harrow, Middlesex, the other night did I realize the extent of the 'Teddy Boy' cult. The streets of this middle-class town were swarming with youths in outlandish, so-called Edwardian suits.

They walked six abreast on the pavement, they indulged in horseplay, they were noisy, they were a great nuisance. Their chief places of congregation were the milk bars. They swilled coffee and milk shakes inside, they gathered in their noisy groups outside. 'Teddy Boys' are seldom seen in public houses. They cannot afford it. As 'dandies', they have very little money to spend. What they have goes in buying their bizarre clothes which are very expensive and are a good thing for the tailors. Nor can their suits be used for work when they become second-best. There have been clothing vogues before – not so long ago it was the blue blazer and grey slacks – but there can seldom have been one that has been accompanied by such evident vacuity of mind.[34]

Despite being disturbed by certain types of behaviour, none of them particularly uncommon in teenage males, the writer's main objection was to the style of clothes being worn. Many thousands of people across the nation would have been sitting in cafes that day, but it is doubtful if he would have also applied the term 'swilled' to their method of drinking coffee. This journalist may have been a reader of the *Manchester Guardian*, who had recently made the same point about the uselessness of such tailoring as future potential workwear and also managed to strike a similar tone of straight-laced disdain, calling the fashions they observed in London 'a grotesque parody of Edwardian costume':

Having struggled into their tight trousers, fixed their shoestring ties, and patted their expansive coiffures into shape they come 'up West' to stroll and presumably win admiration. But all they achieve is the purposeless slouch of the corner boy throughout the ages. Anything less like the elegance of the Edwardian 'knut' it would be hard to imagine.[35]

It is difficult to avoid the suspicion that regardless of any anti-social behaviour issues, the main thing prompting this adverse reaction on the part of middle-class journalists and commentators was that the 'lower orders' had the effrontery to dress up in well-tailored expensive suits or bright colours – previously the preserve of the wealthier sections of society. As John Cooper Clarke wrote, recalling his days growing up in working-class Salford of the mid-1950s and being the fortunate possessor of a genuine US-manufactured two-tone bowling shirt:

> Clothes were very important. You were judged. To go to school in any shirt that wasn't white singled you out for universal opprobrium, as I discovered to my cost. Coloured shirt – big deal! . . . At that time, men's shirts came in three shades: white, grubby, and filthy. In my highly polluted neighbourhood, that was the colour scheme. Coloured shirts carried the stigma of delinquency: spivs, queers, Latinos, and worst of all, Teddy Boys, who by virtue of their hard-nut reputation as blade artists could wear whatever they liked.[36]

Still, it was not just columnists who were unimpressed. Many readers also weighed in with summary dismissals of the motivations, character and appearance of the new breed, such as the man who wrote in to his local paper deploring the fact that the Edwardian trend had spread from the well-heeled to the working class and 'now we have our errand boys, apprentices, etc. wearing some hybrid dress'.[37] One woman in another city declared that 'a Teddy Boy is an apology for a man and his only aim in life is to make an impression on the girls'.[38] Perish the thought.

Hooligans, Juvenile Gangsters and Delinquents

In the midst of this war of words, a more even-handed response came in an investigative article by the former war correspondent Hilde Marchant in the *Picture Post*; in an article entitled 'The Truth About the "Teddy Boys" and the Teddy Girls', she acknowledged the contradictory impressions people had already acquired of such teenagers. 'The "Edwardians", or "Teddy Boys", have been branded as hooligans, juvenile gangsters and delinquents,' she wrote. 'They have also been called dandies and mother's darlings.' Above all, Marchant was keen to point out that there was no such thing as a typical Ted, despite all the generalisations about them:

> The first thing that struck me was that their clothes are deceptive. This Edwardian fashion gives a uniformity to a group of young people who are far from uniform. They are as varied, diverse and informal as any other group of human beings. They set a pattern in their velvet collars, dog-tooth checks and moccasin shoes. But there is no such standard pattern about their lives or behaviour.[39]

Photographs taken by Joseph McKeown accompanied the piece, showing a selection of teenagers at the Mecca Dance Hall in Tottenham, neatly dressed in Edwardian fashions. There is no hint that knife fights or bike chain assaults were about to break out. Indeed, having also spoken to police officers and magistrates, while admitting that some of the young people troubling

A teenage Ted couple dancing in Tottenham, *Picture Post*, 29 May 1954

the courts habitually wore Teddy boy suits, the article closed by saying 'there is a vast majority of young men who merely wish to wear Edwardian clothes as a change from boiler suits and factory overalls.'[40]

Picture Post had since 1938 built an enviable reputation for documenting both everyday life and world events through a combination of high-quality photography and thoughtful reportage, so it is not surprising that the articles they devoted to the Teddy boy phenomenon in the 1950s are among the most valuable to have appeared in print.

For her article, Marchant talked to a number of teenagers, all of whom had left school a year or two earlier, and now had jobs that helped fund their clothing choices and social lives:

> One is a toy maker, one a glass cutter, another a electric welder and, surprisingly, another a national Serviceman on leave – back in his Teddy Boy civilian 'uniform'. (His hair was shorter than the others, but would still have horrified the Sergeant-major.) Their wages were good – ranging from the £4 17s 6d a week apprentice, to just over £12 a week for the skilled cabinet maker. Their suits cost between £17 and £20. All of them agreed that a good poplin shirt was just under £2 and that a pair of shoes was around the £3 mark. Most of them 'kept themselves'; which means they pay their parents something towards the rent and the household budget. Even so, pocket money was never less than £2 a week, and often double. They were not interested in drink, but more likely mineral water.[41]

This last point about Teds supposedly shunning alcohol – which was repeated in various interviews of the time – might simply have been an acknowledgement of the fact that you could be a wage-earner from fifteen, but the licensing laws meant that the pubs were not supposed to serve you if you were under eighteen. It is also possible that those being interviewed might not wish to admit to an illicit drink habit in a public forum, but could still find ways of consuming alcohol on the quiet. Back then, if you were an under-age drinker, you might not be happy to have your parents and their friends reading about it in the newspaper.

Drain-Pipe Trousers and a Long Hair Style

Now that this new species known as the Teddy boy had become the subject of public discussion, there was still debate about who exactly fitted the bill. Unsurprisingly, the finer distinctions of the breed sometimes had to be spelled out in court for the benefit of confused magistrates, such as the one in Great Yarmouth who was informed by a policeman that a Ted 'is a youth who is normally dressed in Edwardian style, with a draped jacket, drain-pipe trousers, and a long hair style'.[42] The sixteen-year-old defendant had been discovered by police incapably drunk and being propped up by a friend, following a report that Teddy boys were damaging parked cars. In this instance, the fact that the teenager's 'long hair was all over his face' was somehow thought to be relevant to the case, as was his mode of dress. This story appeared alongside a report of another case concerning two men thrown out of a pub for drunkenness and fighting; despite their prior convictions for causing bodily harm and gang fighting, no space was found for any description of their clothing or the state of their hair.[43]

Given that in our own time almost any sartorial choice is usually met with indifference, it is sobering to note how even quite a minor deviation from mainstream styles in the 1950s could provoke offence. The headmaster of a school in Canvey Island, Essex, told his male pupils who had their hair combed into a 'DA' or a Tony Curtis in the summer of 1954 that 'these flashy American styles must stop. Have your hair cut in the ordinary English way.' Speaking to a national press reporter afterwards, he commented, 'I think we can agree that we don't want them looking like Teddy boys.'[44]

Time for Some Modifications

In truth, it did not take much in order to stand out at school in the 1950s; uniforms were often the norm and a teacher's word was law. Even minor differences in clothing and hairstyle would be noted, not just by the staff but also by fellow pupils. Ted Carroll was a schoolboy in mid-1950s Dublin at a time when a choice of hairstyle and the width of a trouser could be crucial signifiers. Because of one such instance, he acquired the name by which he has been known ever since, as he told me:

> I had a DA greased up, well, that's how I got the name Ted, 'cause my name is David, and one Wednesday afternoon when I wasn't out playing rugby and my mum was out somewhere, I got my trousers – I had a pair of terylene and cotton charcoal grey trousers that I wore to school – and I thought, 'Time for some modifications.' I got a sewing-machine out and took them in to about fourteen-inch bottoms, and I turned them inside out to sew the inside seam and then ironed them and stuff, then I found that the creases had moved from here to here. It was obvious it was a home-made job, you know, but I had to wear them to school, so that's how I got the name Teddy boy, because I was a Ted for taking in my trousers.[45]

Increasingly, by autumn 1954, Teddy boys were no longer simply a London phenomenon, but could be found in many places across the British Isles and the Irish Republic. In the public mind, however, they were not yet associated with the emerging musical movement from America which became known as 'rock'n'roll'. That process would take a few more months, but a report in the *Daily Mirror* of 30 October 1954 shows that there was still some way to go. Turning to the sports pages, US visitors familiar with the record charts back home might have raised an eyebrow when informed that Second Division football club West Ham United had signed a promising young player called Bill Haley.[46]

6

THE BEAT! THE BEAT! THE BEAT!

I Don't Sound Like Nobody

While the UK was worrying about juvenile delinquents, cosh boys and Teddy boys in the early 1950s, across the Atlantic the first stirrings of a music which would dominate British youth culture half a decade later were making themselves known. In January 1950, a former radio announcer in Memphis, Tennessee, opened a small recording studio at 706 Union Avenue. He called it the Memphis Recording Service, and from there he went on to found the Sun record label.[1] In that tiny space, Sam Phillips would launch the careers of Howlin' Wolf, BB King, Johnny Cash, Carl Perkins, Jerry Lee Lewis, Roy Orbison and numerous others. One day in 1953 a kid with sideburns walked in to cut a one-off demonstration disc for his mother. His name was Elvis Presley. When asked who he sounded like, he is said to have replied, 'I don't sound like nobody.'[2]

On 8 April 1950, a month before Victor Thompson's 'Rising Generation' series painted a picture of Britain's bop-crazed youth, a US music outfit with a hillbilly flavour released two 78s. Appearing on the short-lived Keystone label out of Philadelphia, one of the songs, 'Ten Gallon Stetson', was a jaunty up-tempo number co-written by a local songwriter named Jimmy DeKnight. It wasn't exactly a million-seller – which explains why an original copy these days will set you back upwards of $200 – but the band who performed it, Bill Haley and the Saddle Men, morphed into Bill Haley and His Comets and released another song in May 1954 co-written by Jimmy DeKnight, entitled '(We're Gonna) Rock Around the Clock'. That one sold rather better.

Taking a look at the 8 April 1950 edition of US music magazine *Billboard*, it's clear that many of the signs of the coming storm were already there. Just released or hovering somewhere in the charts that week were versions of songs which would be taken up by the new generation of rock'n'roll stars a few years later. Ernest Tubb's new record was 'I Love You Because', and Patti Page had a hit with 'I Don't Care If the Sun Don't Shine' – both of which were recorded by Elvis at Sun in 1954. Lonnie Johnson appeared with 'Blues Stay Away from Me', later recorded by Gene Vincent and His Blue Caps in 1956. Grand Ole Opry star Little Jimmy Dickens was enjoying one of the biggest hits of his career with 'Hillbilly Fever', and Moon Mullican had 'I'll Sail My Ship Alone'; both of these songs would be covered by Jerry Lee Lewis.[3]

The seeds were being sown, and a new musical wind was about to blow in from the West, by which time the velvet collars would be fully in place, the drapes in shape, the trousers suitably narrowed, and the haircut exactly right.

Delta Cats

In the US in April 1951 – the same week that *Cosh Boy* premiered at the Embassy Theatre in London[4] – a jumping R&B boogie tune was released on the Chess label out of Chicago. It wasn't all that much to do with either that town or that company, however; it had been recorded at the Sun Studio in Memphis by Sam Phillips, who leased it to Chess. At that stage, Sam didn't have the financial muscle or distribution to get behind a hit record, and this particular song rode all the way to number one in the *Billboard* R&B charts.[5] 'Rocket 88' was credited to Jackie Brenston & His Delta Cats – a name that disguised Ike Turner and His Kings of Rhythm, for whom Brenston was the sax player. This recording is frequently cited whenever people are discussing exactly what constitutes the first genuine rock'n'roll record. It probably has a better claim than most, and was swiftly picked up and covered by a certain white outfit called Bill Haley and the Saddle Men.

To contrast these developments with the songs that were popular in the UK at that time, it is worth investigating an eight-minute newsreel made by Pathé about Denmark Street, London's 'Tin Pan Alley'. This short stretch of road was the traditional location of many of the songwriters and music publishers around which the British music industry was still centred; as the film's commentary suggested, it was the 'Birthplace of melodies which have kept Britain singing in good times and in bad'.[6]

Although in America some future rock'n'roll stars were already making tentative moves into the business – Little Richard, for instance, secured his first record contract in 1951 – the Pathé film reveals a British industry still locked into an almost pre-war ideal of musical styles. Big bands and ballads were the name of the game – hardly surprising, given that many of the household names who appear in the newsreel, including bandleaders Geraldo, Lew Stone and Billy Cotton, made their reputations two decades earlier. Among the vocalists who featured were former 'forces sweethearts' Vera Lynn and Anne Shelton, and also the Beverley Sisters, all of whose careers began in the 1930s or early 1940s. There was little sign that rock'n'roll was just around the corner, apart from a couple of subtle clues. Geordie vocal group the Five Smith Brothers could be seen harmonising around a piano on a version of the 1937 standard, 'Harbour Lights', while the one genuine teenager featured was nineteen-year-old Petula Clark, who turned in a fine rendition of the much-covered 1945 tune 'Have I Told You Lately That I Love You?' The young Elvis recorded a version of 'Harbour Lights' at his first proper session at Sun Records, and he would also record 'Have I Told You . . .' for RCA a couple of years later. The new world was being put together using pieces of the old one.

An Odd Mixture of C&W and R&B

When the English singer Vera Lynn topped the US charts in 1952, a broadsheet newspaper that had changed its name months earlier from *Accordion Times & Musical Express* to the *New Musical Express*, devoted its front page to a photo of the lady in question.[7] Vera had been releasing singles on the Decca label for seventeen years, but reaching the number one spot in America, as the paper pointed out, was 'a feat never before achieved by a British artist, not even by Gracie Fields in her prime'. The song itself, 'Auf Wiederseh'n, Sweetheart', however, looked far more to the past than the future, with its chorus of massed ranks of servicemen on backing vocals.

If there was a US chart of the most popular songs, it occurred to the *New Musical Express* that Britain ought to have one as well; in their 14 November 1952 issue they published the nation's first, which they claimed to be 'an authentic weekly survey of the best-selling "pop" records . . . which we know will be of the greatest interest and benefit to all our readers'.[8] The Italian-American crooner Al Martino was at number one with the string-heavy ballad 'Here in My Heart' and Vera herself showed up three times, but there was no hint of rock'n'roll. Even so, elsewhere in the same issue there were listings for the current UK shows by US blues and boogie star Big Bill Broonzy – due at Southampton Guildhall on 16 November – who had been helping lay down some of the key building blocks for the new music since the 1930s.[9]

Melody Maker was read by most of the dance band and jazz musicians in the business, but some of their key staff writers would spend most of the rest of the 1950s sniping at rock, calling it variously 'a monstrous threat'[10] and voicing their fears of 'abject surrender to the lumbering dictates of the masses and grim prospects of a musical 1984'.[11] The paper only felt the need to bother with its own singles chart four years after the *New Musical Express* launched theirs, when they justified their decision as follows:

> With this issue, the *Melody Maker* introduces a regular weekly listing of the best-selling 'popular' records in Great Britain. Despite many requests in the past from all branches of the British music industry we have refused to jeopardise the integrity of the *Melody Maker* by publishing any list of which we could not be assured of the complete and utter integrity.[12]

Even so, and probably much to some of their journalists' disgust, Bill Haley and His Comets were included at number seven with 'See You Later, Alligator'. By that time, Haley was an international star, yet even in 1952, just as Vera Lynn had her US chart success, he was making an impact in his home country. Haley's breakthrough hit at the time, 'Rock the Joint', had attitude to spare, with lyrics that talked of joyously smashing windows and kicking down doors. Directly inspired by the hard-rocking 1949 recording of the same tune by fellow

Philadelphia band Chris Powell and the Five Blue Flames, this had all the hallmarks of his classic sound that would spread like wildfire within two years. Yet for the reviewers at *Billboard*, it had been just one new record out of many that week in April 1952, and the singer's name was so relatively unfamiliar that the paper credited it to 'Billy Haley'.[13] This was the last time Bill's band appeared as the Saddlemen; by the autumn, they were renamed the Comets.

Sweet and Pert Voiced

In January 1953, the American music magazine *Cash Box* ran a heartfelt tribute to the giant figure of country music Hank Williams, who had died on New Year's Day in the back seat of his Cadillac on the way to a show. He was just twenty-nine, but the songs he had written would be covered by many of the first-generation rock'n'rollers that followed in his footsteps, not least among them Jerry Lee Lewis, Gene Vincent, Fats Domino, Elvis Presley, Johnny Cash, Chuck Berry, Roy Orbison, Wanda Jackson, Little Richard and Bill Haley. As *Cash Box* rightly said:

> He showed that a song being sung to the accompaniment of a single guitar could get its message across the same as one being done with a thirty piece orchestra. And he showed moreover that a song written for a single guitar could also sound great with a thirty piece orchestra ... He widened the horizons of American music by opening up the entire folk field for popular enjoyment.[14]

Turning to the reviews of new singles, however, the world looked a very different place, with a very positive review for a record due out that week which in popular mythology has come to symbolise all that was supposedly wrong with music prior to the advent of rock'n'roll – 'How Much Is That Doggie in the Window?' by Patti Page. Calling it 'a sweet and pert voiced dainty reading that makes you feel warm inside', they correctly predicted that it would go on to great success, saying 'we look for the cute little novelty on top to do a bang up job for all concerned'.[15]

For decades this recording with its determinedly tongue-in-cheek lyrics has been held up by certain critics as dividing the culturally significant and worthwhile hits that came after from the alleged sea of saccharine nonsense which prevailed before. All of which is, of course, demonstrably false. To take just a couple of examples, the previous year had seen the release of full-blooded rocking hits like 'Lawdy Miss Clawdy' by Lloyd Price and the pounding, boogie piano-led R&B vocal group smash 'Rock Me All Night Long' by the Ravens. These were not obscure songs, and they sold across the US in very large numbers.

If you only consider the very same month in which Patti's unstoppable canine chorus was unleashed, two records were available to the supposedly innocent listening public in which the entendres were verging on the single. There was 'Drive, Daddy, Drive', a salacious R&B boogie by Little Sylvia, who told her partner that if he didn't know how to drive he should 'get out of the driver's seat'. If that didn't appeal, there was always the new record from the Treniers – one of the most successful R&B groups of the 1950s, who would later appear in the rock'n'roll films *The Girl Can't Help It* and *Don't Knock the Rock*. It was a catchy up-tempo tune entitled 'Poon-Tang', reviewed favourably in the 3 January edition of the magazine,[16] but with absolutely no hint that the title was a very well-known word, especially in the Southern states, that was defined in Wentworth & Flexner's

Dictionary of American Slang (1960) as 'The vagina of a Negress or mulatto'.[17]

Wild About This Jolter

Out of left field comes a sleeper that could burst wide open and take the country by storm. With the popular use of the new bop slang expression, 'CRAZY', this house rocking tune tagged 'Crazy Man, Crazy' could become a universal novelty. Handing in the fabulous job on the rhythmic beaty item is Bill Haley with a sock assist from his Haley Comets. Bill had a terrific success with another jumper dubbed 'Rock the Joint', and this one tops it by far. The rhythm sent out by the aggregation makes you bounce in your seat, and the jitterbugs are sure to go wild about this jolter.[18]

By the summer of 1953, although it was not yet on everyone's radar, genuine rock'n'roll already existed in America – just as the first Teds were walking the London streets. With the benefit of hindsight, it is clear there were numerous indicators if you knew where to look for them, but still, the move from wall-to-wall dance bands and crooners came as an almighty shock to the establishment, as did the sight of working-class flash boys narrowing their strides and giving it the full Edwardian.

It is not hard to see why such things became popular. In terms of music, the above Bill Haley review goes a long way towards capturing the sheer joy that came through in these recordings. They made teenagers want to get up and dance in a very different way than they might have to the smooth sounds of reigning hit-makers in Britain like Dickie Valentine or Mantovani.

Haley's single shifted over 80,000 copies across America in its first couple of weeks, dwarfing his previous success and making the record industry sit up and take notice.[19] Exactly one year later, Bill and the Comets released their worldwide smash, '(We're Gonna) Rock Around the Clock'.

Four to a Bar, All the Way

In America as 1953 drew to a close, the genuine rock spirit was coming through in hits such as 'Honey Hush' by Joe Turner or the 'Rock-a-bye Boogie' by the Davis Sisters – the former an R&B boogie vocalist, the latter a singing duo from the country-music field. There were similar new releases arriving in shops as the festive season ended, like the pounding 'Taxi, Taxi 6963' by Piano Red, or the honkytonk stomp of 'Give Me a Red Hot Mama and an Ice Cold Beer' by Smiley Maxedon.

On this side of the Atlantic, what did the 18 December issue of the *New Musical Express* have to offer? At the hipper end of the market, home-grown jazz ruled the roost, but the big money was still in glutinous ballads sung by comfy, non-threatening twenty-something men in sensible jumpers who were presented as pin-up fodder for Britain's teenage girls.

An advert for one of the biggest song publishers, Campbell Connolly & Co., pushed the merits of 'our new British hit', 'Kiss & Cuddle Polka', alongside 'I Want a Hippopotamus for Christmas', 'the gayest of Christmas songs'[20] – both of which were actually US imports – but balanced against this was a comedy article by Norman Stevens designed to appeal to any readers with a knowledge of more authentic types of American roots music such as jazz and blues, with their fondness for suitably frank adult language:

Give your record collector friend the new 'Pornograph' – a phonograph for playing ripe race records. A built-in thermostat keeps the temperature well up to boiling point and there is an automatic cut-off which springs into action immediately a maiden aunt comes within smelling distance. And the deluxe model has a circular attachment for squares – a device which explains all the obscure double-entendre lyrics in words of one syllable.[21]

Of particular interest was the article's headline, 'It's Crazy, Man, Crazy', the phrase used by Bill Haley for the title of his recent self-penned American rock'n'roll hit back in the summer.

There was also a small sign in that week's issue that Britain would eventually develop its own rock'n'roll subculture. A new and modestly sized independent recording studio in London's Denmark Street, just off Charing Cross Road, was mentioned in the same issue's 'Ad Lib' column: 'Chatting with Ralph Elman, who has Regent Sound Studios, he told me he recently recorded a double-sided disc of a drummer playing four to a bar, all the way. The record was for Lord Rothschild to play piano to at home!'[22]

Victor Rothschild had a lifelong enthusiasm for jazz piano, so it is logical that he would have sought assistance in London's Tin Pan Alley. A decade later almost to the month, Regent Sound was where the Rolling Stones cut their debut album in a London which by then had a markedly different musical environment.

In 1954, many of the readers of the *New Musical Express*, like its rival *Melody Maker*, were musicians themselves. Indeed, a quiz that appeared six years earlier in what was then still called the *Accordion Times & Musical Express* would have been unthinkable in the music papers of the late 1950s or 1960s. As opposed to questions about Ringo's fondness for jelly babies or Elvis's favourite breakfast pancake, the average 1948 subscriber was thought capable of fielding the following enquiries:[23]

1. Who is the composer of 'Roses of Picardy'?
2. What time-signatures can a March be written in?
3. What is the usual bass arrangement of 2 24-bass accordion?
4. Which is quicker: 'allegro' or 'allegretto'?

Within a decade, the new teenage market became a force to be reckoned with; rock'n'roll gradually dominated the pop charts, and music papers had to considerably alter their editorial policies to take account of it.

Everybody Razzle Dazzle

In May 1954, the American branch of the Decca Record Company signed Bill Haley and His Comets, bringing the resources of a much larger organisation behind the band. *Cash Box* announced the deal in the 8 May issue, stating that the contract would guarantee the Comets 'full disk jockey coverage of Decca's 1800 name dee jay list, plus coverage of 500 juke box operators with 100 or more boxes, and other considerations'.[24] All that remained was for Haley to deliver the goods, and the signs were hopeful: 'The group's first release for Decca is due out this week. It includes "Rock Around the Clock" b/w [backed with] "13 Women and 1 Man".'

The Comets had recorded the song which would prove to be their calling card a few weeks earlier on 12 April, at the Pythian Temple studio in New York. Little did they know that three and a half thousand miles away a group of velvet-collared teenagers would prove to be some of their staunchest supporters when the song lit a worldwide fuse the following year as the main title music of a film shot in November and December of '54, *Blackboard Jungle*. But perhaps it was fitting, given that Bill's mother was originally from Ulverston in Lancashire, the town which also gave the world Stan Laurel.

May 1954 was also the month when the young Elvis Presley was contacted by Marion Keisker of the Sun Studio in Memphis to drop by and audition for its owner, Sam Phillips. Things moved fast in music circles in those days, and by 19 July his debut single 'That's All Right' / 'Blue Moon of Kentucky' was in the shops and causing a sensation in the American South. *Billboard* liked the single, calling him 'a potent new chanter who can sock over a tune for either the country or the R&B markets',[25] and *Cash Box* highlighted Presley in their 'Folk and Western Round-Up' column as 'completely new to the business' but reckoned that he 'should be around for awhile'.[26]

Two years later, Elvis was arguably the biggest thing in the entire field of popular music, worldwide, and his impact among the drape-suited teenagers of Britain was immense. As the former Liverpool Ted John Lennon told biographer Hunter Davies in 1968, 'Nothing affected me until I heard Elvis.' Forming a Liverpool skiffle band with some friends in 1956, Lennon was unmistakeably one of the new breed, as Davies noted: 'They called themselves the Quarrymen, naturally enough. They all wore Teddy-boy clothes, had their hair piled high and sleeked back like Elvis. John was the biggest Ted of all.'[27]

7

PUBLIC ENEMY NUMBER ONE

A Jiving, Thriving, Twenty-Four-Carat Ted

Once a visible section of British youth had adopted the new clothing style, it was inevitable that among those who became involved in the usual catalogue of petty thievery, drunken vandalism, and fighting which had long been a feature of normal court proceedings, there would be some who made the customary morning-after court appearance still clothed in their Edwardian finery. This in turn gave rise to a regular flow of newspaper reports which now felt the need to provide detailed clothing descriptions alongside the usual moralistic hand-wringing about the crime itself. Yet in a blindfold test of successive punches delivered to the same victim by someone wearing a bus driver's uniform, another in pyjamas and the third clad in the full Edwardian, surely the strength of the blow would be the distinguishing factor, and the mode of dress an irrelevance?

Of course, another side of the same coin was that if any teenager fancied their reputation as a hard case, or simply wanted to assert their feelings of independence, they might be tempted to adopt Ted clothing as a badge of outlaw status. In his fine autobiography, Tom Jones recalled his younger days in the Wales of the mid-fifties when he was still Tom Woodward, a decade before he became an international singing star:

Early in my childhood I longed to dress like my father but at this point, sixteen going on seventeen, I want – and in fact need – to be a teddy boy, with the drainpipe trousers and the beetle-crusher shoes. As of now, the desired look is exactly the opposite of what my father, and everybody else's father, is wearing. They're in short jackets? We'll go for long jackets. They're in baggy trousers? We'll have tight trousers. They're wearing wide ties? We'll wear our ties bootlace thin. They're in slight, thin-soled shoes? We'll have big, clonking ones, thank you. It's revolution in its crudest form, in a way. See that? Do the exact opposite.[1]

This is an excellent summary of the impulses that drove a generation to start refining their sense of themselves via clothes and music. If you could not afford the prices of a tailor in the 1950s, a few simple items could be used to mark you out as one of the new breed. The first rock'n'roll generation found that everyday cast-offs could be simply customised and then pressed into service. In Tom's case the starting point was an old outsize jacket of his father's which reached far enough down the leg in the approved drape manner, as he recalled:

But it's not quite there. So one day I lift a patch of velvet from the glove factory, take it home and plead with my mother to sew it on the collar for me. The effect is trans-formative: without the velvet, I was just some bloke in a too-big jacket that used to be his dad's. With the velvet, I am a bona fide, dyed-in-the-wool, jiving, thriving, twenty-four-carat Ted, and you'd better fucking watch it.[2]

Jones, like many of those who would later rise to fame in the 1960s British beat boom, was drawn to the working-class flash of the Teddy boy look and also the developing rock'n'roll scene. In many cases, long before they tried stepping onto a stage and claiming the attention of an audience, they had experienced the sensation of leaving their parents' house and strolling through their neighbourhood dressed up in their new controversial finery which could attract anything from admiration to mild disapproval or physical assaults. Not bad training for a life in the spotlight.

Putting the Boot In

Of course, many commentators in the press felt that a Ted costume was a stepping stone to a career as a criminal rather than an entertainer. Some official publications helped reinforce this view, such as the *Home Office Report of the Commissioners of Prisons for the Year 1954*, which stated:

> With such an age group as 17–21 there was naturally a wide variety of types and personalities among the inmates committed. These ranged between first offenders, ex-Approved School boys, delinquent soldiers, young men who fail to comply with the requirements of the National Service Acts, and the notorious 'Edwardians'. So far as fears of contamination may arise, happily the warden is able to report: 'I am confident this inter-mixing does not have a detrimental effect; there is very little time for friendship to mature and each man is so dependent upon his own effort that he cannot afford to be influenced.' With regard to the 'Teddy Boy', the Warden says: 'The opening of a Detention Centre was an unfortunate blow to the undisciplined "Edwardian" but an ideal answer to the Court that had to deal with these irresponsible exhibitionists. One very noticeable factor has

been, the more exaggerated the dress, the greater degree of illiteracy; rarely do we see an intelligent "Teddy".[3]

One man who claimed to have the answer to the supposed Ted problem was the latest in a seemingly endless parade of Church of England vicars attempting to distract drape-wearing youths from going off the rails. The Reverend Douglas Griffiths of Lambeth held well-publicised meetings with groups of London Teds in the summer of 1954.[4] However, by the following January he was complaining to the press that he could not find an assistant willing to help him run a youth club, because all the potential 'liaison officers' were simply too scared: 'Whoever takes on the job – a paid one – will have his own office. I will supply my secret list of telephone numbers of London's Teddy boy gangs and their passwords.'[5] A bold claim, given that Teds were almost overwhelmingly working-class, and a mere 10 per cent of the nation had a telephone in that decade. Griffiths was a regular on British TV at the time, and this sounds as if he was trying a little too hard to play up his supposed insider knowledge. Yet these were teenagers he was talking about, many of them still schoolchildren, rather than a multi-million-pound adult organisation like the Costa Nostra.

Nevertheless, many shared the idea that youth clubs might be an effective counter-measure to incipient crime. The Chairman of the East London Juvenile Court, Sir Basil Henriques, wrote that 'the natural reaction of young men who are today asked to come and help one or other of the youth organisations is: "Why should I give up my leisure time to help youngsters who are more expensively dressed than I, and who are probably earning much more money?"' Henriques, who was also a magistrate and philanthropist, had founded a boys' club of his own in the East End in 1914, which is perhaps why he appeared more measured and less judgmental than some other commentators of the time:

> The ragged street urchin of the past roused one's pity. His appearance and obvious poverty and hunger touched our hearts. His present-day counterpart is the over-dressed 'Teddy Boy', or spiv, who certainly does not arouse our pity or touch our hearts. Yet beneath the external changes boy nature today is the same as it ever was, and he is as much in need of further education and discipline between the ages of 14 and 18 as he ever was.[6]

Discipline was not necessarily in short supply at the time, and there were a string of Teddy boy court appearances up and down the country in early 1955, all documented by a regional and national press that delighted in itemising the colour and style of clothing worn in the dock. If three teenagers appeared in the dock, two in what passed for 'normal' dress but the other in full Ted gear – as they did in a household burglary case brought before Crewe magistrates in January 1955 – it was the latter that made the headlines. In this instance, the youths were charged with the theft of a half-full bottle of brandy, a pair of rubber boots, a purse, a birth certificate, a death certificate, a nail file and £7 in cash – all presumably essential ingredients for a wild evening.[7] Meanwhile police in Southampton investigating another burglary felt that the nature of the stolen item might provide a clue to the thief's identity, speculating that whoever broke into the city's Tudor House Museum and escaped with a black satin waistcoat from 1847 embroidered with colourful flowers might have been a Teddy boy looking 'to add an early Victorian touch to his Edwardian attire'.[8]

The Sins of the Children

In March 1955, Sir Hartley Shawcross – former Attorney General and future chairman of the Press Council and Thames Television – suggested in a speech that parents should be held directly responsible for the actions of their delinquent offspring:

> The Teddy boys we hear about, the youths who deliberately make themselves look like toughs and who behave like toughs, are an unhappy product of the materialism and lowering of moral standards which are a feature of these days . . . Visiting the punishment for the sins of the children upon their parents would often produce salutary results.[9]

Of course, such proposals are never likely to be vote winners, given that the adults who might be footing the bill also have the right to go to the ballot box, whereas their children do not.

Nineteen-year-old Eddie Cochran famously sang in his hit 'Summertime Blues' (1958) that he would take up his concerns with the United Nations, but three years earlier Britain's Teddy boys were one of the subjects discussed at a UN congress on crime prevention held in Geneva.[10] Another organisation which had taken notice of the new trend was the British Army, who routinely called up thousands of teenagers each year into compulsory National Service. This could be problematic. One new soldier in Hereford was court-martialled and sentenced to twenty-eight days in detention for refusing to get his Ted haircut trimmed, claiming he had spent over £70 cultivating it over the previous two years.[11] The military authorities also began holding clothing inspection parades; if troops were wearing anything resembling Ted outfits when off duty, their 'walking out' leave passes would be cancelled. After reports in the *Daily Express* of the streets of Bicester in Oxfordshire allegedly 'swarming' with young men dressed in 'the more extreme, bootlace-tie type of Edwardian dress', they were identified as off-duty National Service soldiers from a nearby garrison. Monthly parades were therefore instituted to check the suitability of recruits' clothing; as the lieutenant colonel in charge claimed, 'We've looked into it very carefully and there's no doubt about it, the man who dresses like that is eight times out of ten the chief troublemaker.'[12]

These inspection parades were apparently the result of an official directive regarding Edwardian-style clothing that came from on high, because when three hundred soldiers of the Royal Engineers were lined up in their civilian clothes at Merebrook Camp in Worcestershire to be checked, an officer explained to the press that this was being done 'on the orders and under the guidance of Western Command'. It prompted an objection from Birmingham MP Victor Yates, who said, 'I don't like Edwardian suits any more than American-style ties but this is a question of the liberty of the individual. It isn't just the wearing of a suit that indicates bad character.'[13] A conference of probation officers from the East Midlands in September 1955, all of whom would have had plenty of experience in working with young offenders, reached the same conclusion. As one delegate from Nottingham responded when asked about Teddy boys, 'We know that they are not a serious problem. Merely because they wear unusual clothes, the press and the public have blamed them for juvenile delinquency. I admit that a lot of them start fights at dances but then the same type of people have always done so; it is simply that they are dressed rather differently.'[14]

Someone who might well have agreed with this point of view was the then Foreign Secretary Harold Macmillan – a man old enough to have lived through the original Edwardian era. In addition to his government responsibilities, Macmillan was also vice-president of the Bromley and Downham Boys' Club, which had a fair number of young Teddy boy members. He told them when paying the club a visit, 'My family think I am a bit old-fashioned, so maybe we are all Edwardians together.'[15]

As open-minded as this seems, at the same time the nation's 'paper of record' *The Times* was still not above running a headline about a criminal trial which read '"KING OF TEDDY BOYS" – Five Years for Man Who Wounded Constable'. An article detailed the brutal assaults in 1955 by a twenty-four-year-old from Walworth in South London on two women and various police officers, only to conclude with a statement from his defence council that there was no evidence the accused had ever worn Edwardian clothing.[16] And even if he had, what difference would that have made to the crimes committed?

The Garb of the Devil

Despite voices occasionally being raised in defence of those who dressed in Edwardian fashion, the constant barrage of negative publicity inevitably affected the way that the general public pre-judged anyone who chose to wear it. A typical reaction came from the parents from Luton whose sixteen-year-old daughter ran away from the family home with her Ted boyfriend in an unsuccessful attempt to get married at Gretna Green. According to her father, four months earlier she had begun 'hanging around with Teddy boys'. The girl's mother had not liked the look of this strangely dressed person initially, but her attitude had since changed: 'What I objected to was the Teddy clothes. Now I think he has acted like a gentleman. You can't judge anybody by their clothes. I would rather they got married right away now.'[17] Nevertheless, the times being what they were, her daughter had already been sent by the court to a remand home for a medical and psychiatric report.

Other parents had a different response to the clothing. Reg Brice, a pub landlord from Bristol, blamed his son's recent conviction for drunkenly kicking in two plate glass shop windows on the teenager's fondness for wearing a seventeen-guinea Ted suit: 'Since my son bought that thing a year ago his personality has changed. From a good, well-behaved lad he's become a Teddy Boy, mixing with others who wear this sort of stuff. I blame the suit for getting him into trouble.'[18]

Reg's solution was to take the clothing into the cellar of his pub and carve it up with a bread knife, before 'donating' the remnants to some local children who were making a Guy Fawkes effigy for Bonfire Night. He invoked a sense of medieval superstition by adding, 'I hope the end of that suit means the end of the family's bad luck.'[19] Coincidentally, another Bristol resident interviewed earlier that year by Charles Hamblett of the *Picture Post* put it in even stronger terms: Bill Wigmore, a seventy-six-year-old Christian, declared that 'Teddy Boys wear the garb of the Devil'. Hamblett had come in search of the new breed, and found some at the city's Palais de Danse:

> In a roped-off jive enclosure we obtained close-ups of pink-faced bumpkins, wearing parodies of Bond Street suitings of 1950 and addressing each other as 'Duke', 'Earl' and 'Prince' in Gloucestershire accents. And when I put what Heywood Magee by now was calling the sixty-four dollar question, their initial impulse to brazen things collapsed and I found 'King' of the Teddy-boys, Alan Chaffey, nineteen, telling me: 'Truth? What *can* you believe? We come here because it makes us feel good. During the week I work underground at Pensford Colliery and keep racing pigeons. When me and my mate first put these suits on, our faces weren't half red. But they're lovely suits, really. In a year or

two I suppose we'll be married and that will be the end of jiving. We'll be too busy getting our homes together.'[20]

Chaffey's friend John Reed had the final word: 'Call this the Devil's garb? It's smashing cloth, brother.'

Tearaway Tony

If these suits were a sure-fire route to damnation, what were a group of four Teddy boys doing among the 90,000-strong crowd watching the American evangelist preacher Billy Graham speak at Wembley Stadium in May 1955? Their presence caught the attention of a national press photographer,[21] and a week later a reporter from *The People* tracked three of them down in a pub. Had they suddenly found religion?

'We just went for a giggle,' said one of the seventeen-year-olds. 'Billy Graham doesn't mean anything to me. But he's a shrewd spieler right enough.'

'Sure,' said another, 'but he didn't make me believe in God. Last time I touched the Bible was when they made me read the lesson at Borstal.'[22]

Perhaps equally inevitably, the story continued by noting that their friend 'Tearaway Tony' Reuter – with five convictions, including three for assault – claimed that after seeing the preacher he was turning over a new leaf, paving the way for the article to conclude: 'Next Sunday, "The People" will print Reuter's own confession that will open the public's eyes to the extent of the Teddy Boy menace.'[23] Of course they would.

Billy Graham had even found time to mention those of an Edwardian persuasion during his Wembley appearance, telling the crowd, 'We have Teddy boys in America. They are trying to run away from the responsibilities of life.'[24] It is hardly surprising that they had come to the attention of an American Southern Baptist preacher like Graham, since their novel appearance and reputation for violence had also proved popular with newspaper commissioning editors across the Atlantic. Often these reports seemed to have been written out of a belief that American readers would find it comforting that their own problems with juvenile delinquency were trivial compared to the situation overseas. For example, the citizens of Cape Girardeau, Missouri, were treated to an article in their local newspaper that summer which claimed to have the lowdown on London's Teddy boys and Teddy girls – although the unnamed writer shot themselves in the foot right at the start by asserting that the word 'Edwardian becomes "Teddy" in cockney rhyming slang'. Nevertheless, the author confidently asserted that Britain's juvenile delinquents were every bit as fearsome as those in the USA. Here, apparently, is a typical Ted:

> He wears a fancy, brocaded waistcoat and a velvet collar on his high-buttoned coat, but the scars on his cheek are razor slashes put there by a rival gang. His hair is 'permed' and frizzed to make him look like a French poodle, but he carries a knife with an eight-inch spring blade in his pocket. He likes to show off a well-turned calf in 15-inch drainpipe trousers, but he swings a wicked bicycle chain in a street fight . . . Taken alone, the Teddy Boy, with his long hair and scarecrow clothes, is pretty much the cream puff he looks. But in a gang he becomes mean. Suddenly, at a signal from its leader, the gang may start moving along the sidewalk in phalanx formation, knocking everyone in its path into the gutter. This is the Teddy Boys' idea of 'fun', yet there is nothing joyful about these hoodlums.[25]

The author also stated that wrecking churches was one of their favourite pastimes, dropped several more hints about their supposed effeminacy, and roped in the January 1953 execution of the innocent Derek Bentley to supposedly strengthen his argument, saying that 'an 18-year-old Teddy Boy went to the gallows not long ago for his part in the brutal slaying of a London bobby'.[26] The Bentley case was a notorious miscarriage of justice. His murder conviction was finally posthumously overturned in 1998,[27] and to call him a Ted was stretching the point considerably. This article was standard tabloid fare, and probably intended to provide relief for any Missourian tired of the endless reports, books and films about home-grown juvenile delinquents that were something of a growth industry in America at the time.

Strong Drink and Fine Clothes

Any teenager who took a fancy to the new Edwardian style was typically earning a wage of perhaps £7 or £8 a week. However, a man named K. D. Robinson, the head of Birkenhead School, told the London conference of the Incorporated Association of Headmasters that everyone under twenty-one deserved a 50 per cent pay cut: 'It is a bad system which provides a teen-ager with the price of a strong drink and fine clothes. We could halve our difficulties if we could halve his pay.'[28]

To be clear about this, he was suggesting that people who were doing an adult job having left school at fifteen should not be allowed to choose how they spent their own wages for the first six years of their working lives, and that a significant fraction of what they earned should be denied them by some kind of central government legislation. It is hard to imagine that he and his fellow conference delegates would have responded well to their own wages being slashed by 50 per cent, yet Robinson's proposal was uncritically reported in both national and local media. No one seems to have bothered to ask any Teds what they thought of it.

If everyone appeared to have an opinion about Teddy boys, the nation had also woken up to the existence of their female equivalent. Given the social constraints placed on teenage girls at the time, their acts of rebellion in clothing and behaviour were seen as even more daring than those of their male contemporaries. Half a century before tattoos became commonplace among the general public of both sexes, a columnist calling himself the Old Stager in the December 1955 issue of *The Sphere* magazine heaped scorn on an apparent new trend among Teddy girls in the Midlands for having them on their legs:

> Girls' legs are not always pretty, and tattooing them is calling attention to them as a large, false diamond or ruby ring calls attention to dirty, ugly hands. Your great-aunts didn't do these things, but had much more justification for doing them, because in their day the secrets of the bathroom *were* secrets. They washed in private, and in public bathed in serge drawers off-shore. You girls do not. You lie almost naked on the beaches, turning yourselves into lobsters, and I don't think that crude tattoos improve the sun's work on your legs.[29]

It is not hard to imagine the likely reaction of any Teddy girl if they chanced to run into the Old Stager after reading this. Indeed, they might perhaps have been tempted to follow the example of a nineteen-year-old from Mildenhall in Suffolk who appeared on charges of being drunk and disorderly having assaulted three policemen, one of whom would remember her

A variety of self-devised Ted styles captured by photographer Juliette Lasserre in 1955, the year that rock'n'roll first started properly taking hold in Britain

Newly paroled prisoner Danny Hughes in front of a poster showing 'Forces No. 1 Pin-up' Joan Collins in the film *Cosh Boy*, May 1953

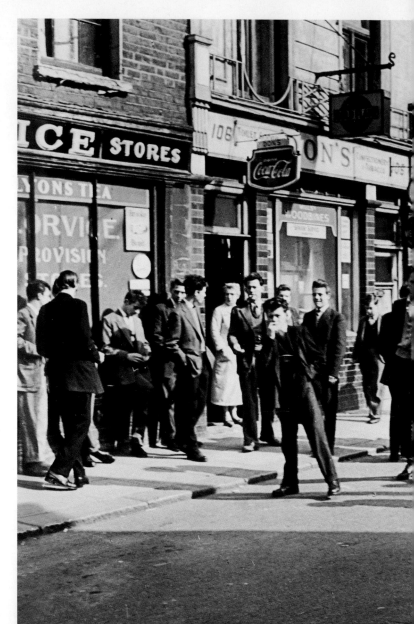

Roger Mayne's classic photograph of a group of youthful
Teds in Princedale Road, North Kensington, 1956

'Call this the Devil's garb? It's smashing cloth, brother.' Teenage jivers in Bristol, April 1955

Sharp-dressed teenagers at a Tottenham Dancehall, 1954 – from the *Picture Post* article, 'The Truth About the "Teddy Boys" and the Teddy Girls'

Teddy girls Rose Hendon and Mary Toovey photographed by Ken Russell in Southam Street, North Kensington, January 1955

Eileen Lewis of Bethnal Green, plus two Teddy boys duelling with toy guns – a Ken Russell photo from the 1955 *Picture Post* article, 'What's Wrong With Teddy Girls?'

Marie Imiah from Glasgow in her 'Rock Around the Clock' skirt awaiting the train carrying Bill Haley and His Comets, Waterloo Station, 5 February 1957

Police on the lookout for signs of trouble from the supposedly dangerous crowd queuing obediently to see *Rock Around the Clock*, Manchester, 21 September 1956

Bill Haley and His Comets at the Dominion Theatre, Tottenham Court Road,
on the opening day of their ground-breaking UK tour, 6 February 1957

The Boys – novelisation of
the film script by John Burke,
1962, released into a world
in which Teds were already
becoming yesterday's news

'When the "juke" goes wrong they start
walking out. No "juke" – no business.'
Teds in a London café, 13 July 1955

Four of the accused on their way to West London Police Court where they were remanded on charges relating to the Notting Hill race riots, 4 September 1958

Notting Hill race riots – scuffles with the police in Bramley Road, which resulted in several arrests that night, 31 August 1958

with little fondness, as the court heard: 'He was obliged to restrain her, and she spat in his face and brought her knee up forcibly into his body.'[30] Having punched another officer and spat in the face of a third, she then threatened to throw herself out of the moving police car while being taken into custody. A probation officer told the magistrates that the defendant had 'announced in 1954 that she was a Teddy girl',[31] and subsequently been sent to a psychiatrist.

That was of course one way of making it into the newspapers, but there were others. Once again, it was the reporters from *Picture Post* magazine who attempted to provide a more balanced view of these young people, and took the trouble to ask them in detail about their lives. The magazine ran a feature article on 4 June 1955, entitled *What's Wrong With Teddy Girls?* which proved to be one of the most historically significant of the era. Illustrated with superb black and white photographs by future film director Ken Russell, it delved into the lives and attitudes of various London teenagers who had adopted the Teddy girl style, while taking note of the controversy which already surrounded them: 'Teddy clothes, it has been said, can cover a multitude of sins – or juvenile delinquencies. But we found that some Teddy Girls were hard-working girls with a fashion sense which has brought a welcome flash of mass-elegance into the British scene.'[32]

Teenagers like Iris Thornton, Pat Wiles, Mary Toovey, Jean Rayner, Grace Living, Vera Harrison, identical twins Elsie and Rosie Hendon, Josie Buchan, and Barbara Wood – whose ages ranged from fourteen to nineteen – were photographed by Russell in often bomb-damaged London locations such as North Kensington, Tottenham, Stepney, Poplar, Walthamstow and Canning Town. Not all of them were named in the photo captions, but half a century later some of them were interviewed for a research project by Eve Dawoud about their memories of having appeared in that article.[33]

Despite the fact that Teddy girls had often been painted by the sensationalist press of the day as desperate characters who were handy with a flick-knife, the women who spoke to Dawoud came across as normal fun-loving teenagers who had mostly married shortly afterwards. Mary Toovey, for instance, struck up a conversation at the cinema with a boy when she was fifteen, and they married three years later; in a similar fashion, Iris Thornton started going out with her future husband at the age of sixteen and they wed after five years, while Grace Living married at the age of twenty. Another thing they all appeared to share was a good recall of the precise details of their clothing and hairstyles and the motivations behind their choice of them. They all seem to have been drawn to the Teddy girl fashion as a means of asserting their identity.

As Grace Living recalled,

> I had black pencil skirts and black trousers too. I also had a shawl-collared jacket, mine was black with a yellow trim, drainpipe trousers, little ballet pumps, a clutch and clip on circle earrings. I used to make and customise things, stitch a rose onto a blouse or cover a clutch bag in a fabric to match your earrings. I'd paint my earrings with nail varnish to have them match your outfit.[34]

Iris Thornton was able to afford hand-tailored clothes, and the look she opted for was close to that of her male companions: 'All the jackets I had made were a finger tip drape. Two flap pockets on one side, one on the other. Velvet collar, vent up the back.'[35] So much did tastes cross over, that not only did some of these interviewed say that they regularly wore each other's clothing, but also that of male friends, as Rosie Hendon explained: 'I was always buying clothes, I was terrible. You'd share clothes too, with your friends and sisters, used to borrow the boys' jackets sometimes.'[36]

It was a similar story with hairstyles, in that often the girls chose something relatively short which the boys might also have worn. Cameo brooches were popular as accessories, as were Chinese-style straw hats, the occasional turban, gloves and rolled umbrellas. Like their male counterparts, Teddy girls had a look which was both smart and distinctive, and almost guaranteed to attract attention. The more specific aim was to get the boys to notice them, but there was also the simple pleasure of causing a reaction. As Iris Thornton put it: 'You would walk past people on the street and hear them saying, "Oh god, look at what they are wearing!" Which made me chuckle.'[37]

Whether public opinion was favourable or negative, people were well aware of their existence. Teds and Teddy girls across the nation were all dressed up. Now they just needed somewhere to go.

8

ON THE TOWN

My Kingdom for Some Horseplay

If you were a post-war teenager, with a little money in your pocket from a job, or from your parents if you were still at school, you would naturally be looking for some fun once the evening rolled around. This often meant the cinema or a dance hall – a place to meet the opposite sex, or somewhere to go with them once you had struck up an acquaintance. However, many of the adults who ran such establishments often had a jaundiced view of their youthful patrons, usually based on experience.

Some decades ago I worked at one of London's oldest cinemas, the Screen On The Green on Upper Street in Islington. The staff gradually became used to the fact that while most of those who walked through the door just wanted a ticket and some entertainment, a certain percentage were simply looking for trouble, especially at the late shows which typically started after the pubs had closed for the evening. We would be sworn at, threatened, and then every year around Guy Fawkes Night, as an added bonus, we would have fireworks thrown at us as we stood behind the counter by feral twelve-year-olds running in off the street. Anyone who has worked with the public will tell you that most people you deal with are absolutely fine, but the few that are not can be scary.

All of which is a roundabout way of saying that I can

completely understand the wary reactions of anyone who worked in the nation's cinemas directly after the war, when many people made multiple visits in the same week and television was not yet any form of serious competition. Among so many customers, there were bound to be troublemakers, and the litany of disturbances and vandalism in such places was a well-established fact of life long before the first Ted carved up a cinema seat. To take a single random example, the residents of Uxbridge were informed in 1949 by a regular columnist of the *Uxbridge and West Drayton Gazette* that hooligans were stalking the district: 'The High-street entrance to the Underground Station appears to be a meeting place for some of them; in the evenings it echoes their strident voices, and bona fide travellers are embarrassed by their nonsensical shouting and stupid horseplay.'[1]

The writer identified cinemas as a particular focus for such troublemakers, because, 'like all bullies, our local "toughs" are much braver in the dark'. In this instance, they proved his point a few weeks later by bringing stones and catapults into the auditorium of the art deco Odeon cinema on the High Street and piercing the screen in eight places, after which the evening performance was abandoned.[2]

Unruly Toilets and Non-Stop Plumbing

It was not only London cinemas that were attracting trouble at the close of the 1940s. In the Cumberland market town of Penrith, the manager of the Regent cinema reported that numerous seats had been slashed with knives, while toilet fittings were 'considerably damaged and removed'.[3] In Hull, cinema doormen were said to be 'constantly on guard against the organized gangs, who, especially in the company of girl friends, try to show their he-man abilities by shouting and general rowdyism'.[4] Here, as in

Penrith, an apparently sure-fire way to impress the ladies was to smash up the gents: 'One of the favourite haunts of the unruly is the toilet, and a West Hull cinema employs a plumber almost non-stop to cope with such damage.'[5]

Occasional disturbances at cinemas were an established fact of life, and by 1954, many in the adult world viewed any teenagers adopting the new Edwardian styles as potential troublemakers. 'Cinemas to Act Against "Teddy Boys"' said a front-page headline on the *Portsmouth Evening News* that October, but in this instance, a few proprietors whose opinions were canvassed were not unduly worried – hardly surprising in a dockyard city well used to groups of sailors on shore leave. Also, as one manager pointed out, so many local teenagers were following this clothing trend that if he banned them all, 'at my cinema, this step would mean playing to empty houses'.[6]

Cinema-going Teds even attracted the attention of future Poet Laureate John Betjeman, who took issue with their behaviour in one of his regular articles for *The Spectator* in February 1955:

> Some friends, on my advice, went to see the wonders of Cinerama at the London Casino. They booked their seats beforehand because it is important, in order to get the full effect of Cinerama, to be sitting as near to the middle of the theatre as possible. When they arrived, a row of Teddy Boys and their girls (average age about fifteen) were occupying their seats. They said to them, 'Get along now, move off,' in an authoritative way, and the whole lot darted off terror-struck, like minnows from a man's shadow. Two old ladies who were sitting near said how glad they were someone had had the courage to shift the Teddy Boys away. I mention this incident because I have known similar

happenings in other cinemas. Toughs, or pseudo-toughs, will buy a cheap seat and occupy an expensive one, and neither usherette nor patron will have the courage to tell them to go away.[7]

Punch-Drunk Morons

The precise moment when British cinemas and Teddy boys were linked with the emergence of rock'n'roll occurred in September 1955, with the UK release of the film *Blackboard Jungle*, based on Evan Hunter's autobiographical novel about his experiences as a teacher at a school in New York. At the beginning of the month, the film had been controversially withdrawn from the prestigious Venice Film Festival by its makers, MGM, in response to a special request from the US ambassador to Italy, reportedly because 'she did not think that it gave a sympathetic view of American life'.[8] A staunch Republican, Clare Booth Luce was also the wife of multi-millionaire publisher Henry Luce, whose magazines such as *Life*, *Time* and *Sports Illustrated* did much to project an image internationally of what America represented, and teenage juvenile delinquents smashing up an inner-city classroom were not necessarily a desirable part of that picture.

This politically motivated censorship was widely criticised in film circles, both at the festival itself and internationally, and when the picture was released two weeks later in Britain it opened to a barrage of publicity as a result. 'Anthony Carthew Sees the Film That Was Banned at the Venice Festival' read the headline of an article in the *Daily Herald* a few days before the UK premiere, which pulled few punches: 'I saw a film yesterday which horrified me. As I came out into a drizzling London afternoon, I felt physically sick . . . From the evidence of the picture

I can only conclude that many American male teenagers are either mentally deficient, or brutal thugs.'[9]

Reg Whitley in the *Daily Mirror* made the same points in a similar article a few days later headlined 'A School Where Stilettos Flash!'[10] Yet in among all their talk of knife fights, alcoholism, beatings, attempted rape, and attempted murder, neither writer mentioned the element that was to really fire up the Teddy boys and Teddy girls when they saw the film: its opening title music, 'Rock Around the Clock'. It is one thing playing a song in your bedroom at home, but quite another having it blasting out at ten times the volume in a cinema auditorium among a crowd of your fellow teenagers. The sheer power of that tune, with Billy Gussak's snare drum cracking out and Marshall Lytle's slapping double bass driving the whole tune along as Haley's joyous vocals rode over the whole thing, would have been something quite unprecedented in most young listeners' lives. And then there was the guitar, an amped-up, scene-stealing electric magnificently played by Danny Cedrone.

In a post-war Britain where reassuring family-friendly crooners still dominated the BBC airwaves, this was definitely something new.

Ah, Did You Hear That Music, Man?

Kent schoolboy and future Rolling Stone Keith Richards was approaching his twelfth birthday when the film started out on the national release circuit, and when asked by journalist Robert Greenfield in 1971 about his memories of rock'n'roll first making an impact in Britain, he identified this particular moment as the spark that lit the fuse:

The music from *Blackboard Jungle*, 'Rock Around the

Clock', hit first. Not the movie, just the music. People saying, 'Ah, did you hear that music, man?' Because in England, we had never heard anything. It's still the same scene: BBC controls it. Then, everybody stood up for that music. I didn't think of playing it. I just wanted to go and listen to it. It took 'em a year or two before anyone in England could make that music.[11]

The film did incredible business at the box office around London, and then across the nation when it went to wider release, carrying with it the sound of genuine rock'n'roll to tens of thousands of young people.

The few British record reviewers who called attention to the film's use of 'Rock Around the Clock' seemed to much prefer the vocal group treatment of the tune by the Deep River Boys, released as a single in those days when multiple versions of any tune would compete for a place in the charts. 'I doubt if there is a better recording by any other combination', wrote Reg Exton in the *Norwood News*,[12] while the respected jazz critic Max Jones concluded in his regular column in the *Daily Herald* that the version by the Deep River Boys was 'the most entertaining'.[13] This was hardly surprising, given that the American group had been living and performing in Britain for some years and were a well-known live act across the nation. Despite the opinions of these critics, it seemed that the kids had other ideas; a quick look at the weekly pop charts in the *New Musical Express* for 9 December[14] shows the Haley version firmly ensconced at number one, just ahead of British crooner Dickie Valentine with 'The Christmas Alphabet', currently starring nightly as Wishee-Washee in the pantomime *Aladdin* at the Theatre Royal, Newcastle.[15]

Meanwhile, as things were taking off for the Comets in Britain, the news from America was even more stellar, as the

NME's US correspondent Nat Hentoff noted in the same issue: 'Bill Haley's remarkably prosperous career continues to flourish. It looks, as of present counting, that his recording of "Rock Around The Clock" will sell 2,000,000 copies. Bill is also set to star in a Columbia picture with the hit song doubling as its title.'[16]

Cinema screenings of *Blackboard Jungle* had gone a long way towards lighting the rock'n'roll fuse in Britain, but the as-yet unmade feature film mentioned here by Hentoff would cause unprecedented mayhem at screenings the length of the UK when it finally hit these shores.

Sullen, Pathological, Embryonic Criminals

Inevitably, comparisons were drawn between the American classroom violence depicted in *Blackboard Jungle* and the actions of British Teddy boys – with a film reviewer in Dublin newspaper the *Catholic Standard* leading the charge. A lengthy appraisal of the film on 4 November made much of Clare Booth Luce's decision to ban it and concluded that despite the director Richard Brooks's good intentions, the resulting film strained credibility:

'TEDDY-BOYS' AT SCHOOL

The entire student body, it seems, is composed of sullen, pathological, embryonic criminals; polyglot, illiterate, juvenile desperadoes, physically well-developed by constant all-in combat, their brain power seems about equal to a dinosaur's . . . The Irish Film Censor, Dr Brennan, has used his scissors to delete some of the activities of these American 'Teddy Boys'.[17]

This message was amplified nationally by an anonymous teacher in a January 1956 *Daily Mirror* article headlined 'Britain's Blackboard Jungle': 'We are scared of the thugs who are growing up in our schoolrooms. We are scared of the Teddy Boy rule they are trying to clamp on the schoolroom – and of the threats to teachers outside it.'[18]

The film itself, and in particular the rock music on its soundtrack, was soon being directly blamed for violent incidents at picture houses, such as in this February 1956 report from the Midlands:

'TROUBLE FILM' CINEMAS SEEK POLICE AID

Several Birmingham cinema managers have asked local police to stand by to deal with expected outbreaks of hooliganism at their theatres this week during the showing of the film, *The Blackboard Jungle*. Since the film, which depicts juvenile delinquency at an American school, was released to suburban cinemas three weeks ago, it has left a trail of broken seats, say managers. At one cinema, the Clifton, Great Barr, last week, the film attracted Teddy Boys and noisy teen-agers. After every performance staff found seats and woodwork smashed and loosened from fittings. Mr Eric Walls, the manager, said last night: 'The main trouble is when the song, "Rock Around the Clock", is played during the film. It is a "hot bop" record and it causes a form of mass hysteria among the teen-age element in the audience.'[19]

All of which might well have encouraged some of those whose idea of a good night out was the prospect of a fistfight or some vandalism to pay a call to their local cinema and see what all the fuss was about.

We Don't Want You in Here

By now a reasonable number of young people habitually wore Edwardian styles when going out for the evening, so it followed that some of those causing trouble in cinemas would be dressed in that style. The same went for disturbances at coffee bars, dance halls, bus-stops or anywhere that teenagers might be found.

In March 1956, following a well-publicised fight at a North London church youth club in Edgware involving some Teds,[20] Britain's newly established second television channel ITV interviewed a small group of the boys themselves. This short piece of footage has survived,[21] and it is fascinating decades later to watch such people speak for themselves. Not that the television journalist with the microphone sounds remotely sympathetic – on the contrary, he asks more leading questions than a hostile prosecution counsel, barking them out in a patrician voice – while the Teds, like the vast majority of the population at the time, would never have had a film camera pointed at them in their lives. It is a shame that he did not let them talk a little more freely:

> Interviewer (to Ted 1): 'You went down to make trouble?'
> Ted 1: 'No, you know, it was just more for a giggle more or less.'
> Interviewer: 'You just got involved?'
> Ted 1: 'Yeah, we just got involved, you know.'
> Interviewer: 'Have you been "involved" in other sorts of things like this?'
> Ted 1: 'Well yeah, we've been involved in quite a few, you know.'
> Interviewer (to Ted 2): 'What do you do in your spare time down here?'
> Ted 2: 'Well, we just hang about, like.'

Interviewer: 'Nothing else to do?'

Ted 2: 'Nah, nothing else to do, just hang about.'

Interviewer: 'You go to the pictures?'

Ted 2: 'Yeah, go to the pictures twice a week, three times a week, like.'

Interviewer: 'Dances?'

Ted 2: 'No, don't go to many dances. Really, we're barred from a lot of dances.'

Interviewer: 'Why's that? Because you make trouble?'

Ted 2: 'I don't know. They just look at your gear, like, and then look at your hair, and say, No, we don't want you in here.'

The boys seem to have had little difficulty visiting their local cinemas dressed in Ted clothing, whereas gaining entrance to dances had already become a problem. However, four months later when the low-budget musical film starring Bill Haley and His Comets opened to widely reported scare stories of riot and disorder, that too would change.

Rock Around the Clock also featured pioneering US rock deejay Alan Freed, and other musical outfits such as Freddie Bell and the Bell Boys. The script may have been thin, but it gave teenagers a chance to see the faces behind the records in action – and it arrived in July 1956, in a week when the *New Musical Express* charts showed ample evidence of the rock revolution which had taken place in the UK Top Thirty that year. The Teenagers were at number one with 'Why Do Fools Fall in Love', Elvis's recent chart-topper 'Heartbreak Hotel' was still at number four and Britain's own Lonnie Donegan was at number ten with 'Lost John'. A little further down, Bill himself was at seventeen with 'The Saints Rock'n'Roll', Elvis was at twenty-five with 'I Want You, I Need You, I Love You' and the magisterial

Gene Vincent was at number thirty with his debut hit, 'Be Bop a Lula'.[22]

Hooting, Yelling, Hissing, Booing and Jeering

Former Liverpool Teddy boy John Lennon recalled the Haley film's release in an interview with *Rave* magazine in 1964: 'I read that everybody danced in the aisles during that film, *Rock Around the Clock*. It must have all been done before I went. I was all set to tear up the seats, too, but nobody joined in.'[23] Its well-publicised progress as it gradually moved across the country might have done more than anything else to link Teddy boys and rock'n'roll in the popular imagination. Six months earlier, *Blackboard Jungle*'s controversial British reputation had been largely down to the depiction of juvenile delinquent behaviour onscreen, but in the new film it was the rock music that was said to be stirring young people into frenzies of destruction. There was even a leader column devoted to it in *The Times* on 15 September, which while reasonably even-handed was under the impression that these disturbances were somehow the work of a new breed of jazz fan:

> For those social critics who are quick to detect every sign of decadence and ill-discipline in the youth of the welfare state, this latest instalment of transatlantic rhythm is no less exciting than it is for the boys and girls whose enthusiasm lands them in court. The reactions of six chimpanzees from the Liverpool zoo, who are reported to have given no more than 'mild applause' to the film, may be compared favourably, by some censors of contemporary behaviours, with those of jiving teenagers ... But then the amateurs of music in this heady *genre* tell us that, in the best Teddy-boy

circles, rocking and rolling is regarded as non-U, except for children. It is also said, to add to the confusion, that the true jazz expert discovers decadence, deviation, and reaction in this particular music.[24]

Leopard-Skin Shirt and Crêpe-Soled Shoes

Perhaps unsurprisingly, the box-office success of *Blackboard Jungle* also helped inspire a fine British juvenile delinquent film of the era. *Violent Playground* was partly shot at Pinewood Studios in the early summer of 1957, but also on the streets of Liverpool, the city whose police initiative to help prevent youth crime became a key part of the plot, as the local paper noted: 'Liverpool's pioneering juvenile liaison officer scheme, which is now being adopted all over the world, will form the basis for a drama to be filmed by the Rank Organisation. A film unit will arrive in Liverpool during the week-end to begin five weeks location filming on Monday.'[25]

Producer Michael Relph said at the time, 'The story is like *Blackboard Jungle* in texture, only we are playing it on a wider canvas.'[26] But where the latter film's American school-age cast had been mistakenly labelled Teddy boys by British reviewers, the teenage gang in *Violent Playground* are unquestionably Teds. One of the most convincing was a genuine Teddy boy called Gibbo who had been spotted observing the filming, as the *Leicester Evening Mail* reported:

'Take my clothes – take me,' said 19-year-old Gerrard Gibson and he was IN the film *Violent Playground*. He was OUT within a week. In Liverpool – his home town – Gerrard, wearing his best Edwardian suit, leopard-skin shirt and crêpe-soled shoes, was watching the film unit at work. When asked to sell his 'outfit', he replied: 'You can't have my best clothes unless I'm inside them.' Landed with a part, he took the other boy actors on a shopping spree and to the local barber's. All worked out fine until shooting in Liverpool finished and 'Gibbo' went back to Pinewood for finishing shots. After a week he had had enough – and caught the next train back to Liverpool.[27]

In the run-up to its release, the press repeatedly identified the group as a 'Teddy boy gang', with promotional pictures taken by the publicity department featuring some of the young actors posing alongside genuine Liverpool Teds.[28] *Violent Playground* was given a Royal Charity Premiere at the Odeon, Marble Arch on 3 March 1958, at which the chief guest was that well-known aficionado of crêpe-soled creepers, Prince Philip, Duke of Edinburgh, although he seems to have restrained himself from carving up the furnishings with a flick-knife.[29]

NO Bloodshed and NO Unpleasantness

It is hard to establish how much serious trouble occurred in and around early UK cinema showings of *Rock Around the Clock*. For every local council banning the film out of fears of some kind of imminent youth Armageddon, others claimed it was a fuss about nothing. One typical report in *The Times* from 7 September specifically blamed Teds while also namechecking the new music:

'ROCK AND ROLL' BAN IN BLACKPOOL

The Blackpool Tower Company, after their decision to deal with the 'Teddy boy' problem by excluding elements who might interfere with the enjoyment of patrons in their ballrooms and cinemas, have decided not to show the film *Rock Around the Clock* which had been booked for the Palace Cinema next week. The management have been disturbed by reports from various parts of the country of noisy behaviour by young people in places where the film has been shown.[30]

By now the link between Teds, trouble and rock'n'roll was firmly established in people's minds, and bans were put in place before the events could be staged. Yet the veracity of some of the original cinema scare stories which prompted councils to ban *Rock Around the Clock* was also sometimes called into question. A mid-August 1956 showing at the Gaumont in Shepherd's Bush resulted in claims in the national press of Teddy boy violence, staff members being assaulted and of the police being called, but a few days later the assistant manager who had been on duty that afternoon went public to deny that there had been any trouble:

CINEMA RIOT REPORTS 'RUBBISH'

Theatre spokesman and assistant manager, Mr Peter Corneille, was emphatic on different points raised in the reports. Firstly, they were NOT 'Teddy Boys'. They were NOT jiving. There was [*sic*] NO policemen present at any part of the performance. NO police were called. There was NO bloodshed and NO unpleasantness.[31]

News of such disturbances spread to America; *Billboard* magazine noted the apparent riots that had taken place at showings of the film in England, and quoted the moderate views of the *New Musical Express*. The British music weekly had written that 'hooligans were hooligans before *Rock Around the Clock* was ever exhibited', and asked if Beethoven and Bach should therefore be held responsible for the raucous behaviour of the Albert Hall crowd during the Last Night of the Proms.[32] Bill Haley himself waded into the debate in Britain that October with an article published in *The People*, just as plans were being formulated to bring him over for a tour early the following year.

> I've been reading that my movie *Rock Around the Clock* has been causing a little commotion in your neck of the woods ... Almost all of it is harmless. It's what we call 'letting off steam'. For no matter what the country or the place, whether they be Teddy Boys or undergrads, boys do like to let off steam. So do girls.[33]

Although very likely written on behalf of the man himself, these were some of the more sensible thoughts expressed on the subject that year.

Razors in the Dance Halls

If reports of Teddy boy rioting at cinemas were sometimes overstated, the scale of the threat posed by such people in the nation's dance halls is equally hard to judge. In 1971, Keith Richards recalled his own schooldays and the perceived dangers of a night at the local hop:

> I was just into Little Richard. I was rockin' away, avoidin' the bicycle chains and the razors in those dance halls. The English get crazy. They're calm, but they were really violent then, those cats. Those suits cost them $150, which is a lot of money. Jackets down to here. Waistcoats. Leopardskin

lapels ... amazing. It was really 'Don't step on mah blue suede shoes.' It was down to that.[34]

Of course, not every working-class youth was a Teddy boy, and many actively disliked them. I asked a man named Ken, a South London teenager in the late 1950s, about his experiences going to dance halls at the time:

> I used to go every Saturday night, sometimes Friday nights when I could afford two days. In those days you had two bands on and everything, and when I say bands I mean orchestras. That's the way it was in those days: the Lyceum in the Strand, the Locarno in Streatham, the Orchid Ballroom, Purley. I danced at them all. Nine times out of ten you would have trouble. That was the days of the open face razor, razor blades stitched into caps, but to be honest I was never a Teddy boy, never wanted to be a Teddy boy. I didn't like the hairstyle, it was called a duck's arse. My father was very Victorian, and he would have knocked the hell out of me if I'd be likely to do anything like that, so I never actually got into those things. That's the way that the fathers were in those days.[35]

No sooner had the general public become aware of the clothing and hairstyles favoured by Teddy boys, notices began appearing outside dance halls barring entry to those in Edwardian clothing. Anyone adopting this style was pre-emptively found guilty by some proprietors and dismissed as a troublemaker. When fifty Teds were turned away from a dance in Luton in December 1954, the local paper reported this under the headline 'TEDDY BOYS BANNED', making much of their Edwardian suits.[36] Yet no clothing restrictions were in place at the venue;

the teenagers had, in fact, failed to gain entry because tickets had long since sold out, and the youths dispersed peacefully when asked to do so by a lone policeman. Soon, however, the wearing of a Ted suit became a problem in itself; when a different ball-room in the same town brought in a new manager, his plans were approvingly reported:

> The extreme Edwardian get-up is BANNED ... Jiving and jitterbugging are BANNED (except for one or two numbers during the evening). He's bringing some bright spots into his dances, though. There will be 'knobbly knees' and 'slimmest waist' contests; competitions to find 'Mr Heart Throb' and a 'Cover Girl'.[37]

All of which presumably left any number of Edwardian-garbed, knobbly-kneed heart-throbs weeping in despair at not being allowed inside to join the fun.

The Long Hair Style Affected by This Cult

There were certainly some dance-hall incidents linked to those who had adopted the fashion. In June 1954, scuffles occurred one night in Edenbridge, near Sevenoaks, prompting an article in the *Kent & Sussex Courier* with the headline '"TEDDY BOYS" CRASH RURAL DANCE'. Some locals blamed 'teenage gangs' who were 'wearing the drain-pipe trousers and long hair style affected by this cult'.[38] They said that beer glasses were thrown, windows smashed, police summoned and that fighting had spilled out into the street. Yet the member of the constabulary approached by the newspaper for comment criticised residents for exaggerating the problem. 'Some of the people who have the most to say about it ... do not actually see anything at all – they were asleep in their beds all the time.'[39] Indeed, the police went even further in their attempt to counteract the received wisdom about such clothing:

[Teddy boys] dislike fighting because it spoils their elegant attire. The suit alone can cost up to £25. 'If anything they are less trouble than some of the other youths,' was a police officer's observation to the *Courier*. 'It seems rather unfair on the youths who do affect the Edwardian dress to paint them all with the same brush because some of their number get into trouble. Remember that the general public has its black sheep as well.'[40]

Trouble occurred in July 1954 at a dance in Irvine on the Firth of Clyde among a group of forty Teds, some of whom were said to have come down from nearby Glasgow looking for a fight. Knives were found by the police, and two received short prison sentences.[41] Presumably they were wearing what was described at another Glasgow trial as 'the draped jacket, stove-pipe trousers and huge shoes favoured by many of the youthful patrons of our dance halls'.[42] Later that year, a series of Saturday night dances at a hall in Wimbledon were reluctantly cancelled when the organiser acknowledged that they had been attracting teenage gangs in Edwardian clothing from various parts of London, with regular fights, and wine and gin bottles left around afterwards.[43] A month later, a news item in the *Daily Herald* managed to imply that those in drapes had caused the problem: 'TEAR-GAS FLOORS THE DANCERS IN A WEEPING FOX-TROT – Bristol, Sunday: Teen-age girls screamed and collapsed. Their partners sagged to the floor. Fights broke out among youths, some in "Teddy boy" suits.'[44]

Sitting happily on the fence, the same newspaper also ran

a story about the dance-hall proprietors banning people from doing the popular dance the Creep because it supposedly 'attracts Teddy Boys – and trouble',[45] while directly beneath it printing another one which offered a solution proposed by the Assistant Education Officer for Lancashire, who felt that 'well-chosen poetry well read at youth clubs would make even Teddy Boys come to enjoy it'.[46]

Maybe, but then again, maybe not.

Old Farts Everywhere

In 1955, fifteen-year-old Tom Jones had just left school and was marking time earning £2 a week as an apprentice glove-cutter in South Wales. After attempting to convince an older saxophone-playing work colleague of the merits of 'Rock Around the Clock', he accepted the man's invitation to come along and listen to some 'proper music':

> I go to see his dance band in Caerphilly. And then I very quickly wish I hadn't. Old farts everywhere. Foxtrots and waltzes. Boring. Safe. This thing is horrible to me. 'Now, ladies and gentlemen, it's time for an excuse-me.' Give over. On the Monday at work, I go for the glove-cutters: 'You're condemning "Rock Around the Clock" and you're playing that crap?'[47]

Even so, not every teenager seems to have been quite so willing to embrace the new. One young Londoner who wrote to *Picture Post* in February 1956 complained of feeling positively old-fashioned after a night out on the town:

> I am mystified. I am a young man who likes dancing,

though I am not, I hasten to add, one of the Edwardian type. I went into a dance hall in the West End recently. I sat down at a table and began to 'survey the talent' (that is, I understand, the term used nowadays). Having spotted a 'real crazy doll', I asked her for a dance. After we had been on the floor for a few moments she expressed surprise at my manner of approach. Most of 'them boys', she said, just tapped her on the arm and jerked their heads towards the floor. Am I just too 'square'?[48]

Yet given the bans on Teddy boy clothing at many venues, how did such people gain admittance? Given that groups of them were photographed in such places as the Mecca Dance Hall in Tottenham, it is hard to say how seriously such restrictions were enforced. Narrowness of trouser alone was sometimes held to be an indicator, which in 1958 led to Blackburn Rovers and England football international Bryan Douglas being denied entry by a bouncer at the Blackpool Tower Ballroom, despite the fact that the suit he was wearing – which had nineteen-inch-wide trouser legs – was one of a formal set bought for him and the rest of the national team by the Football Association to wear to that year's World Cup in Sweden. 'I felt I was being branded as a Teddy boy,' Douglas said afterwards. 'I was hopping mad.'[49]

In 1955, the year in which 'Rock Around the Clock' caused a seismic wave in the music landscape of the UK, Richard was a sixteen-year-old Londoner with a powder-blue, velvet-collared Ted suit. I asked him about the dance halls he and his friends used to go to in those days, and the difficulty when encountering signs which said 'No Edwardian Clothing, No Drape Jackets': 'Well, we used to beat that. We used to put an old mac on, long, you know, like Columbo wears, one of them. Put a pair of glasses on and look respectable. You know, it's like anything – it was there for the taking.'[50]

Once inside, the disguise could be left in the cloakroom, and the risk of then being ejected was apparently small. Richard's crowd would travel around the wider London area in search of entertainment, and venturing onto another group's home turf could be a risky business. Even on presumably neutral ground such as a centrally located dance hall near Oxford Circus that Richard recalls, fights could be sparked:

> I think it was called The Locarno, and that used to be a great place for pulling birds. It was always women that caused the problems between the Teds, because it became very territorial. You know, if you went across the river. I had a fight at the Elephant and Castle where I glassed a bloke. I'm not proud of it, but it was one of them silly occasions where the guy said to me, 'Get yourself back across the river by the time I've finished this pint or I'm gonna chin ya.' So he raised the glass up to his mouth and I smacked the bottom of the glass. Got out of there very rapid. But that's what you did when you were kids, you had no fear.[51]

The average non-Teddy boy or Teddy girl enjoying a night out would have been aware that such outbreaks of violence might suddenly intrude upon their evening, during which they were either spectators or unwilling participants. Margaret was a teenager in mid-1950s Berkshire, who enjoyed going to the weekly village-hall dances where she lived. These were generally peaceful events run by a local man named Simmy who also acted as doorman. She told me her memories of the night that a group of Teds showed up from a nearby town – either Reading or Slough:

They tried to push their way in without paying. We'd never seen them before. It was obvious they were there to cause trouble, and thought it would be easy in a quiet village, but they didn't know Simmy, he was very strong. He knocked two of them out with just one punch each and then they all ran away. I think they got the shock of their lives.[52]

A Few Bob on a New Whistle and Flute

As far as teenage Teddy boys and Teddy girls were concerned, public halls were only part of the story. Much of their dancing took place in less formal places – youth clubs and cafes where dress codes were less strict or non-existent, and the music sometimes came from a record player or a jukebox. If so, you could dance to the genuine rock'n'roll of Elvis, Bill Haley or Little Richard, as opposed to a pale imitation served up by the local palais orchestra. There were even record clubs which met at local dance halls, such as the one at the Mayfair Ballroom in Long Eaton, Nottinghamshire in 1956 where teenagers were encouraged to bring along their own records for a dance session one night a week. Basil Halliday, one of the people in charge, told local paper the *Stapleton & Sandiacre News*: 'We started this scheme with the idea of catering for the town's young record fans. They buy up so many discs and it's only fair they get a chance to share them and listen to records they haven't got themselves.'[53]

One of those enjoying these evenings was seventeen-year-old Mick May who appreciated the chance to dance to authentic sounds and avoid the ban on Edwardian clothing in some regular dance halls:

> Rock'n'roll is just what we want. It's got a terrific rhythm – and now we've got a chance to use it to the best advantage.

This town's got nothing else for us to do and we've waited a long time for this club. Another good thing is that they don't mind what you wear. When we get dressed up on a Saturday and go to Derby we're not allowed in some dance halls ... They must think I become a different character when I change my clothes. I even had to take off my silver brocade waistcoat and leave it in the office before I could get into one dance hall. There's none of that here.[54]

A rare glimpse into the life at a youth club was preserved by film-maker Karel Reisz, who captured a part of the lives of a group of young people that met regularly at the Alford House Youth Club in Kennington in the summer of 1958. The finished documentary was released the following year under the title *We Are the Lambeth Boys*,[55] by which time Reisz was well into his next project – *Saturday Night & Sunday Morning* – the fiction-alised story of a Nottingham Teddy boy factory hand, which would make his reputation internationally.

We Are the Lambeth Boys contains a long sequence of a dance taking place at the club, and there is a close-up of a hand-written sign chalked on a blackboard which reads:

SATURDAY

DANCE

THE

MICKEY WILLIAMS

GROUP

BRING GUESTS

2/6

The band does a creditable job of mimicking the sax-led Bill Haley sound, playing a decent version of the previous year's skiffle hit, 'Puttin' on the Style' by Lonnie Donegan, to a dance-floor full of teenage jivers. Girls sit watching the action from one side of the room while the boys line the other wall, weighing their chances and smoking intently. The latter have slicked-back quiffs, and wear jackets of varying length, straight trousers, shirts and ties. Although they generally live in the local council blocks and would have come from homes where money was tight, they look smart and have paid attention to their appearance. Elsewhere in the documentary, when asked about how much they might spend on a suit, one replies 'about fifteen guineas' (roughly £16), which they estimate would give them less than a year of use: 'After about eight months to a year it don't look smart anymore, so you've gotta buy a new one.'[56]

Many of the teenagers who appeared in Reisz's film were reunited in 1985 for a follow-up documentary, *We Were the Lambeth Boys*,[57] in which they reflected on the younger versions of themselves as seen in the 1958 original. One of them, Percy, talked about the violent reputation which was still clinging to the Ted movement three decades later:

I had the haircut, and the big long drape coat and the drain-pipe trousers. Oh yeah, it was in my era, the Teddy boy. There was lots of them that used to congregate in different places, outside coffee bars and stalls and things like that, but a lot of them you didn't know. You was with your particular little group, possibly around about four, five or six of you, and you would see some others there. That's when the trouble sometimes started. Few punch ups here and there. See, I was never really cut up or anything like that, scarred in any way – specially when you went out and you'd spent a few bob on a new whistle, a whistle and flute, you didn't want all blood all over that and your sleeves ripped off, so you tended to avoid having them slashed. When they turn round and say Teds carried bicycle chains – that was only a few. I never carried a bike chain, or a razor or anything. Never had to.[58]

Under Their Legs and Over Their Shoulders

All this talk of fighting tends to obscure the fact that a great proportion of the millions of young people who attended dances up and down the country during that era would have had an enjoyable time and finished the evening safely at home, never going anywhere near an accident and emergency department or a magistrates' court. The simple joy of dancing to rock'n'roll comes through vividly in the recollections of one 1950s teenager interviewed for the 1986 BBC radio series *You'll Never Be 16 Again*, who spoke of lunchtime sessions sandwiched into their working week:

> Everybody was throwing everybody under their legs and over their shoulders ... I used to go to the Plaza every dinner time. It cost us sixpence for two hours. The thousands that used to go there! They had it on from twelve till two, and I only had an hour for my dinner. I used to sneak the two hours and creep into work so that nobody would see me. But I wasn't on my own – everybody else was doing the same, and of course at that time you could walk in a job and get sacked, then go and get another job in the afternoon.[59]

Despite such examples of innocent enjoyment, in the second half of the 1950s the perceived image of Teddy boys as dance-hall troublemakers and weapon-carrying thugs was enough of a cliché that such figures had begun making their way into novels, plays and radio dramas. For instance, in his 1958 London-based novel, *The Gigantic Shadow*, the great crime writer Julian Symons has a scene in which the protagonist Bill Hunter ventures out from his cheap boarding house in Pimlico for a night's entertainment at the nearby Victoria Dance Rooms:

> Two teddy boys lounged by the entrance. They wore long draped jackets and narrow trousers beneath which bright pink socks showed. As Hunter turned the corner of the street a long low car pulled up and two couples got out, young men and women in evening clothes. The teddy boys whistled appreciatively and said something as the couples went in. One of the young men, short, dark and sullen, turned back as if to speak to them, but the girl with him pulled him on. Hunter gave the boys a savage scowl as he passed.[60]

Predictably, inside the hall a short while later, one of these same Teds pulls a knife on someone and a fight breaks out. If the book had been written a decade earlier – or later – another type of hooligan would have been pressed into service. For the moment, Teds filled that role, and the fear of picking a fight with someone who might have a concealed weapon somewhere in their Edwardian finery was understandable.

At the Plaza Ballroom in Manchester in 1958, described locally as the 'rock'n'roll spot for thousands of teenagers', the manager was happy to explain to the press his series of procedures designed to weed out potential troublemakers:

1. All Teddy boys are spoken to before entering
2. If replies are not very encouraging they are searched

3.   If someone is found to carry a pocket knife, out he goes[61]

That particular manager, so keen to preserve the peace, landed a job as a deejay with Radio Luxembourg later the same year, and would become one of the best-known household names on British radio and television. Had Manchester parents of the time been aware of what is now known about him, they would have had far more worries about letting their teenage daughters go to the Plaza than the fact that they might encounter a Ted carrying a penknife; the manager in question was Jimmy Savile, revealed after his death in 2011 to be a prolific abuser of children.

A Bit of a Ruckus

Of course, teenage Teds on a night out might be carrying other concealed items which were less easy to spot. When I asked Richard about such measures, he had this to say:

> Well, to be perfectly honest, as a young man, I was a total hooligan. You know, we didn't carry knives, but we used to carry bike chains underneath the lapels of our long coats, and another little trick we used – I don't know if you know what a perch hook is? – a triple hook, what you catch perch on. We used to sew them at the back of our lapels. The first time the police grabbed you, when there was a bit of a ruckus, they'd grab you by the lapels. Of course, they got the shock of their lives when they found they'd got three or four hooks in their fingers . . .[62]

Whatever was causing the trouble at dance halls and ballrooms, it was unlikely to have been rock'n'roll. The typical evening's entertainment was usually provided by a local band or orchestra that would have routinely played their own interpretations of the hits of the day, mixed in with popular standards from times gone by. This was ten years before the discotheque boom of the mid-1960s in which vinyl records provided the entertainment; live music still prevailed, and performers were judged by their ability to mimic the sounds broadcast on radio and on television. There was often no definitive recording of many popular songs, and the charts regularly accommodated two or three competing versions of the same tune. A year or so later as rock became a fixture in the charts, most combos would single out one of the regular vocalists in their line-up to attempt to be their town's 'answer to Elvis' for a couple of numbers, while still serving up more traditional material to please a wide age range of paying customers. As Ted Carroll told me, recalling dances he attended in late 1950s Ireland at which the showbands reigned supreme:

> Brendan Boyer, the lead singer of the Royal Showband, was like Ireland's Elvis Presley, he could leap around and he did fabulous voices, he was a wonderful singer, he could do the Presley stuff really well. They were basically kind of living jukeboxes, they played the charts, played a little bit of Dixieland because trad was very popular then, bit of Latin American, a bit of everything.[63]

Various clues to the music likely to be encountered in dance halls of 1954 can be found in the edition of the *New Musical Express* from 17 December, which shows that the big bands that had held sway since before the war were still dominant. The front page was devoted to an advert for a new record by American singer Billy Daniels (born 1915), singing 'Bye Bye Blackbird' (a song from 1924) and 'She's Funny That Way' (written in 1929).[64] Large adverts for upcoming attractions that month tell their own story: Ken Mackintosh and His Orchestra at the Trocadero, Elephant and Castle; the Lou Preager Orchestra at Hammersmith Palais; Frank Weir and His Orchestra at Clapham Baths (tickets four shillings from Bassett's newsagents opposite the venue); Geraldo and His Orchestra at the Dudley Hippodrome, and Gracie Cole's all-female orchestra at the Ritz Ballroom, Swindon. Away from the big bands, you could also seek out more traditional New Orleans-inspired sounds at the Cy Laurie Jazz Club in Soho's Great Windmill Street, or Humphrey Lyttelton's regular gig at 100 Oxford Street, a historic venue that's still going more than six decades later.[65]

Shake, Rattle and Role-Play

Still, on closer examination, there were signs of change to be found in that well-thumbed music paper as 1954 drew to a close, such as the advert from the UK song publishing firm Campbell Connelly for a tune whose rights they had acquired, 'Shake, Rattle and Roll'. In fact, this was the week that Haley first broke into the British charts[66] – and a few pages further on, his version of the song was shown as having gone straight in at number thirteen.[67] By the first week of January, the Comets would have two records in the listings, as 'Rock Around the Clock' followed it up the charts. For the moment, Haley was still trailing seven places behind the Big Ben Banjo Band, but British record buyers were only just starting to propel rock'n'roll into the hit parade, an area that this genre would come to dominate for the rest of the decade.

Looking at the equivalent issue of US trade paper *Cash Box* for the same week, Haley's single was at number six in the Top Ten Juke Box Tunes listing, and in just about every regional

American top ten[68]. In *Billboard*, it was the nation's number ten best-selling record[69]. This is not to say that rock had yet conquered all in the States – the recent mambo craze was still going strong, and early fifties heart-throb Johnnie Ray's new single was a version of the standard 'Alexander's Ragtime Band', written by Irving Berlin in 1911.[70] Even so, out in the clubs and juke joints, something was definitely stirring, and soon many older British band musicians would decide that the way to revitalise a flagging career was to try and imitate Bill and play something called rock, whatever exactly *that* might turn out to be.

9

WE'RE GONNA TEACH YOU TO ROCK

Don't Say You Haven't Been Warned

Teddy boys acquired their name in the summer of 1953. American rock'n'roll arrived in Britain in the autumn of 1954 and gained public awareness a year later, following the use of the song 'Rock Around the Clock' in the film *Blackboard Jungle*. However, it was not until the release of Bill Haley's own film in the summer of 1956 that Teds and rock'n'roll started to become indelibly linked in the popular imagination. Prior to that, although Teds were known to love dancing, it was most often stated that they did so to some kind of jazz.

What really helped cement things was the double blow of Elvis entering the UK charts in May (with the game-changing multi-million-seller 'Heartbreak Hotel') followed in June by the release of *Rock Around the Clock* in British cinemas. On the day that Bill's film opened for its initial run at the London Pavilion on Piccadilly Circus, it received a lengthy condescending review in the *New Musical Express* by Charles Govey – clearly not an admirer of rock – who managed to convey the impression that it was beneath someone of his superior intelligence, concluding with, 'the "little people" are coming your way. Don't say you haven't been warned!'[1] With that attitude, he must have been having a difficult time, given that the *NME*'s own Top Thirty was suddenly awash with the new music.

Over the next few months, as even more rock'n'roll appeared in the charts and varying degrees of trouble accompanied the Haley film around the UK, specific links were drawn between this type of music and the country's pre-existing Teddy boy and Teddy girl population. Their name and exploits had long since become known in America, and regularly provided ammunition for commentators making barbed comments about juvenile delinquency, such as Robert C. Ruark, who wrote an article with the headline 'Insufferable Set' for the *Pittsburgh Press* in November 1956:

> I have tried desperately to plumb the thinking of the youths of today, mixing in all the possible excuses – cold wars, overcrowding, TV, psychiatry or lack of it, 'tween war frustrations, speeded-up living, and the rest of it – and I still don't dig it. When I was in England lately the teddy-boys – zoot-suiters – were getting their faces tattooed to resemble knife scars … The dark streets and parks from New York to London to Sydney, Australia are jungles peopled by duck-tailed hairdo, pimpled, leather-jacketed, blue-jeaned, young thugs who steal for fun, attack strangers for fun, kill each other for fun, conduct riots for fun, use lame excuses such as rock'n'roll music for their loutish behaviour and are altogether the most insufferable bunch of young swine, male and female, that I have ever observed.[2]

If you believed half of what the newspapers and the politicians told you, Teds already had a reputation only slightly less dubious than that of Dr Crippen, and as for this new thing called rock'n'roll, well, *Daily Mirror* columnist Patrick Doncaster was here to help you protect yourself and your family against it:

Can it happen here – the trouble that goes with rock'n'roll music in the United States? Over there it has been blamed for starting riots, rape and alcoholism among the youngsters ... Most adults in America lay the blame for the 'rock' craze at the ungainly feet of a white singer, a sidewhiskered drool of a lad named Elvis Presley.[3]

Making much of the racial background to the music, Doncaster described it as 'this stimulating rhythm of the coloured people' which had 'been taken up commercially and is now becoming a white man's burden'.[4] Indeed, he quoted a US deejay named James Dillon Burks, from St Louis, who called it 'an ignorant type of music', and backed up this devastating verdict by pointing out, twice in the course of the article, that 'Mr Burks is a Negro'.[5] However, a search of the files of both US trade magazines, *Billboard* and *Cash Box*, yields precisely zero results for any deejay of that name, which suggests his fame was somewhat limited. Had Doncaster sought the advice of genuinely well-known black deejays of that era, such as Tommy 'Dr Jive' Smalls of New York City, or Lavada 'Dr Hepcat' Durst of Austin, Texas – both of whom helped spread the popularity of rock'n'roll in America – he would have received a very different answer, but that was not what he wanted. 'Personally,' Doncaster concluded, 'I think this rhythm is about as musical as the flushing of a sewer. I hope it soon gets the "thumbs down" over here.'[6]

Six months later, readers of the *Daily Mirror* might have felt confused about the fact that the same newspaper had discovered a wild enthusiasm for this new music, and was promoting Bill Haley's impending debut UK tour:

Well, cats, this is your last chance! The response to the *Daily Mirror*'s competitions and other plans for the visit to Britain of rock'n'roll king Bill Haley and his sizzling Comets has been FANTASTIC! ... Our rock'n'roll night at the Hammersmith Palais on February 7, two days after Haley arrives, is a sell-out ... There are also some seats left on the Mirror Rock'n'Roll Special that will pull out of Waterloo at 12.35 p.m. on February 5 to welcome King Haley and his men when they dock at Southampton. This is going to be the trip of a lifetime.[7]

Who was the proud author of this article, giving rock an enthusiastic 'thumbs up'? None other than Patrick Doncaster, who went on to enjoy a long career as a pop music pundit at the paper. In the early 1960s Beat Boom era, he was one of the key national tabloid music columnists plugging the latest hits; he was billed by the paper as 'The *Mirror*'s DJ', and stayed with them long enough to write an article in 1974 celebrating the twentieth anniversary of the day Bill Haley recorded 'Rock Around the Clock'. In a January 1963 article recommending that readers keep an eye out for 'The Beatles, a guitar-based instrumental quartet from Liverpool', Doncaster also praised the 'sidewhiskered drool of a lad', whose new single 'Return to Sender' was judged to be 'first-rate'.[8] Whether it was also likely to provoke the youth of the nation into a frenzy of riots, rape and alcoholism he strangely neglected to mention.

String Ties, Peculiar Hair Cuts and Drainpipe Trousers

Patrick Doncaster was a genuine jazz fan who earlier in 1956 had written glowingly of Stan Kenton's landmark Albert Hall show and Louis Armstrong's visit. However, within a month of his initial denunciation of rock'n'roll, he was turning in far more conciliatory pieces. Indeed, his editor probably reasoned that if the kids with disposable income were sending numerous rock records into the charts, there was probably little mileage in having your regular music columnist knocking the trend each week. In any case, reports of the music's capacity for inciting Hellfire Club-style degradation were perhaps a little over-stated, as a columnist in the *Midland Counties Tribune* noted on 7 September 1956:

> I have seen that film, *Rock Around the Clock*, which is causing riots in London by the teenagers and teddy boys. Youngsters in the audience beat their hands in time to the music and there was some dancing in the aisles in the sedate town where I was watching. String ties, peculiar hair cuts and drainpipe trousers were the wear by the noisy males, while the girls, equally noisy, wore jeans and horse's tail hair styles. I have never seen such a demonstration in a cinema before, but it was certainly no riot.[9]

As for the film itself, he found it 'very ordinary, but with some clever wise cracks, and excellent sound'.

Jazz had long enjoyed a respectability in Britain, having been the new sensation following the First World War. Nick La Rocca's Original Dixieland Jazz Band came over from America in 1919 for an extended West End engagement, and even gave a performance in front of King George V at Buckingham Palace. This was the music of rebellion, born in the brothels and juke joints of New Orleans, but it quickly gained a foothold among the British middle and upper classes, and many public schoolboys of the 1920s and 1930s grew up passionately fond of the music. This helped ensure that it did not receive the rough ride which rock later encountered from the newspaper and radio commentators; many of those schoolboys went on to hold influential positions in the media, and great artists such as Louis Armstrong and Cab Calloway were given respectful coverage when visiting Britain.

Despite everything that jazz and rock'n'roll had in common, there were those of the slightly older generation who drew a sharp line between the two, and heaped scorn upon the new style. In August 1956, following a ban on that type of dancing and on Edwardian clothing imposed in Whitby, an article appeared in the *Halifax Daily Courier* under the outwardly sympathetic headline, 'Why All This Fuss About a Little Jiving?' The writer began by expressing the reasonable view that 'the ban strikes me as rather pointless and narrow-minded. A particular style of dress does not make a boy into a hooligan and jiving seems to be nothing more than a harmless sort of way for teenagers to release surplus energy.' So far so good, but while the writer had no prejudice against those in Edwardian clothing, when it came to their choice of music, it was quite a different story:

> The 'pop' music that is so attractive to teenagers has been getting steadily worse over a period of years and now with 'Rock and Roll' it has plumbed the depths. I am appalled that teenagers want this kind of music, which seems to be little more than the cheapest of cheap commercialism . . . Why not go back for a little cool modern jazz, or to the past for some old-fashioned swing?[10]

By that logic, why not push the boat out properly and go back even further all the way to the tenth century for some old-fashioned Gregorian chanting?

The Antics of the Jungle

This dislike of rock'n'roll, even as the music was taking a firm hold on Britain's teenagers during the summer of 1956, was widespread among many sections of society, and it blended with the pre-existing antipathy towards Teddy boys and Teddy girls. For nearly three years, Teds had been regularly referenced – in everything from satirical articles, comedy sketches and radio shows to court reports, newspaper columns and political speeches – in terms of their clothing choices and their behaviour, rather than their listening habits. Now, for the first time, they were linked in the public mind with rock'n'roll – and the same insulting terms which had been flung at them were directed towards the music. The council in Reading had banned showings of *Rock Around the Clock* in the town, but that did not stop the *Reading Standard* publishing a smug and condescending column entitled 'Antics of the Jungle' that attacked the music, a film which they clearly had not even seen, and the mental capabilities of everyone involved:

> What is the peculiar quality of *Rock Around the Clock* that it should provoke our young people to such a frenzy that they behave like savages? By all accounts it is not a particularly good film, as films go, but it 'has something' and that 'something' is a rhythmic din known as Rock'n'Roll which is admittedly exhilarating and moves the immature and less intelligent in the audience to displays of unrestrained exuberance. The dominating feature of the 'music' is the insistent beating of a drum, primitive and barbaric in its effect, and suggestive of the jungle ... It is true that wherever it has been shown there has usually been trouble, but it is also possible that the Teddy Boys, egged on by their admiring female counterparts, have deliberately seized upon the occasion for a more spectacular parade of that exhibitionism which is their sole claim to notoriety. Their

love of showing off – hence their peculiar clothes and long hair, and the swaggering gait of their spindly legs and enormous feet.[11]

References to the jungle and the use of words like 'primitive' were commonplace among those attacking rock'n'roll when it first appeared in the UK. Jeremy Thorpe, MP for North Devon – regular 1950s television pundit and future leader of the Liberal Party, whose career would resoundingly hit the buffers two decades later, after a notorious Old Bailey trial – dismissed rock as 'musical Mau Mau',[12] which to a British audience at the time would have conjured up images of violence, torture and death. Although he was only in his twenties himself, Thorpe came from a world of privilege. Ironically, when he arrived fresh from Eton to study at Trinity College, Oxford, he became known for his dandified adoption of Edwardian-styled clothing.

Jukeboxes had been a fixture of American life for decades, but there were only an estimated 300 in Britain in 1950. By 1956, however, the figure had risen to 5,000; as one owner told the *Daily Mirror*, 'when the "juke" goes wrong they start walking out. No "juke" – no business.' Although the journalist claimed that 'the customers are NOT only Teddy boys, NOT only rock'n'roll teenagers',[13] the association in many people's minds between such groups was clearly established. Indeed, the following year magistrates in the Warwickshire market town of Coleshill ruled against granting cafe owners Thomas and Attracta Blount the required music licence for a jukebox. Mrs Blount claimed that her young customers were 'not all Teddy boys', but the town clerk objected that 'normal café trade doesn't seem to go with a jukebox', asking, in some bafflement, 'Do they want rock'n'roll with their sandwiches?'[14] An officer from the local constabulary, Inspector T. H. Everitt, backed up the objections of several local residents, saying that he knew from experience of other juke-boxes in the area that they attracted troublemakers.

I Didn't Like It and I Didn't Understand It

In the summer of 1956, the UK record industry was faced with a choice: they could either see the new music as a threat, or realise that it represented a business opportunity. The teenagers who might spend a month or more's wages on a hand-made Ted suit clearly had disposable income left over for rock records; the search was soon on to provide them with home-grown bands who could make some attempt at the new style, with the extra benefit of being available for live gigs, TV and radio appearances, newspaper interviews and other fringe benefits. If you owned 10 per cent or more of such a performer, or had them signed exclusively to your record label, this could bring in significant wealth while the good times lasted, whether or not you liked the music yourself.

Rock'n'roll was frequently dismissed as a short-lived gimmick that would soon go the same way as other transient but hugely popular fads like Davy Crockett hats and hula hoops. Nevertheless, there were those with a few years' experience who were prepared to take a punt on the latest craze and try selling a home-grown facsimile of the US original version in the hope that the kids on the street could not tell the difference. Most countries outside America in which rock'n'roll developed a foothold would sooner or later produce their own native imitations of the key rock innovators. In Germany, there was Ted Herold, who began recording in 1958; Italy had Adriano Celentano, whose debut single in 1958 was a cover of 'Jailhouse Rock', and one of whose 1959 singles was called 'Teddy Girl'; in France there was Johnny Hallyday, who cut his first disc in 1960. All of the latter were heavily influenced by Elvis and marketed in their home countries as a local 'answer' to the King – a title which in Britain would be visited on Cliff Richard, although he resisted it.

It was 'Heartbreak Hotel' that introduced Presley to the UK record-buying public in May 1956, but the fact that it had already hit the number one spot in America was no guarantee that it would even see a British release. That decision lay in the hands of one very powerful man in the UK music business, Walter J. Ridley at EMI's HMV label. He alone chose which of the company's US recordings would be marketed in the UK, and when he first heard 'Heartbreak Hotel', his natural instinct was to give it a miss. 'I didn't like it and I didn't understand it,' he recalled in a 1998 interview.[15] However, Ridley's advance copy of the disc came with a personal note from Steve Sholes – the man who had signed Elvis to RCA in 1955 – explaining why he felt it was an important recording, and this tipped the balance.

Presley's own label might have been temporarily blind to the financial benefits of rock'n'roll, but there were many in the established British entertainment business who scented an opportunity and began to take action, sometimes regardless of their own music preferences. Many of them didn't like or understand it, but that was hardly going to stop them.

This Commissionaire Geezer Shouts 'You're Barred'

Apart from all the records being bought, another obvious signifier was the continuing success of the *Rock Around the Clock* film as it made its way around the country that summer, despite all the bans. *Picture Post*, which was generally well-informed about new trends, specifically linked the Ted movement to rock'n'roll alongside a large photo of Elvis on-stage in a 22 September 1956 article entitled 'Presley Fever Hits Britain', in which they but-tonholed a teenager in a drape suit who had just been ejected from a London cinema:

'Well it was this way,' said the diminutive Teddy-Boy with the big black dog. 'I'm sitting down near the front, clapping and stamping my feet and singing a bit, when this commis-sionaire geezer comes up and shoves his arm across in front of me and shouts: "You're barred." So I grab hold of his arm and pull it and give him a twistie – you know, start the old jive. And then, before I know anything, I'm outside.' We were talking outside an East End cinema, underneath a huge poster advertising 'Rocking, rolling Bill Haley and His Comets in *Rock Around the Clock*.[16]

Jeff Kruger was an entrepreneur in his mid-twenties who had opened London's Flamingo Club in 1952. Having seen a New York showing of *Rock Around the Clock* some months ahead of its British release – and secretly recorded the songs in the cinema[17] – Kruger approached established British jazz drummer Tony Crombie with a view to him getting a rock band together, thereby taking advantage of the fact that the likes of Haley, Presley, Little Richard and Gene Vincent had never played shows in Britain. The idea was that any teenagers wanting the live rock'n'roll experience would provide a ready-made audience. Crombie was a serious musician with a heavyweight reputation who had been leading his own successful jazz orchestra for some years, gigging with US stars like Duke Ellington and Lena Horne. He had also seen hard bop at first hand in New York in the 1940s, but had little use for Haley's sound, so asking him and his fellow jazz players to form a teen-friendly rock band seems to have been a cynical and purely commercial move. Nevertheless, the deal was done, and Kruger called in some favourable early press in the *Melody Maker* even before the band had played any shows, knowing that the readership would be aware of Crombie's career to date. Indeed, that initial announcement was judged by the paper to be front-page news:

CROMBIE FORMS ROCK-AND-ROLL OUTFIT

Britain's first full-time rock-and-roll group hits the road at the end of this month. Fronted by drummer-composer-arranger Tony Crombie, it will comprise tenor, guitar, piano, bass, drums and vocalist. Names cannot yet be divulged for contractual reasons ... Agent Jeff Kruger on rock-and-roll package they're putting together: 'We plan eventually to carry a complete dance team to demonstrate a rock-and-roll dance.'[18]

To reinforce the message, Crombie had 'TONY R'N'R CROMBIE' written on the front of his bass drum. A few weeks later – despite him still appearing that month in his jazz persona at Kruger's Flamingo Club – the press build-up designed to change his image continued with a carefully placed news item in the *Melody Maker* explicitly linking Crombie to the new music:

ROCK AND RIOT BOYS DON'T WORRY CROMBIE

Teddy Boy riots at London cinemas showing Bill Haley's *Rock Around the Clock* are not going to deter the Delfont Agency from putting on their touring show starring Tony Crombie and his new rock-and-roll package show.[19]

Violence, Arson, *Murder* . . .

Finally, on 10 September, the newly configured outfit, Tony Crombie and His Rockets – despite being largely composed of seasoned musicians who would rather have been playing jazz – made history by playing the first ever show by a home-grown rock band at the Theatre Royal in Portsmouth. This was the opening salvo in a week of dates at that venue, followed by a week apiece in Nottingham, Birmingham, Sheffield, London, Liverpool, Edinburgh, Glasgow, Leeds and Stoke.[20] Portsmouth was a shrewd choice for the start of the tour; an early Ted stronghold, it was far enough from London that only a few national critics would consider it worth the trip, thus giving the band time to find their feet before reaching the capital a month later. Unsurprisingly, someone from the Kruger-friendly *Melody Maker* was there to give the debut performance a cautious welcome, and also to reassure readers that no riots had taken place, especially after he had spotted policemen in attendance as he arrived, and thought 'Anything might be happening: violence, arson, *murder* . . .'[21] In fact, the two constables in question were in the habit of dropping by every evening, regardless of the programme, and the show went off without incident, seemingly to the reviewer's disappointment: 'After the first house, one might have expected a deluge of delirious rockers-and-rollers, dancing on the pavements, spilling over to stop the traffic. The crowd that issued was sober and sedate, older folk smiling faintly, the younger element contented, perhaps even sated.'[22]

This should hardly have come as much of a surprise, since the band were playing a version of rock which was really not so far from their own jazz orchestra roots. Their repertoire included the obligatory bloodless covers of US hits like 'Teach You to Rock', mixed in with home-grown froth like 'Brighton Rock' – a made-over version of the 1907 singalong music hall number 'I Do Like to Be Beside the Seaside', which was only likely to cause a dance-hall riot if it started with punters demanding their money back. Even so, the pace at which this particular bandwagon began to move was impressive: less than a week later it was announced that this new band had been booked for an appearance on the prestigious national ITV television show *Sunday Night at the London Palladium*,[23] and that Decca Records had thrown their hat in the ring by signing nineteen-year-old Bermondsey rocker Tommy Steele to a three-year contract.[24]

Steele was not, incidentally, managed by Jeff Kruger, whose approach was to find older established musicians and attempt to shoe-horn them into the new trend for financial benefit. Having made a splash with Tony Crombie, before the month was through the manager followed up by announcing another act he had created, Art Baxter and His Rockin' Sinners.[25] However, the market for British rockers was swiftly becoming crowded, and the average big-beat-hungry Ted would have needed his wits about him to keep track of developments in the two weeks between Crombie's live debut and the formation of Baxter's group. The club impresario Rik Gunnell – who with his brother John would soon assume responsibility for the day-to-day running of Kruger's Flamingo Club – took out adverts for a new venture of his own involving themed evenings at the Tavistock Ballroom on Charing Cross Road which he grandly named Club Haley, starring another new outfit, Rory Black-well's Rock'n'Rollars (*sic*).[26]

In an obvious bid to attract the teenage rocking crowd, the popular UK jazz outfit the Mick Mulligan Band announced that they were hiring twenty-two-year-old 'skiffle singer' Jimmy Jackson to supplement their regular front man George Melly.[27] Further intrusions into that scene prompted the headline 'ROCK'N'ROLL BANDS AT JAZZ WEEKEND' accompanying a report that the line-up for the Jazz Festival Weekend at Butlin's Holiday Camp in Clacton-on-Sea would include Tony Crombie's Rockets and also the Kirchin Band, a long-established jazz orchestra, who now claimed to be playing 'big band rock'n'roll'. Meanwhile, BBC TV broadcast a programme that month featuring singing group the Keynotes entertaining the viewers while wearing Victorian clothing in a broadcast entitled 'Rock and Roll 1856'.[28] What the average teenager would have made of it is anybody's guess.

That Kind of Trash

The overwhelming impression conveyed by such developments is that rock was being seized on by jazz and big band musicians as some kind of temporary career boost, while long-term fans of these artists voiced complaints that they were betraying their roots and compromising their art. The news that jazz giant Lionel Hampton and his orchestra would be tailoring the performances on their British tour in November 1956 to take account of the new trend – 'HAMP SLANTS SHOW ON ROCK'N'ROLL'[29] ran one headline – was greeted with disgust in some quarters. 'Doesn't Hamp realise that it isn't necessary to resort to that kind of trash to pack fans in?' asked one *Melody Maker* reader, while another letter signed by eleven readers from Yorkshire simply said, 'If this is the sort of noise we are to expect, please don't bother to come to Bradford, Hamp.'[30] All of which makes one wonder how such people felt when the following year one of deejay Alan Freed's musical films arrived at their local cinemas under the unambiguous title *Mister Rock'n'Roll*, starring the likes of Little Richard and Chuck Berry, shoulder to shoulder with Lionel Hampton and His Orchestra.[31]

In the same week that Hampton's fans were loudly

denouncing 'that kind of trash', Jeff Kruger unveiled yet another new British rock'n'roll band which he had conjured into existence, Don Sollash and His Rockin' Horses – his third in a matter of weeks.[32] Once again, these musicians were not beat-crazy teens driven by Elvis or Gene Vincent to pick up a guitar and cut loose – quite the opposite. As Kruger revealed in a December interview that was largely concerned with the money his new acts were pulling in, 'Don Sollash was leading a mambo band in Brighton six weeks ago,'[33] but mambo, by then, was last year's craze. Sollash was a similar age to his fellow recruits Tony Crombie and Art Baxter, and it is not hard to see why he chose to throw in his lot with them. As Kruger explained to journalist Bob Dawbarn,'Within twelve short weeks in Variety with the Rockets, Tony owns a Daimler . . . In twelve weeks the Rockets have grossed the fantastic sum of £20,000.'[34] Art Baxter had been working as a £5-a-week meat porter 'when Rock'n'Roll came into his life', said the manager. 'Now he is earning £200 a week.' As Dawbarn wrote in the introduction to his article, it seemed to some people like a get-rich-quick scheme and nothing more: 'If you want Willy to earn lots of lovely lolly, provide for Mum in her old age, become the idol of British girlhood and star at the Palladium, then teach the lad to Rock-'n'-Roll.'[35]

New convert Tony Crombie was happy to write a full-page article about his new outfit for *The People* in which he was billed as 'the East End wild cat who likes his music tough'. Blithely brushing aside the fact that his latest direction was something he had been talked into, he wrote: 'Rock'n'roll has made some youngsters more than a little frisky. But juvenile delinquency can't be blamed on me and the other rock'n'rollers. It existed long before we began to beat it out.'[36]

Claiming that he had formed the Rockets long before he ever heard of *Rock Around the Clock* – 'Then came Bill Haley's rock'n'roll film in America. The Tony Crombie Rockets were soon causing as much rumpus as Bill did'[37] – he sketched out a version of his past which had him as an originator of the rock sound, a dyed-in-the-wool disciple of the big beat. Rory Blackwell did much the same a few months later, claiming to have been playing rock'n'roll when he was a prisoner of war in Korea. On the other hand, a month later Rory was telling the press that he was Canadian – despite coming from Battersea; as with many of these encounters, it seemed to be largely a case of just telling the papers a good old yarn. This was showbusiness, not real life, in a world where British chart-toppers also appeared in pantomime.

The activities of managers like Kruger, and more specifically, Larry Parnes (who specialised in 'discovering' teenage performers rather than re-branding seasoned jazz musicians), soon attracted attention as ripe subjects for fictional portrayal. Robert Hancock's knowing insider novel of the late-1950s British music business, *The A&R Man* (published in 1958), features a cynical record company operative who moulds the career of the young working-class singer Margaret Love, having discovered her at a talent contest in the North of England and witnessed the reaction of local Teds:

> The contest was judged by the manager of the dance hall, and he picked the winner by listening to the noise made by the watching dancers as each contestant came to the front of the stage and bowed at the end of the contest. Margaret won easily. The hot-faced adolescents, the boys in narrow trousers and the girls in cobweb nylons crescendoed their approval of Margaret.[38]

Rock managers were also lovingly skewered by Wolf

Mankowitz and Julian More's musical *Expresso Bongo*, which became a West End hit on opening in April 1958,[39] and went on to tour the country the following year. The title character Bongo Herbert – a youthful singing prodigy ripe for exploitation – was played in the original stage run by none other than James Kenney, the former star of *Cosh Boy* and now somewhat long in the tooth for a teenager at twenty-six. When the great director Val Guest shot his film version in the summer of 1959, Kenney was out, and the new British rock sensation Cliff Richard, then eighteen, appeared as Herbert.[40] Made in the closing months of the 1950s, and released that December, it depicted a Soho that was strangely Ted-free, with not a drape or velvet collar in sight – but then a fair amount of what appeared to be location shooting was actually filmed on studio sets at Shepperton. At one point in the script, Richard's character is referred to scathingly as a 'snotty-nosed little Teddy boy', and the moment at which his hustler of a manager tells him backstage before a live television broadcast to 'go out there and kill 'em – tonight, eight million telly-hugging imbeciles are going to fall in love with you, simultaneously'[41] invites parallels with some of the real-life sharks who had been attempting to make money out of this musical bandwagon.

The Hottest Bands in the Land

Once rock proved to have a significant audience, the nation's mainstream film magazines like *Photoplay* and *Picturegoer* also began including several pages of music coverage, in the hope that this might bring in more teenage readers. The former had a regular column entitled *Pop Parade*, written by Ken Ferguson, who clearly had good connections to Jeff Kruger, and was happy to help spread the word about his latest signings. One article was more transparent than usual about the motivations involved:

A new outfit to jump on the rock'n'roll band wagon is Art Baxter and his Rock'n'Roll Sinners. They're causing a mild sensation up and down the country. Art used to sing with the Ronnie Scott Band, but gradually faded out of the limelight – and went back to driving a lorry. One day he received a phone call from Jeff Kruger (Tony Crombie's manager) who asked if he would be interested in leading a new group. Art was interested. But when he heard that it was a rock'n'roll outfit, he began to have doubts. Art is a ballad singer with a style like Eckstine's. 'I wasn't well up on this new trend,' Art said to me. 'I decided it was worth a try, though. Within a few days I found myself with a bunch of boys who had never seen each other in their lives.'[42]

Little did Art realise that this would also briefly make him a film star of sorts. Kruger had obviously noticed the advantages of having a rock'n'roll movie to market alongside your act's recordings, and immediately set about producing his own – a cheaply shot one-hour B-picture called *Rock You Sinners*, featuring what an over-excited headline writer at the *South Yorkshire Times* called 'the hottest bands in the land'.[43] By a strange coincidence, the top three outfits in the billing turned out to be Tony Crombie's Rockets, Art Baxter and His Rockin' Sinners and Don Sollash and His Rockin' Horses. Nineteen-year-old Jackie Collins was the female star, appearing in a similar role to the one played by her sister Joan four years earlier in *Cosh Boy*. As she told the press in a promotional interview at the time of the film's release in June 1957, 'I'm always Teddy Girls, juvenile delinquents, girls-gone-wrong or rock'n'rollers'.[44] Frustrated by such type-casting, she now claimed to want to 'show I can be an adult comedienne', but eventually went on to make a fortune writing romance novels.

Rock You Sinners did respectable business as a supporting feature at cinemas across the country, yet its time had essentially passed, since many of the rock fans of the nation had experienced the authentic live-on-stage onslaught of Bill Haley and His Comets, who toured Britain amid scenes of unprecedented but good-natured mayhem during February and March 1957, kicking off with a three-night run at the Dominion, Tottenham Court Road.[45]

You'd Never Seen Anything Like It

It is hard to overstate the impact of Bill Haley's UK tour in 1957, both in terms of the avalanche of publicity it generated, and its pivotal role in helping inspire young people in Britain to form bands of their own. Yet perhaps it needs to be said again, given that in February 2022 *The Guardian* published an article concerning '50 Gigs That Changed Music' which, when discussing the 1958 UK tour by Buddy Holly and the Crickets, stated that 'Britain had never seen a rock band before March 1958'.[46] Holly's outfit introduced UK musicians to the classic two guitars, bass and drums line-up, and showed that singers could write their own songs – both of which messages the Beatles later took to heart – but the Comets had blown crowds away night after night a whole year earlier, and they were unquestionably a rock band – one of the earliest and finest that ever hit the stage.

Bill Haley's ground-breaking spring 1957 itinerary comprised multiple engagements in London, Coventry, Nottingham, Birmingham, Manchester, Leeds, Sunderland, Newcastle, Bradford, Glasgow, Liverpool, Cardiff, Plymouth and Southampton. There then followed three more nights in London, then Belfast, Edmonton, Croydon, Norwich, Doncaster, Wolverhampton, Cheltenham and London yet again. In the middle of these dates, the Comets broke off to play four shows over two nights at the Theatre Royal in Dublin.[47] Fourteen-year-old Ted Carroll watched one of the Dublin gigs while wearing home-tailored drainpipe strides, and more than sixty years later the sheer power and impact of the show that he witnessed comes through in the marvellous description of that night which he gave me: 'So anyway, I went to see Bill Haley and the Comets. Saw it advertised, saved up, sent away the twelve and sixpence, which was the best ticket I could afford. It came back in the post, and I went, on my own. I went to the first night, second show, on the first balcony.'[48]

The support act for the tour was the unthreatening sounds of the Vic Lewis Dance Orchestra, seasoned professionals who gave little hint of the seismic force that was to follow, as Ted told me:

> They just played a crowd-pleasing bunch of standards and Latin things. I remember they turned the lights down and they had all these maracas and percussion things that were luminous. So that was the support. They finished, and then curtains came across, and then there was a great big fireproof curtain that came down, real heavy, with slogans advertising local businesses.
>
> Anyway, second half, up goes that thing, and then the main big heavy red velvet curtains come across and there's just one curtain left, and you can hear little noises, so you know they're onstage, and the anticipation is just ... And then, they start with 'Razzle Dazzle': 'On your marks, get set, *ready* ...' and on the first two or three bars, the curtain jumped up about two feet, so you could see all the legs across the stage, and then 'Ready, steady, go!' – up went the curtain, fuckin' place erupted.

It was amazing. You can imagine, because they were a fucking great band. They were fantastic, they were so slick, they looked great – I forget whether they were wearing the tartan plaid jackets or whatever. There was none of this fuckin' fat avuncular dad figure. I mean, Bill Haley was a great singer, had a big fuck-off guitar, he moved around. He wasn't Elvis – nobody wanted Elvis – we wanted Bill Haley and the Comets who made the best rock'n'roll records which were great to dance to, the A and B sides were fantastic. The place went fucking wild. Luckily I was near the front [of the balcony] and there were tiers, so I could see. Fantastic. It probably lasted for about forty minutes, maximum, but it was amazing, and I remember looking up at one stage and thinking this fuckin' balcony above is gonna come down because of feet thumping, and the excitement was just fuckin' insane. This was in the Theatre Royal in Dublin, about a two-and-a-half-thousand seater, so he played to ten thousand fucking people in two days.

And afterwards the punters came out onto the street. People were so fucking high, they rioted, they overturned a few cars, nothing serious, you know, not the end of the world. It was an amazing thing.

I'd seen a few local rock'n'roll bands, but that was the first, a world star who made fantastic records, I mean it was magical to be able to see that. I was so high I wasn't able to go to school the next day. And I mean I've been to the Beatles' first show in Dublin, and the Stones, I've seen amazing shows, Ike and Tina Turner in the Royal Ballroom in Tottenham, but *that* one, because I was only fourteen, it was just totally fucking mind-blowing. You'd never seen anything like it.[49]

From Here to Obscurity

All of this goes a long way towards explaining why Tony Crombie was later that year billing his outfit as 'Britain's Versatile Show Band', saying 'Rock'n'roll is finished in Britain. I thoroughly enjoyed it and we did very well out of it. I earn my living as a musician and will go any way the public wants.'[50] By 1958, he had resumed his jazz career full time, and Don Sollash was back mamboing the night away in Brighton as Don Sollash and His Latin Rhythm.[51] Art Baxter, meanwhile, had been given the boot by Jeff Kruger; he went on to bemoan his fate in a self-flagellating May 1957 *Sunday Pictorial* article headlined 'I Was a Mug – From Here to Obscurity in 240 Days', which finished with him saying, 'Rock'n'Roll is dead in Britain. And as far as the teenagers and public who clamoured for me are concerned, I am dead, too.'[52]

The reality was far more complex. Pundits had been loudly claiming that the rock craze was dead almost as soon as it began, but the truth was that Kruger's bands were mostly just filling the gap until the real thing came along. As John Peel told me when I interviewed him in 2004, recalling the days when such outfits were being foisted on teenagers like him who had already heard genuine US rockers on disc: 'It was such a good time to live through, because you just knew at the time that it was shite. That it was opportunist – you wouldn't have known the word opportunist – but you kind of knew that Gene Vincent was right and that all of this other stuff was wrong. It was exactly that, Musician's Union people and jazzers thinking, "Fuck me, we'd better get into this ..."'[53]

Decent home-grown British rockers would emerge in the later years of the 1950s, and unsurprisingly they tended to be almost half the age of Kruger's hopefuls, drawn from the same generation as the Teds themselves, and who were rock'n'roll fans before they first picked up an instrument. At the time that *Rock You Sinners* was being committed to celluloid, Tony Crombie was thirty-one, and Art Baxter was thirty, while the as-yet-unknown Billy Fury and Cliff Richard were both sixteen, and new sensation Tommy Steele still only twenty. If you were a school-age rock'n'roll fan, the Baxters of this world were only a year or two younger than your parents.

10

THROUGH THE LOOKING GLASS

Nuthin' but a Hound Dog

Back in late 1953, when the name 'Teddy boy' first took root in the media and was swiftly employed as a catch-all term for a variety of troublemakers, the negative and often very violent imagery associated with cosh boys of the previous few years had also devolved onto them by association. By comparison, the 140-year-old term 'juvenile delinquent' was a relatively mild description, sometimes only implying misdemeanours as common as graffiti-writing or the vandalising of phone boxes, rather than life-endangering assaults. The headlines prompted by July's Clapham Common murder cast a very long shadow.

Three months before that brutal stabbing, a reader of the *Portsmouth Evening News* had placed an advert with the following description, during the last days when its name would carry no other connotation: 'LOST – Pure chocolate Alsatian Dog; answers "Teddy Boy," timid, gentle; last seen Tuesday p.m.'[1]

The Job's on Tonight, with Razors

Over the next two or three years – as the British population were being instructed how to recognise a Teddy boy and identify their supposed criminal tendencies – many radio and television scriptwriters, comedians, playwrights and novelists began to refer to them in their work. Even if you had yet to see one walking down the street or loitering in a local cafe, the caricature was gradually being reinforced, just as it would be a decade later when the clothing and hairstyles of hippies became prime fodder for the media.

The new breed with their distinctive look were certainly a godsend to the nation's cartoonists. In June 1954, Roy Ullyett in the *Daily Express* drew a fine pair of Teds in the full gear – drainpipes, long velvet-collared jackets, fancy waistcoats and creepers – slouching over a pinball table amid clouds of cigarette smoke.[2] This was a fairly good-natured example, whereas Arthur Horner in the *News Chronicle* the previous month went for the less subtle approach of depicting a gormless young Ted being fitted for a new velvet-collared drape suit by three grim-looking elderly tailors labelled 'Fear', 'Violence' and 'Apathy'.[3]

It began to seem as if every section of society had an opinion on Teddy boys, whether favourable or otherwise. It was reported for instance that George Pargiter, Labour MP for the West London seat of Southall, had hosted a panel discussion alongside three local councillors in which they had their say about the phenomenon, as well as 'the number of standing passengers allowed on buses, Socialist books, the tendency of having more and more winking lights and the problem of myxomatosis'.[4]

Society photographer Cecil Beaton joked at a Foyles Literary Lunch – one of the regular series of such occasions aimed at showcasing authors which the London bookshop had been presenting since 1930 – that his own Edwardian-style tailoring had led to him being approached in the street by a shifty-looking young Ted who whispered to him conspiratorially, 'The job's on tonight, with razors.'[5] He seems to have felt a kinship with them, as he told a journalist at the same event, 'I like these Edwardian clothes,' pointing to his own outfit. 'The Edwardian gangs and myself have our clothes in common. And these peacocks are only trying to do what you and I would like to do – make a creative splash.'[6]

Meanwhile, the equally well-heeled satirists at *Punch* magazine noted the case of a child arrested for carving the initials 'T.B.' for Teddy Boy into four of his classmates' arms with a penknife, suggesting that he might be invited to contribute a 'working model of a remand home break-out' to the upcoming Schoolboy Art exhibition.[7]

All Aboard for the Dustbin Chorus

In the world of popular entertainment, as early as December 1954, long-established comedy stars the Crazy Gang had a revue show at the Victoria Palace Theatre in London that featured a sketch in which they dressed up as Teddy boys visiting a dance hall.[8] They were hardly the only ones: veteran Scottish music hall star Dave Willis appeared as a distinctly new kind of pantomime dame that month at His Majesty's Theatre, Aberdeen, and he and his sidekick Jack Anthony were given the following rave review in a local paper: 'All Aberdeen is going to get to know the dustbin chorus song which Dave, as a Teddy girl with the most grotesque horse and tail wig ever conceived, and Jack as a Teddy boy in velvet collared jacket, have the audience singing lustily with the aid of words written large on a screen.'[9]

When not poking fun at drape suits and creepers, professional gag-writers were also getting mileage out of the Ted reputation for illegal activities. Long-established film, radio and television star Tommy Trinder claimed to have invented a new party game in which 'all the girls remove their jewellery and put it in my hat in the centre of the room. Then the lights are switched off and all the boys make a grab. The one who

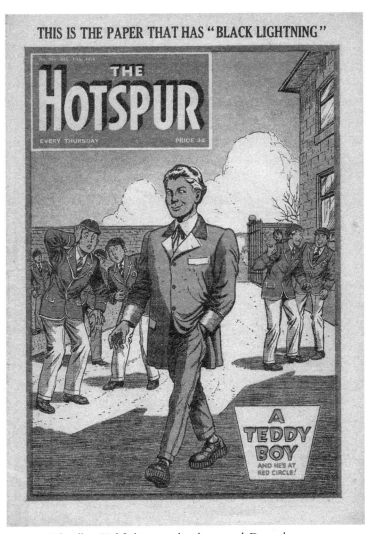

Schoolboy Ted fashions in the playground, December 1954

gets the most loot is the winner.' He called it 'the Teddy boys' Picnic'.[10]

Some theatrical productions seemed to think the mere fact of someone appearing on stage dressed as a Ted would be enough to provoke unstoppable howls of laughter – a prime example being the 'Night of 100 Stars' charity event at the London Palladium in June 1955. Quite what the audience was supposed to make of Laurence Olivier and Danny Kaye performing what was described as a 'Teddy Boy song-and-dance' is hard to say. More to the point, at fifteen guineas a ticket, it is unlikely any genuine Teds were there to witness it.[11]

Children's comics had also woken up to the interest value of these strange creatures, and top-selling boys' weekly title *The Hotspur* featured one on the cover in a full-page colour illustration. Since its foundation in the 1930s, the comic had run serial stories set at a fictional public school called Red Circle, and their 11 December 1954 edition introduced a new character, Edward 'Teddy Boy' Brown. The image on the front depicted the smirking new arrival parading across the playground in a full drape suit, watched by the other pupils, who are wearing regulation school uniforms, either giggling, nudging each other or clapping their hands to their heads in astonishment. 'A Teddy Boy,' said the caption. 'And He's At Red Circle!'[12] More details of his appearance were given inside:

> His long hair was waved and oiled, with two wings brushed back over his ears and round the back of his head ... He was about the same age as the Red Circle Fourth Formers, and he was a well-built lad, but there the resemblance ended. He wore a white shirt, a brightly coloured waistcoat, and a bootlace tie. Over this he had a jacket of expensive material, cut long, with velvet collar, and trimmings to the cuffs

and pocket flaps, and a pair of narrow trousers. The picture was completed by a pair of thick-soled shoes.[13]

This was still a week before Bill Haley and His Comets first entered the UK charts, yet Teddy boys were already such a familiar part of the landscape that even the ten-year-olds who made up the key audience for this mass-market children's weekly were presumed to have known what they looked like and how they behaved. The uncredited artist who provided the cover illustration had apparently observed the real thing in close detail – the finished picture is surprisingly accurate for the time, with little sense of caricature. The new Edwardians were now, quite simply, part of the furniture.

Across the British Isles that year, any village fete or town carnival hosting a fancy dress competition seemed to attract at least one youthful entrant winning a prize in their own approximation of the Teddy boy look – but then, novelty was always an advantage in such contests. Roy Breen, who as a Ted came first in the 'Most Comical' section at the Portrush carnival in County Antrim, shared a platform with other contestants dressed variously as 'The Horror of the House of Wax' and even 'Scott's Porridge Oats'.[14] Sometimes, however, you didn't have to go to a village fete to run into people wearing fancy dress, as reporter Arthur Helliwell discovered in West London in early 1955:

The scene . . . Barnes Common at midnight . . . In a parked car with dimmed lights sit four Teddy boys wearing velvet-collared jackets, stovepipe pants, crêpe-sole shoes and string ties. A police constable stops and flashes his torch into the car. 'Now then, you lot,' he says. 'Get weaving before I pinch you.' The driver produces an identity card, and from the rear seat a gruff voice growls: 'Shove off, fathead. We're CID keeping observation for an escaped prisoner.'[15]

Dandruff, Body Odour and Halitosis

Television played a significant part in raising public awareness about Teds, and once rock'n'roll had been added into the mix, Britain's two television companies – the long-established BBC and ITV, which had only begun broadcasting in 1955 – gradually turned their attention from simply reporting on the Ted phenomenon, to including them as characters in dramas and eventually attempting to produce programmes which might appeal to such teenagers themselves. Quite what the BBC's original Director General Lord Reith might have made of this is not hard to imagine, given that in the parliamentary debates in 1952 concerning the government's proposals for the introduction of a commercial television channel, he warned that it would be similar to unleashing the Black Death.[16] The idea that the same organisation would one day be presenting programmes about rock'n'roll and occasionally interviewing Teddy boys would have seemed quite a stretch at the time, and yet a few tentative signs were there, nevertheless.

Reith was in charge of the BBC from 1922 to 1938, and shaped the ethos of the organisation in ways which were still very much in evidence during the 1950s. They had begun experimental television broadcasts in 1930, and their regular service commenced in 1932. By 1936 the BBC's television operation was established at studios in Alexandra Palace, presenting a wide variety of programmes over the next three years until the service was suspended on the outbreak of war. One highlight was the appearance of New York stride piano master Fats Waller, who broadcast five songs live from Alexandra Palace in a special programme on the evening of 30 September 1938.[17] The previous day he had performed for BBC radio at their Maida Vale Studios – a building now boasting a unique musical history dating back almost a century.

Little Hats and Matching Gloves

Despite the corporation's general lack of sympathy, Teds had been appearing in one form or another on BBC television programmes since 1954, albeit usually as stock figures of fun or as pantomime villains. The Scottish comedian Jimmy Logan put on Ted gear during a television comedy appearance in November 1954,[18] and a week later the hugely popular TV soap opera series *The Grove Family* featured familiar television and film actor Oscar Quitak as a Teddy boy, although at twenty-eight he was arguably a decade too old for the part.[19] Even so, Quitak was younger than Peter Sellers, who at that time had just been cast to play a baby-faced Teddy boy criminal in the Ealing comedy masterpiece *The Ladykillers*, which was filmed during 1955 in and around King's Cross Station, just as Sellers was about to turn thirty.

Someone much closer in age to the actual Teds was the twenty-year-old television ventriloquist Dennis Spicer, who for one programme in July 1955 dressed up his regular dummy James Green in a full Teddy boy outfit, again on the assumption that the general public would have no difficulty recognising such a figure.[20] Later that year, someone at the BBC evidently decided that it might be a good idea to let a couple of genuine Teds speak for themselves as part of a television programme examining the lives of young people from a variety of income brackets. Even the advance filming generated publicity, such as this teaser item which appeared in an October issue of *The People* newspaper:

'Making a documentary on teen-ager life, for screening soon, Lime Grove fixed to film scenes at a Teddy-Boy tailor's shop. Camera crew arrived to find the local populace crushing to get in the picture. The tailor – currently doing big business – had advertised TV's visit!'[21]

However, when it was screened the following month in a prime 9.15 p.m. spot, it carried the suitably loaded title 'The Problem of the Teenager'. The camera crew accompanied five supposedly 'typical' teenagers to their various places of interest, as that week's edition of the *Radio Times* explained: 'The film starts with Mike and his friend Pat, who wear Edwardian suits, and who live and work around Pimlico. We go with them as they visit the barber and tailor, as they play football and cards, as they sit around in pin-table saloons and cafés.'[22]

These were all suitably working-class locations and pastimes, very much conforming to the perceived Teddy boy image. At least two of the other three teenagers, however, were from a more affluent background:

> Next comes Lynette, who works as a photographer's model. Lynette is a debutante, and we visit her Finishing School, her home in Scotland and the London flat she shares with her sister. We go with her to her agent's office, and to a theatre and a party. Teenager number four is Philip, who's a student at the London School of Economics. He lives in Teddington, and is a keen amateur actor and motorist, and takes a confident and optimistic attitude to life.[23]

Fair enough, and it is reasonable to assume that like Philip, most other car-owning teenage college students also felt suitably optimistic about their prospects in an era when less than 4 per cent of the population attended university and 80 per cent of Britons of whatever age had no car at all. As for Lynette, the brief description places her firmly in the upper echelons of society, which still clung on to the rituals of the debutante season until 1958, involving a presentation at Court to curtsy before the Queen, up to three or four formal balls a night and countless expenses to be underwritten by parents or relatives, as one 1950s deb later recalled: 'Well, you had to have something totally original for your own party. You also had to have several ball dresses, several cocktail dresses, things you were going out to lunch in and out to tea in, little hats and matching gloves.'[24]

It is relatively obvious which of these five were supposed to represent the 'problem' referred to in the title of the documentary – unless the strain of wondering which Paris couturier to approach when ordering their next consignment of ball gowns had pushed some of the wealthier teenagers over the edge into a life of juvenile delinquency.

Wicked Leers and Nasty Innuendo

The new commercial station, Independent Television, then weighed in with *Teddy Gang*, a Saturday night prime-time play about a leadership struggle among a group of teenage car thieves. Director David MacDonald claimed in advance of the broadcast that 'this is tough, near X-certificate television.'[25] A reviewer the following day, while agreeing that it was 'a strong meaty drama about Teddy-boys and Teddy-girls', went on to complain that 'the girls' wicked leers spoke volumes of nasty innuendo', and finished by saying 'it looks as though commercial TV is really going to the bad!'[26]

The new channel was a popular target for columnists who claimed that the station was appealing to the lowest common denominator; even so, BBC TV followed two months later with a

Teddy boy in a drama of their own. It was hardly intended as gritty social realism, however, given that it featured the forty-eight-year-old portly and balding Robert Morley as both a father and his Teddy boy son. This was a televised forty-five-minute excerpt from a new full-length comedy play by Gerald Savory called *A Likely Tale*, previewed in that week's edition of the *Radio Times*:

> Playing a double role – that of the ageing widower Oswald, who once succeeded in getting a slender book of poems published, and of his son Jonah, an outsize in Teddy Boys, Robert Morley switches from fading gentility to brash opportunism with astonishing skill, while his sister Mira-belle, played by Margaret Rutherford, gives an enchanting performance as an elderly, sentimental spinster with her dreams and her crochet for consolation.[27]

Savory was only a year younger than Robert Morley – making both of them genuine Edwardians – and had recently returned from years of living in the USA, so his acquaintance with genuine Teds would have probably been sketchy at best, but he had obviously recognised their value as a new cultural stereotype, as did many others in the arts that year.

Existentialist Storm-Troopers and Ape-Adolescents

The casting of Morley as a Ted was a clear case of playing for laughs, whereas in March 1957, BBC TV once again had their 'concerned' hat on when creating the latest in a series of what they termed 'dramatised documentaries' made by the team of producer Gilchrist Calder and author Colin Morris. These were billed as having been 'drawn from the hard core of the social dis-eases which they have sought to examine, [which] have included strikes, mal-adjusted children, hooliganism, and prostitution.'[28] Unsurprisingly, they now turned their attention to the world of the Teddy boy in a one-hour play called *The Wharf Road Mob*, previewed in that week's edition of the *Radio Times*:

> Thursday's addition to this list of memorable productions turns the spotlight on those gallant oases to be found in the grimy deserts behind every city's glittering façade, the Youth Clubs. Bravely they open their doors to the millions of boys and girls in the half-resolved status of adolescence, accepting the rough and the smooth, the bold and the meek, the cocksure and the diffident, in an effort to provide them not only with a link, however tenuous, with the church, but also with a sense of community and responsibility. But in an era of 'Rock'n'Roll', in an age of bigger pay-packets and flashy clothes, in an atmosphere where the good intentions of the welfare worker seem unrealistic and, to the peacock-proud young men who have found a new and more adventurous club for themselves in the Teddy-boy fraternity, the attractions of the 'tea-and-cakes' Youth Clubs have inevitably paled.[29]

Ironically, the writer of this article was another BBC producer, Rowan Ayers, whose son Kevin grew up to have a lengthy and highly respected rock career from the late 1960s. This preview appeared below a shot of four young men from the cast looking suitably sinister, one with slicked-back hair, sideburns and a velvet-trimmed drape jacket, an impression reinforced by a specially drawn cartoon on the listings page showing various drape-suited layabouts hanging around threateningly under a lamp-post. The show's producer, Gilchrist Calder, displayed little affection for the play nearly four decades later, dismissing it as 'just a so-so sort of show'.[30] As for the reaction at the time, it prompted a lengthy response from *The Observer*'s regular television reviewer, Maurice Richardson, melodramatically entitled 'Death is a Teddy Boy', which began:

> I admit to being terrified of Teddy-boys. Not so much physically – for I am convinced that only a tiny minority of these who wear the gear, or the latest style of all, known as the 'county look', are delinquents who would wish to do me with nut or cosh and put the leather in (thank God for the 'elephant's tread', those thick crêpe soles) when they had me down yelling 'Don't! Don't!' on the pavement – as mentally and spiritually. I see the Teddy as a kind of existentialist storm-trooper in the age-war; he is coming for you as sure as Death.[31]

After this strangely incoherent introduction, he went on to praise the direction and the acting highly. In the play, the young vicar of an East End church invites the teenage members of the Wharf Road Mob to his club, only to be 'set upon outside his own church, kicked *and* stabbed'. As with most fictional depictions of Teddy boys at that time, violence was a foregone conclusion, with them inevitably cast in the role of the aggressor. Yet despite labelling them as 'ape-adolescents', he acknowledged that on television, 'the Teddy-boy is a natural. You can always rely on him to steal the screen'. Noting the tendency for TV companies to round up supposedly tame examples of the species for earnest documentary programmes, he observed that 'those live and virtuous Teddys whom we have seen on ITV as well as BBC scoring points off parsons and scoutmasters, these seem to me to be the real witty nihilists'.[32]

Tony Lyons, the actor who had played gang leader Ron in

The Wharf Road Mob, was back on the small screen in October as one of a gang of Teddy boys and Teddy girls whiling away their time at a south coast seaside resort in a one-hour ITV play *The Pier*,[33] written by James Forsyth (and indeed, he showed up as yet another fictional Teddy boy in the 1958 TV series *Quatermass & the Pit*[34]). Such dramas functioned as something of an informal training ground for up-and-coming young actors who could convincingly play working-class toughs, although some were a little long in the tooth by genuine Ted standards. Peter O'Toole – a twenty-five-year-old member of the regular company at the Bristol Old Vic – was listed a long way down the cast list in that week's edition of the *TV Times*,[35] still five years away from the international stardom that would result from his starring role in *Lawrence of Arabia*, and was sufficiently below the radar that the magazine credited him as 'Peter O'Poole'. Still, he fared better than another member of the cast, twenty-year-old Michael Hastings, who was taken to hospital after the live broadcast, having been accidentally stabbed in the leg with a Teddy boy flick-knife during the performance.[36]

Hail! Hail! Rock'n'Roll

On the face of it, ITV had been trendsetters in launching the nation's first pop music television show, *Cool for Cats*, in December 1956.[37] However, the format – which mostly involved the Dougie Squires Dancers performing decorous moves to a selection of new songs introduced by the smooth tones of commentator Kent Walton – was unlikely to provoke outbursts of frenzied jiving in any Teds or Teddy girls who happened to be viewing. These days, Walton is most famous for having been ITV's wrestling commentator between 1955 and 1988, but he was also a Radio Luxembourg deejay in the fifties.

A year after the debut of *Cool for Cats*, Howard Thomas, the managing director of one of ITV's main companies, ABC Television, wrote a lengthy article praising what he saw as the many successes of the new network; in the two years since its launch it had increased its initial audience of 250,000 London region households to 5,000,000 nationwide by the end of 1957: 'The key question was whether Britain would accept the "commercials." They were not only accepted, but enjoyed, and the jingles and cartoons especially are as entertaining as many of the programmes.'[38]

Of course, this final unsupported assertion could be taken as a damning criticism of the programme quality, but while he was banging the drum for the new age of television advertising, he also found time to mention what he termed the 'rapid decline and fall of fads like "rock'n'roll".'[39]

Thomas wrote this piece for that year's edition of the *Television Annual*, but even as he was consigning such music to the dustbin of history, a picture article on an earlier page of the same book noted another highlight of the year just gone, saying: 'Six-five Special was a new BBC bid to provide "teenager" entertainment on Saturday evenings. Filling a new period of TV transmission, it did not overlook rock'n'roller Tommy Steele.' Alongside this was a shot of the man himself performing on the set of the programme, surrounded by a group of suitably wholesome-looking young people, with not a drape suit in sight.[40]

Six-Five Special, a weekly Saturday evening music show first broadcast on 16 February 1957,[41] was the BBC's direct response to *Cool for Cats*, and had the advantage of being produced by Jack Good, the force of nature who went on to stage the best live 1950s British TV show, *Oh Boy!*, and in the mid-1960s crossed the Atlantic and achieved great success in America, creating and producing the vastly influential show *Shindig!* (1964–5). He also wrote the script for the key episode, 'Hail! Hail! Rock'n'Roll!', in *All You Need Is Love* (1977), Tony Palmer's superb television documentary series about popular music, which features some of the best footage of Jerry Lee Lewis ever filmed. Interviewed himself in that episode, Good recalled his dealings with senior television executives at the start of his career when they first approached him to work on *Six-Five Special*:

> Since I was the youngest member of the BBC team of producers, and had never done anything – they couldn't think of anything I could adequately do – they decided to unleash me on this programme, which would include such items as 'whether to wear lipstick before six o'clock' for young ladies, and 'how to do mountain climbing for Boy Scouts in only hilly areas'.[42]

Such 'educational' pieces were brought in at the insistence of senior management, whereas Good's instinct was to focus on musical performances, which would certainly have been more appealing to the Ted fraternity. As for the Corporation's attitude to rock'n'roll itself – despite having made the decision to feature it as a key part of their weekend television schedules – Jack had this to say:

> The head of light entertainment at BBC asked me how long I gave it, and I could see no end to it and he gave it three months – I think it was three months, might have been two. And then I met him six years later, it was at the Beatles' first concert at the Carnegie Hall, and I walked up to him and then I said, 'Well now how long do you give it?' and he regretted that he now believed me and that he could see no end to it. He was very sad about that. He's dead now. It lasted longer than he did.[43]

Good produced thirty-three episodes of the weekly show, but left out of frustration with the format changes, resurfacing in June 1958 on ITV with *Oh Boy!*, an all-music show performed live in front of a packed teenage audience at the Hackney Empire. This, finally, was the real deal.

As for *Six-Five Special*, despite the fact that early episodes had at least featured occasional showings of short clips from current US motion pictures like the Alan Freed extravaganza *Don't Knock the Rock* (1956) – and they also landed a live performance by Philadelphia rockabilly artist Charlie Gracie – it mostly fell to the regular ITV variety programme, *Sunday Night at the London Palladium,* to present visiting American rockers live on British television. These included Bill Haley and His Comets (24 February 1957), the Teenagers (14 April 1957), the Platters (19 May 1957), and Buddy Holly and the Crickets (2 March 1958).[44] Even the staid *Cool for Cats* managed to bring in the occasional gem like Buddy Holly, or the Everly Brothers, but *Six-Five Special* had long been moving more in the direction of traditional jazz, as its rock-averse new producer, Dennis Main Wilson, proudly recalled many years later:

> It was a dreadful time, skiffle was in, kids playing guitars were in, they used to go into music shops and a guy would sell you a guitar shall we say for twenty quid and then charge you five quid to tune it for you, it really was that bad. And I have a horror of ever playing down to a public in order to make money out of it, I think it's bad manners, it is bad for the nation and it is shitty from every point of view. I tried, maybe it's cocky of me but I tried to bring a bit of quality into *Six-Five Special*.[45]

All of which suggests that the prevailing BBC attitude even

among those making programmes supposedly aimed at teenagers was just to keep their heads down in the confident expectation that rock'n'roll and the Teddy boys would soon be gone. Teds were objects of curiosity, vaguely newsworthy but unworthy of deeper consideration.

11

A DRIP IN A DRAINPIPE

Literary Teddy Boys

It cannot have been easy to be a clergyman in 1950s Britain, forever scanning the weekly headlines in search of themes for your latest sermon – especially since a proportion of what was said by men of the cloth was picked up in the pages of national newspapers in a way that is far less common today. The Reverend Walter Lazenby gave a speech in April 1959, quoted in the *Manchester Guardian*,[1] in which he managed – despite six years of blanket Ted coverage via the press, radio, books, television and motion pictures – to conflate the more recent US-derived bearded beatnik styles favoured by the anti-nuclear CND Aldermaston marchers or modern jazz aficionados with elements of the classic Teddy boy look. Not to miss a trick, he also lumped in the Angry Young Men, who had been obsessing the press since the 1956 appearance of John Osborne's play *Look Back in Anger*, but such people also had precious little to do with Teddy boys.

> The teddy-boy contemptuously dismissed as a 'drip in a drainpipe' is really the frustrated child of an insecure age. This description was applied last night by the Rev Walter Lazenby, chairman of the Lancashire Congregational Union, who said that the 'angry young men' were of the same mould. Speaking at the union's annual assembly at

Crosby, Liverpool, Mr Lazenby (of the Ormskirk Street Church, St Helens) said that the faithlessness and fear of the modern world were found in every nation in the subconsciousness of the 'beat' generation. The teddy boy wore his jeans, his thick-soled shoes, his string tie, and his unkempt hair and beard as a gesture of defiance, but he protested too much.[2]

Anyone searching for bearded Teds in the East End would have retired disappointed; nevertheless, confused declarations such as Lazenby's were frequently reported seriously by the mainstream press. Yet the reverend was hardly alone in in conflating the Teddy boy with the Angry Young Men as portrayed in novels since the mid-1950s, and it had not taken long after the first appearances in the press of youths in Edwardian dress before writers of fiction began including such characters in their works.

In the summer of 1955, the writer Kingsley Amis – whose debut novel *Lucky Jim* had been published to great acclaim the previous year – was described by reviewer V. S. Pritchett in the *New Statesman* as a 'literary Teddy Boy',[3] an eye-catching turn of phrase that had little deeper meaning. A few weeks earlier Evelyn Waugh had written something similarly condescending in a private letter to his friend, the author Christopher Sykes, using terms of reference several light years removed from the Elephant & Castle: 'I have a theory about the modern Teddy-boy school of novelist and critic – [John] Wain, [Kingsley] Ames, [*sic*] etc. It is that they all read English Literature for schools and so take against it, while good critics & writers read as a treat and a relaxation from Latin & Greek.'[4]

It's Smart, Sis

Amis and Wain were in their early thirties, and Osborne and Wilson their mid-twenties, and they had all been lumped together by critics as 'Angry Young Men'. Teddy boys were even younger; some of them were undoubtedly angry on occasion, but there the similarity ends. Nevertheless, once commentators had sunk their teeth into the idea, it refused to lie down and die. A full two years later, Frederick Lumley wrote an article for *The Spectator* considering the options available for younger Scottish authors: 'Out of the new bourgeoisie in England has arisen the intellectual Teddy Boy such as Jimmy Porter. Scottish Teddy Boys are far from being intellectuals, while our angry young men can always become militant nationalists, taking care, of course, that they don't have to suffer for the cause.'[5]

Eventually, however, the genuine working-class Ted became of interest to the nation's novelists. 1958 stands out as the year when representations of Teds became commonplace in highbrow fiction, but unsurprisingly, the pulp novelists – whose books were sometimes knocked out in a matter of weeks – had been there several years earlier.

One of the earliest attempts to incorporate the new breed into crime fiction was the novella *The Teddy Boy Mystery* by John Drummond, published in April 1955. Billed as a '64-Page Thrilling Detective Story', it was number 334 in the Sexton Blake Library series which had been running since 1915.[6] Drummond was one of various pseudonyms used by forty-four-year-old prolific pulp and genre author John Newton Chance, who also published under the names John Lymington, Desmond Reid and David C. Newton. It would be another couple of years before established authors began giving brief walk-on roles to caricatures of thuggish Teds in the kinds of novel that were routinely praised in the Sunday papers, but Drummond set a

'It's smart, sis, it's the latest thing.' A crime-solving teenage Ted gang, 1955

Teddy boy gang at the heart of his story, and gave a flavour of the popular perception of such teenagers during the spring of 1955.

As *The Teddy Boy Mystery* begins, its protagonist Johnny Harris has acquired his first Edwardian suit of 'narrow trousers and long jacket with velvet collar'[7] which he wears with a bootlace tie, much to his sister's disapproval. 'It's smart, sis,' he tells her, 'it's the latest thing. All the chaps wear suits like this now.' She is unconvinced, and is especially worried about his membership of local Ted gang the Denbury Lot. Sure enough, they dare him to break into a scary mansion as an initiation test, and the owner is conveniently murdered by an unknown assailant while Johnny is in the building. He escapes, but leaves behind multiple traces of his forced entry, and has no choice but to go on the run, disposing of his bloodstained Teddy boy suit in the process. All this within the first few pages – amply demonstrating the perils of adopting drape suits and hanging out with the ruffians down at a place called Harry's Milk Bar.

There was a message here for any real-life Teds appearing in court on criminal charges: it helps if your loyal sister calls in a world-famous private detective to pluckily ferret out the evidence proving your innocence. Johnny, of course, is not a bad boy really – indeed, even the police sergeant at one point expresses the view that most Teds are simply in need of guidance or something to do. The Denbury Lot help round up the real murderers at the end; a surprisingly enlightened plot twist, given the prevailing attitudes of the day. However, despite being written during the months when Bill Haley and His Comets were first staking a decisive claim on the UK charts, there was no mention in the story of rock'n'roll.

By the time James Wood came to write his Glasgow-set espionage novel *The Shop in Loch Street* (1958), the connection between Teds and music was well established in the public mind. It would be reflected in the narrator's description of the following scene:

> I began to saunter down Loch Street. Several folks were about; and there was a pin-table and amusement arcade, where a bunch of kids in bottle-breeches and long hair-cuts were hanging around the entrance. I looked into the arcade and lit a cigarette. Most of the kids were listening to a juke-box and making comments – mostly adverse, oddly enough – about this guy Presley who was the current guff-craze with a guitar . . . An insolent kid with dirty hands and a velveteen collar to his coat came up to me and said, 'Youse lookin' fur somebuddy, mister?' in a menacing slur.[8]

This is more typical of novels at the time, in which Teds only show up as a form of down-market window-dressing. Crime fiction fans, however, seem to have been kept in the picture better than most, even those overseas. For instance, the American mass-market pulp magazine *True Crime* ran a lengthy sensationalist article in May 1956 entitled *Teddy Boys vs Gang Boys*, illustrated with some excellent photographs of English Teddy boys and Teddy girls taken at a dance halls in London and Birmingham. One picture carried an unsubtle hint at drug use in its caption, despite appearing to show nothing more sinister than a group of friends in a ballroom enjoying a cigarette: 'Teddy Girls puff on "sticks" and swap stories of their escapades.'[9]

Fancy Clothes and a Bicycle Chain

One British crime writer who put drape-suited teenagers at the heart of a story was Guy Cullingford, whose sixth novel, *The Whipping Boys* (1958), featured a group of Teds at a youth

club that murder an elderly lady. Even prior to the revelation of
their homicidal tendencies, the gang hardly seemed likely to win
any popularity contests. In contrast to some who felt that poor
social conditions were to blame for young people's criminality,
one of the book's older characters was having none of it:

> Under-privileged my foot! Those scoundrels have never had
> it so easy. They can pick and choose their job, play hookey
> when they like, get paid the earth and always find some
> mu – beg pardon, sir, some well-meaning person like your-
> self to provide them with the sort of equipment that would
> make a public schoolboy green with envy. And out of this
> Paradise on earth slouches the Teddy boy with his evil face,
> his fancy clothes and a bicycle chain in his pocket.[10]

Here, in one paragraph, are many of the commonly held
criticisms of Teds that surface time and again: they have too
much money, and the ease of finding a job gives them an
arrogance unknown to older generations who had suffered
through the era of mass unemployment during the Depression of the 1930s. It is hard to say how far this speech reflected
the author's own views. Guy Cullingford was the pen-name
of Constance Lindsay Dowdy; fifty-one when *The Whipping
Boys* appeared, she would certainly have had first-hand knowledge of the deprivations of earlier years, but it is dangerous to
ascribe opinions to authors based on their characters' words.
Nevertheless, the artist who painted the front cover illustration
for the first edition duly served up a stylised image of a gang
of sinister-looking young men in drape suits, waistcoats and
quiffed hair loitering in a narrow street, one of them casually
swinging a bicycle chain. The message was clear – if you see
them approaching, run.

Another female author who wrote about Teds that year was Elizabeth Stucley; her book was a memoir of her past few years getting to know a group of teenagers who lived in a block of flats near her large seventeenth-century house overlooking Clapham Common in South London. 'Couldn't you start a club for us chaps, ma'am?' one of the teenagers asks her, and another adds, 'Don't yer want to keep us orf the streets?'[11] She gave her book the title *Teddy Boys' Picnic*, a play on words which had been used extensively in the previous four years, but in this case was justified – she had taken her small club of ten school-age boys on picnics and camping expeditions. On their first trip away, following a scuffle, she makes them hand over whatever weapons they may have brought with them: 'A huge collection of knives and daggers were produced, but were surrendered without much protest. I was too large to argue with. And the sight of blood had sobered them a little. The cut victim still snivelled. I pocketed the knives and frisked the boys for coshes or bicycle chains. Then did first aid.'[12]

At the start of her book she spends several pages retelling the story of the 1953 Clapham Common stabbing,[13] as if to suggest she was there when it happened. It had certainly occurred on her doorstep, but her world was very different from those who were involved. Born in 1906 to an aristocratic family who had owned Affeton Castle in Devon since the fifteenth century – not to mention their more substantial eighteenth-century country seat, Hartland Abbey – she was the daughter of the late Sir Hugh Nicholas Granville Stucley, fourth baronet. Although the dustjacket of the first edition featured the title spelled out in shapes made from bike chains, flick-knives, a cut-throat razor and some elongated drawings of drape-jacketed characters, her book is mostly the story of a kind-hearted upper-middle-class woman taking some time to expose a group of early teenage kids to the delights of places outside their experience, such as the Tate Gallery. There is little Teddy boy content here at all.

Somethin' Ter Make You Look Different

Young people in Edwardian clothing may have attracted readers to Guy Cullingford and Elizabeth Stucley's works, but another novel published the same year put them more directly in the spotlight. The author was Ernest Ryman, and his book was simply called *Teddy Boy*. It was even given a hardback publication, the dustjacket of which showed a restrained drawing of a slim-jim tie.[14] Two years later, however, when published in paperback, it received the full lurid pulp illustration treatment; a misleading cover illustration of a leather-jacketed, American-style thug was accompanied by the slogan, 'The pathetic story of a teenage criminal whose career ends in murder'.[15] A former Borstal boy, the title character becomes a Ted, carries a flick-knife, and hangs out at 'Teddy Boy cafes' and 'Teddy Boy dancehalls', thus ticking most of the required boxes. Yet Ryman seems to have had a serious purpose in writing the book. An Oxbridge graduate who had served in Royal Navy minesweepers during the war, he spent time in the mid-1950s teaching young people who had been sentenced by the courts to a spell in a residential institution known as an approved school, which mostly forms the setting for the book – some of which is written from the point of view of a staff member dealing with a class:

> I decided to have some discussion and brought up the subject of Teddy-boy clothing. This special uniform of some sections of our youth consisted of black drainpipe trousers, a long, draped jacket, a waistcoat with a pocket to put the thumb in, and a very narrow tie, for which

sometimes a bootlace was substituted. Only a minority of boys in my group had ever worn it, but most of them were in favour of this type of clothing. I started by asking one of them why he liked it, and the following reply was very much to the point.

'Well, when you go out to work, yer want to buy somethin' ter make you look different; and when you've got a Teddy suit on people look at you in the street, 'specially the judies [girls]. Some judies won't look at you if you ain't wearin' 'em.'[16]

Another Ted in the same class, when asked by the teacher if he liked the kind of clothes that the staff wore, replies, 'No, I don't,' before adding, 'You're all peasants – that's what we call fellows who don't wear Teddy clothes.' Others mention that a full Ted suit would cost 'around forty quid', that the cause of gang fights was usually a disagreement 'over some judy', and that carrying knives was normal behaviour – as they put it, 'you've got ter be able to defend yerself, ain't yer?'[17]

Despite such exchanges, the title probably did *Teddy Boy* an injustice; as several reviewers pointed out, it was generally a much less sensationalist book about the lives of a variety of young inmates, many of whom did not really belong in the Ted category at all. Writing in the *Manchester Evening News*, David Brett called it 'the most inspiring – and certainly the most satisfying book I have read this year', while also finding the central Teddy boy character a distraction from the novel's main purpose: 'Running parallel with this absorbing day-to-day study in rehabilitation, is the story of Jimmie Albon, an old boy of Fulwood [the approved school] whose career ends in murder. This is so melodramatic, so wildly out of key with the rest of the book's natural dignity that it seems a pity it was ever included.'[18]

Reviewing the book for *The Observer*, Angus Wilson also felt that 'as an account of the approved school system, it is an interesting and valuable corrective to the sensational popular nonsense talked about juvenile delinquency', and that 'a large percentage of the delinquents were not the Teddy Boy sophisticates we hear so much of, but very simple, low intelligenced boys'. He was far from convinced, however, by the book's literary merits, and said so in somewhat harsh terms: 'Unfortunately, the author's naïve approach to his subject is matched by a completely amateur approach to writing. The narrative reads at times like a schoolboy story of 1920, at times like a prep school magazine account of an outing to Aldershot tattoo.'[19]

As a respected fiction writer himself, Wilson had ventured into Ted territory a few months earlier with the title story of his latest collection, *A Bit off the Map*. Published in October 1957, it received a very favourable review, also in *The Observer*, by the critic John Davenport. Claiming that Wilson's approach to his characters enabled him to 'reveal the fearful vacuity in these impotently mechanical lives', Davenport singled out the title story as 'technically a masterpiece, told partially in the first person by an almost certifiable Teddy-boy, a pathetic creature fed on fantasy'.[20] The Ted character Kennie is adopted as a sort of pet by older men at pretentious house parties where a group of people who call themselves 'The Crowd' speak in 'cultured tones', yet despite his supposed low intelligence, he employs words such as 'bourgeois' in his interior monologues. Other such passages suggest that Wilson has constructed a character based less in reality but rather on the author's fantasies of what such a person might be:

Well, me being dressed as I am – see, when I've got money
I buy my jeans and sweaters at this place where they make

specially for you (so you never see the same on anyone else) and my hair cut at Raymond 15/- with Pour Les Hommes, and my jeans very tight because I've got good legs. Well see, The Crowd thought I might be on to some game (but what have they got to lose?) or a queer (The Crowd is strong against queers, but Susan could tell them different about me) or in with a teddy boy lot (but I'm always alone).[21]

Wilson's characterisation of a Ted here is also about as convincing as a schoolboy story of 1920, simply in a different way to that of Ryman.

Allus Making Trouble

The autumn of 1958 also saw the publication of a book that includes what is still the most effective literary portrayal of a Teddy boy: Alan Sillitoe's debut novel *Saturday Night and Sunday Morning*, which remains one of the most accomplished works of post-war British fiction. Anyone looking at the cover of the first edition, with a fine illustration by the painter Mona Moore,[22] would probably have been able to hazard a guess as to the subject matter: a young couple are pictured inside a pub, the man wearing a drape jacket and high-buttoned waistcoat, his hair slicked up in an elaborate pompadour. The principal character, Arthur Seaton, is a young Nottingham factory worker who identifies as a Ted. He starts the book by getting legless in a pub drinking competition, before vomiting over a man, and shortly afterwards on the man's wife. Just before he throws up on her, she shouts at him to apologise:

> The woman stood a foot away from Arthur. 'Look at him,' she jeered into his face. 'He's senseless. He can't say a word.

He can't even apologise. Why don't yer apologise, eh? *Can't* yer apologise? Dragged-up, I should think, getting drunk like this. Looks like one of them Teddy boys, allus making trouble. Go on, apologise.'[23]

A little later on, it becomes clear how important his clothes are to him, and how much they have cost. Even stumbling in after a night on the sauce, Arthur takes care to put them away neatly before passing out: 'he started laughing, drunk to himself and all the world, until he crept upstairs in his stockinged-feet, set his teddy suit on the number-one hanger, and slept sounder than any log.'[24]

This instinct to look after such items rings more true than when Angus Wilson's Kennie speaks about clothes. Indeed, I recall an original fifties Teddy boy once telling me that he and his friends would deliberately try to avoid fights when out in their best drape suits; they were worried about the risk of them being damaged after paying a significant amount of money to a tailor to have them made in the first place. These valuable clothes were all about self-esteem and personal style, as Sillitoe expressed in the following description of Seaton returning from a day working at the factory:

Upstairs he flung his greasy overalls aside and selected a suit from a line of hangers. Brown paper protected them from dust, and he stood for some minutes in the cold, digging his hands into pockets and turning back lapels, sampling the good hundred pounds' worth of property hanging from an iron-bar. They were his riches, and he told himself that money paid-out on clothes was a sensible investment because it made him feel good as well as look good.[25]

This would have been a sentiment the author knew well – unlike Angus Wilson, educated at Westminster School and Oxford University, Sillitoe had left school at fourteen, and then got a job as a drill operator and a lathe operator in the Raleigh bicycle factory, where his father had also worked. He was thirty when the novel appeared, although for some reason his publisher claimed he was twenty-eight. They also felt the need to explain his background on the inside flap of the dustjacket, commenting that 'he differs from most writers who have sprung from the working classes in that he is not conscious of himself as an intellectual'.

Hailing from the Midlands, Sillitoe was accorded a lengthy interview as a local author with the *Leicester Evening Mail*, which provides an interesting snapshot of him as his career was about to take off:

> Pipe-puffing Alan Sillitoe, who lives in a two-roomed book-lined flat in unfashionable rent-cheap Camden Town, is a compact 10-stone hank of coiled wire with piercing eyes glittering in an alert face. He has a rhythmic sense of spacing his jabbing, jolting talk with expletives redolent of the barrack room. He likes to be excited. He says he is excited by a five-hour opera session, with 'The Trojans' or 'The Iceman Cometh', or equally with a dancing jag to Rock'n'roll ('listen to the words of "Jailhouse Rock" ... sheer poetry ... wish I could do it').[26]

In addition to generally glowing reviews – such as that in the *Daily Telegraph* ('A novel of today with a freshness and raw fury that makes *Room at the Top* look like a vicarage tea-party'[27]) – Sillitoe's book also received some useful publicity on national television one Sunday afternoon that October when he was interviewed on ITV's *The Book Man* show, alongside Brendan Behan, who spoke about his new memoir, *Borstal Boy*. For a debut novelist from his kind of background, this was quite an accolade.[28]

Caught Up in These Teddy-Boy Types

Alan Sillitoe's novel was turned into what was arguably the best film to emerge from the new wave of British 'kitchen sink' dramas, many of which were made by Woodfall, a production company formed by Harry Saltzman, Tony Richardson and John Osborne. Saltzman – who would later strike gold in partnership with Cubby Broccoli, producing the James Bond series – secured the film rights to *Saturday Night and Sunday Morning* in April 1959. In many ways, this was a logical choice for Woodfall, given that they were the people behind the cinema adaptation of *Look Back in Anger*. However, it was the best part of a year before shooting began at Twickenham Studios on 29 February 1960,[29] and almost another year before the completed picture went on general release. Location work took place on the streets of Nottingham, and inside the Raleigh bicycle factory where both Sillitoe and his father had worked. Indeed, the author's mother was still working there at the time of filming.

While Sillitoe was writing *Saturday Night and Sunday Morning* – and when it was published in 1958 – Teddy boys were still a hot topic as far as news stories and the wider culture was concerned. By the time the film adaptation was shot two years later, the world had moved on, fashions and hairstyles had changed, and the central character of Arthur Seaton as portrayed on screen was far less obviously a Ted. The jacket of his best suit which he proudly takes from his wardrobe after changing from his factory clothes before heading for an evening at the

PAN

SATURDAY NIGHT AND SUNDAY MORNING
Alan Sillitoe

A novel of today with a freshness and raw fury that 'makes ROOM AT THE TOP look like a vicarage tea-party'
DAILY TELEGRAPH

Filmed by
WOODFALL PRODUCTIONS
starring
ALBERT FINNEY

Albert Finney on the cover of the 1960 movie tie-in edition
of Sillitoe's novel, no longer wearing Ted clothes

pub is not a fingertip drape with a velvet collar but a shorter, Italian-style item of a type that had recently become popular. Clearly the film-makers were attempting to depict a slice of contemporary life, so the novel's Ted references were downplayed.

Ironically, in the month that shooting began, two of the film's main stars, Albert Finney and Shirley Anne Field, were appearing together at the Royal Court Theatre in London in a play by Harry Cookson called *The Lily White Boys*.[30] Billed as 'A positive play of the prosperous Sixties', it had been briefly staged in 1958 at the Shrewsbury Festival, but was now remodelled as a musical.[31] Finney appeared as the leader of a gang of Teds, while Field was a Teddy girl. The critic J. C. Trewin of the *Illustrated London News* had been one of the few people who had seen the play in its original incarnation, and he had not been impressed:

> It babbled on with a trio of teddy-boys and another of teddy-girls. We were supposed to laugh ourselves pink at the spectacle of the teddy-boys 'getting on in the legitimate racket', the author being quite sure that any kind of success must be a racket ... In its new guise at the Court (where its origin and the Shrewsbury performance are not mentioned in the programme) it has a 'dated' air, almost as if these teddy-boys had been plucked from under misted glass.[32]

Like most of the journalists who reviewed *The Lily White Boys*, Trewin seems to have judged it a failure; even so, he praised some of the cast, and wrote 'I hope Mr Finney will not get caught up in these teddy-boy types: he is too good an actor.'

Animal Virility and Supreme Self-Possession

Interviewed in a pub later that year, a month prior to the London premiere of *Saturday Night and Sunday Morning* at the Warner Theatre, Leicester Square, on 26 October 1960, Finney was described by Thomas Wiseman as having 'the look of a sensitive Teddy Boy, his talk and movements smack of the street corner rather than the stage door'.[33] Yet the near-universally favourable reviews of the film did not mention Teddy boys at all, despite it having been based on what is arguably the most nuanced literary characterisation of a member of the breed. Indeed, although film critics generally admitted that Arthur Seaton had significant character flaws, they saw him as a rounded human being rather than a two-dimensional stereotype. Jympson Harman in the *Liverpool Echo* was keen to define him:

> He is a rebel against convention, tramples on all the rules, not because he is an Angry Young Man but because he just does not care. He is no mixed-up kid. He doesn't – like so many fictional heroes today – worry his little mind about where he is going, or his purpose in being alive. He is a bundle of animal virility and supreme self-possession. Arthur Seaton is very much All Right, Jack, and nobody is going to stop him being that way.[34]

Elspeth Grant in the *Tatler & Bystander* was impressed by the actor's skill in making her care about someone who might otherwise have been completely unlikable: 'Yet, brilliantly played by Mr Albert Finney, Arthur somehow commands one's reluctant respect. He has guts and an individual attitude to life. He is no member of the "beat" generation, of which I am heartily sick.'[35]

Both of these were mainstream reviews, but it is also interesting to note the opinion of the usually more pragmatic film trade press, whose main interest lay in determining a film's prospects as a commercial property. *Kinematograph Weekly* called it an 'outstanding adult entertainment and infallible box-office proposition', but even this review felt the need to define Arthur Seaton and differentiate him from other recent controversial screen anti-heroes.

> Adapted from Alan Sillitoe's sensational bestseller, it concerns a young Midland factory worker, a rebel without a cause, who recklessly opens his big mouth during 'office hours', yet spends his leisure boozing and womanizing until the right girl comes along. The tale crashes a shabby world, but, unlike *Look Back in Anger* and *Room at the Top*, doesn't make dissatisfaction an eroding obsession. Neither does it trade in obscenity, although sex frequently rears its ugly head.[36]

This was a rare case of both book and film delivering satisfying versions of the same story, despite the usual need of the latter to considerably compress the narrative in order to achieve a ninety-minute running time. Sillitoe's novel of a working-class factory hand who likes to dress up in Ted gear brought home the wider point that it was possible to be attracted to such styles and not be pigeonholed by society. Take, for example, the case of one particular teenager from Southend. Born during the Second World War, and fifteen years old when *Saturday Night and Sunday Morning* was published, he loved dancing to the music of Bill Haley and Gene Vincent, and soon acquired a drape and some drainpipes, becoming part of a gang of Teds. He ended up getting involved in street fighting with rival out-of-town mobs near the pier, and falling foul of the law, as he recalled in later life: 'I was said to have hit a policeman with such force he had to be picked off the pavement. It was absolute rubbish but I was found guilty. I had to spend a night in a cell with the light on all the time, and I wasn't allowed to use the lavatory. It was hateful. I think there should be more education for the police.'[37]

As far as many would have been concerned at that time, this lad was a thug and a troublemaker who conformed nicely to the stereotype. Yet dig beneath the surface, and it turned out that one of his hobbies was crochet work – and he went on as an adult not to a life of petty crime interspersed with inevitable stretches in prison, but one of musicianship, singing, songwriting and writing. For this drape-wearing teenager was the great Viv Stanshall, founder member and lead vocalist of the Bonzo Dog Doo-Dah Band, who commemorated his 1950s past in the title of his 1981 solo LP, *Teddy Boys Don't Knit*.

Not everyone fits the convenient stereotype, and labels are to be resisted, just as Sillitoe's Arthur Seaton had maintained in 1958:

What am I? he wondered. A six-foot pit-prop that wants a pint of ale. That's what I am. And if any knowing bastard says that's what I am, I'm a dynamite dealer, Sten-gun seller, hundred-ton tank trader, a capstan-lathe operator waiting to blow the Army to Kingdom Cum [*sic*]. I'm me and nobody else; and whatever people think I am or say I am, that's what I'm not, because they don't know a bloody thing about me.[38]

12

KNIVES IN WEST ELEVEN

The Chic and Bohemian Environs of West London

Anyone strolling through the lovingly restored Georgian terraced streets of Notting Hill today, or perhaps watching Richard Curtis's saccharine 1999 rom-com of the same name, might find it hard to credit that in the fifties some of the residents of these same streets were crowded into decaying, multiple-occupancy buildings owned by vicious, exploitative landlords. Indeed, it is no surprise that in Hugh Clevely's 1953 London crime novel, *Public Enemy*, Mickey – a young wide-boy thief who tries to blackmail the main character – comes from Notting Hill, and lives in what is bluntly described as a 'slum' area off the Portobello Road.[1]

This is all a far cry from the 1990s neighbourhood that inspired Curtis's movie. In recent decades the area has moved even further upmarket, and houses that once sometimes held upwards of fifty people crammed in over four storeys have long since been converted back into single dwellings. In Blenheim Crescent – where hundreds participated in some of the worst of the area's race riots on the night of 1 September 1958 – houses now sell for upwards of £5 million.

Kevin Fitzgerald's fine crime thriller, *Trouble in West Two* (1958), written just before the riots, shone a light upon the area's late-night joints and criminal fraternity. The occasional Ted could be observed hanging around the clubs and bars, although many were not yet old enough to gain admittance to these establishments, so cafes remained their favourite option. In Fitzgerald's book, they are window-dressing rather than any kind of active threat: 'there was the usual little crowd of Teddy boys and girls',[2] he writes at one point, and then later, 'a Teddy boy sat without speaking, staring fixedly at a horsetail of hair which decorated his girlfriend'.[3] Teenagers, doing much the same things as any others of the same age.

After five years of headlines, cartoons, scare stories and sermons, Teds had become a known commodity. Not cosy by any means, but as far as many of the older generation were concerned, it was an adolescent phase which would pass once its adherents discovered the joys of matrimony, child-rearing and adult responsibilities.

Then, in the late summer of 1958, events took a far more sinister turn.

Panting Like a Hippo

In the immediate post-war era, Notting Hill became home to many people who had moved to London from the West Indies or Africa. Colin MacInnes first explored the lives of this section of the Notting Hill community in his 1957 novel, *City of Spades*, which traces the story of the protagonist Johnny Fortune after his arrival from Lagos, Nigeria, told from various perspectives, including that of a white character who seems to embody much of the author's own fascination with that world, and the complexities and rivalries within it. 'Listen to these Ras Tafaris,' says a man from Africa mockingly to a Jamaican. 'All long hair and dirty fingernails.'[4] There is a real sense that the author had spent time getting to know these people, and the book seems to have been written with genuine affection.

MacInnes returned to writing about Notting Hill in his next novel, *Absolute Beginners*, which appeared in 1959, and is more impressionistic in tone. Its climax used the previous year's race riots as a backdrop, but the principal Teddy boy character in the latter is a pathetic, thinly realised, one-dimensional caricature called Ed the Ted. During the first few pages of his initial appearance, the narrator informs the reader that Ed is an 'imbecile', a 'poor goof' and a 'goon', with a 'pasty, scabies-ridden countenance', dirty fingernails, halitosis and smelly, unwashed clothes, who is 'panting like a hippo' and repeatedly cries out 'like a ten-year-old'. Most other characters in the novel are shown speaking relatively normally, but Ed's dialogue consists entirely of sentences like 'You fink I'm sof or sumfink?' (*sic*), presumably designed to make the point that he has – in the words of Tom Waits – the IQ of a fence post.[5]

It is not hard to see why the teenage fans of the Jam in the 1979 mod revival were attracted to this book; its principal character is a young photographer of the loose grouping which in 1958 were just beginning to define themselves under the word *modernist*; he whizzes around town on a Vespa scooter and is living something akin to the Swinging Sixties lifestyle half a decade before it began. Yet by the time the movement had gone mainstream under the shortened name 'mod' the original modernists had long since moved on to newer pastures. By contrast, anyone drawn to the music and style of 1950s rock'n'roll might be justified in dismissing the book as a naïve caricature of youthful poses written by a man whose own teenage years began back in 1927, at the same time that Hitchcock's silent film *The Lodger* was released.

Nevertheless, the simplistic presentation of Teds in *Absolute Beginners*, along with that of another 1958 novel, *Awake For Mourning* by Bernard Kops, in which a sinister pop idol manipulates his gullible Teddy boy followers into embracing fascism, has helped colour their reputation,[6] just as images of mid-1980s King's Road chancers with Mohicans wearing studded leather jackets have distorted the general public's impression of the original punk teenagers of 1976. All this, however, is trivial compared to the media attention Teddy boys attracted in the aftermath of the 1958 riots.

Go On, Boy!

If you were looking for a single image published during the Notting Hill clashes that laid the blame squarely on Teddy boys, the cartoon which occupied the front cover of the *Daily Mirror* on 2 September is as good a candidate as any. It ran alongside the following headline story:

2,000 RIOT
GANGS INVADE 'COLOUR' CLASH AREA

Two thousand teenagers and young children ran riot in the Notting Hill trouble area of London last night, smashing windows at the homes of coloured people.[7]

This was shocking enough, but the cartoon alongside it was even more disturbing. It showed a flabby, gormless thug with high, quiffed-up and slicked-back hair, drape jacket and the narrowest drainpipe trousers, who stares blankly into the distance, his hand holding an outsized flick-knife dripping with blood. On the brick wall next to him was a crudely drawn swastika, above the scrawled words 'RACIAL PERSECUTION, INTOLERANCE & PREJUDICE'. At the top of the picture, Hitler himself is shown as a ghostly presence, whispering in the Ted's ear the words, 'Go on, boy! I may have lost that war, but my ideas seem to be winning ...' In the middle of the youth's bloodstained chest was the label 'Our own racialist thugs', while closer inspection revealed that the figure of Hitler was actually the shadow that the Ted cast on the wall.[8]

All of this was bad news for the thousands of teenagers across the country who were simply into wearing the clothes, listening to rock'n'roll music and trying to impress the opposite sex. This stark image seemed to be saying that being a Teddy boy was the moral equivalent of Nazi Party membership. More importantly, it also absolved other members of the community of whatever age, class or sartorial inclination from any responsibility for what had happened during the riots.

At the time of publication, the *Daily Mirror* was one of the largest-selling newspapers in the world, and their cartoonist, Vicky, among the nation's most popular. A measure of his power was that his contract at the paper granted him complete editorial freedom. Whereas some artists worked in tandem with content writers, both the words and images of Vicky's cartoons were entirely his own creation; in this case, the sentiment so unambiguously expressed left little doubt that with him, this was personal. Given his background, the reasons for this are entirely understandable.

Vicky was the pen-name of Victor Weisz, who was born in Berlin in 1913 to a Hungarian Jewish family. As a teenager he witnessed the growth of the National Socialists during the years of Germany's Weimar Republic, and had drawn cartoons mocking Hitler for the newspaper *12 Uhr Blatt* under its anti-Nazi editor, Walther Steinthal. In 1933, upon Hitler becoming chancellor, Steinthal was summarily replaced and the paper was forced to sack all of its Jewish staff; Weisz himself eventually fled to England in 1935.[9] That he had good cause to hate the Nazis is self-evident, although his first-hand experience of Teddy boys is unclear. The link between Notting Hill and resurgent fascism, however, can mostly be laid at the foot of a man who was Victorian, rather than Edwardian: Sir Oswald Ernald Mosley, sixth baronet, born in 1896.

Two Weddings and a Führer

As his title suggests, Mosley's background was not remotely similar to that of any Teddy boy or Teddy girl. His aristocratic family had lived at Rolleston Hall in Shropshire for centuries, and the sale of this estate in 1919 made him very wealthy. Elected as an MP the previous year, in 1920 he married Cynthia Blanche Curzon, daughter of the Foreign Secretary and a rich woman in her own right. A Ted planning a wedding reception might have opted for a knees-up down the Old Kent Road, whereas the Mosleys' nuptials were attended by King George V and Queen Mary.[10] Previously a Labour MP and Chancellor of the Duchy of Lancaster in the government of Ramsay MacDonald, Mosley formed his own political party in 1932, the British Union of Fascists – whose name was changed four years later to the British Union of Fascists and National Socialists, just in case anyone had missed the point.

Although he had travelled to Italy at the start of that decade for talks with Italian fascist leader Benito Mussolini,[11] Mosley seems to have primarily based his political tactics upon the strategies employed by Hitler and his Brownshirts in the later Weimar years: identify a section of the population to use as a scapegoat, and then march your thugs into a working-class area and stir up resentment among them against this supposed enemy.

In the 1930s, the Jewish population were Mosley's prime target; in the 1950s, he switched his focus to the Jamaican residents of Birmingham, Wolverhampton and Notting Hill. In each instance, this was a cynical attempt to gain political power, and in both decades – despite having some very well-placed friends in high society, in government and in the media (in particular his 1930s supporter and fellow admirer of Hitler, Viscount Rothermere, owner of the *Daily Mail* and *Daily Mirror*[12]) – he failed miserably.

When Mosley's blackshirts planned to march into White-chapel on 4 October 1936 they were guarded by several thousand police and met by an estimated 100,000 counter-demonstrators in what became known as the Battle of Cable Street – nearly all of which consisted of the police charging the barricades of the anti-fascist demonstrators.[13] The following day, as news of the riot made headlines across the country, Mosley flew to Germany with his partner Diana Guinness (his first wife had died of peritonitis in 1933). Oswald and Diana were secretly married the next day in the Berlin home of Joseph Goebbels, Reich Minister of Propaganda; Hitler was in attendance, and presented the happy couple with a framed photograph of himself.[14]

Heckling, Hissing, Foot-Stamping

The public reaction of many commentators following the 1958 race riots in Nottingham and London was one of understandable shock – there was a feeling that such things just did not happen in Britain. Yet the warning signs had been there, and although Mosley did not live in the UK, he had been happy to be photographed by *Picture Post* in a carefully selected spit-and-sawdust East End pub in 1954, surrounded by followers giving him the straight-armed 'Hail Mosley' fascist salute.[15] Clearly, he was once again considering the idea of stirring up trouble in working-class London as a way of achieving political power, despite having spent most of his time since 1951 at one of his two luxurious homes abroad. The first was the neo-classical former residence of one of Napoleon's generals, Jean Victor Marie Moreau, located in its own park in the Paris suburb of Orsay, and which carried the overblown name Le Temple de la Gloire.[16] Mosley's other property was in County Galway; a sixteenth-century country mansion called Clonfert Palace that had been originally built for a bishop.[17] He spent a great deal of time there until it burned to the ground in 1955, after which he resided permanently in Orsay until his death in 1980.

There were signs that Mosley had identified areas with a West Indian population as a likely new target for his rabble-rousing as early as 1956, when, as *The Times* reported, 'there was agitation against the coloured people in Birmingham, and slogans saying "Keep Britain White" had appeared on walls. With the slogans was an emblem – a flash of lightning in the centre of a circle – which was the emblem of the British Fascist party.'[18] This occurred shortly after the local council had voted to employ bus drivers and conductors from Jamaica. There were already bus crew members in nearby Wolverhampton who were originally from India; a year earlier a union dispute had arisen out of tensions between various groups among the staff, during which it was reported by the *Birmingham Daily Post* that the Wolverhampton branch of the Transport and General Workers Union 'passed a resolution that a ceiling of 5 per cent of the traffic staff should be fixed for the employment of coloured labour and that any replacement within that limit should be from Jamaicans only'.[19] This prompted bus workers from Indian backgrounds to object that a discriminatory colour bar was being operated against them.

It came as no surprise when Oswald Mosley opted to hold a large meeting in Birmingham Town Hall in October 1956, prompting a storm of publicity both in the run-up to the event, and afterwards. Multiple calls for a ban, numerous newspaper articles, and predictable verbal and physical conflict at the meeting itself all played into his hands, gaining him the front-page publicity he desired. As the *Birmingham Daily Post* reported:

> Sir Oswald Mosley, leader of the pre-war British Union of Fascists, last night rented Birmingham Town Hall to mourn the passing of Fascism and to try to woo the city with his post-war political brain-child, the Union Movement ... On the coloured immigration issue, Sir Oswald protests that the remarks attributed to him have been 'complete rot'. What he wanted to see was that coloured immigrants were not exploited and that their own countries were developed. However in the next breath, when he replied to a questioner, he said: 'We do not want to live with you, and you do not want to live with us.'[20]

Two years later, Mosley switched his attentions to Notting Hill, where his pathetic strategies would play out on the doorstep of the government and national media. There was speculation in January 1958 that prime minister Harold Macmillan might call a general election in the spring, so this was an opportunistic move on Mosley's part. As it turned out, the election did not happen until October 1959, when Mosley chose to run as a candidate for MP in the Kensington North constituency, right at the heart of the previous year's rioting. He polled so few votes that he lost his deposit, demonstrating that his attempts at stoking divisions in one of London's poorer areas had signally failed to impress local voters.[21]

A Side-Burned Double of Elvis Presley

Notting Hill residents might legitimately have been curious as to what possible connection a titled upper-class long-time resident of Paris might have to their own London district. In fact, there was at least one link, however temporary, as astute readers of the *Daily Herald* on 14 May 1958 may have noticed. In the newspaper's gossip column, alongside thrilling details about the culinary preferences of skiffle player Peter McVey, a candidate in that day's 'Youth-in-the-Kitchen' contest – 'I've given 'em Canapes Lonnie Donegan (they're cut out like guitars)' – there was a cosy chat with a somewhat different representative of the nation's teenagers:

> Behind the polished desk at the Union Movement's London HQ last night sat another Mosley – Alexander, the 6ft 6in son of the man who led Britain's Blackshirt Fascists. Sir Oswald's 19-year-old boy – intensely earnest, wholeheartedly a Mosleyite, and a side-burned double of Elvis Presley – was giving me his first interview.[22]

Questioned about his role in the disturbances that had taken place the previous evening at a political meeting given by Conservative Party chairman Lord Hailsham in Islington – where Alexander and his younger brother Max had been photographed in the middle of a fistfight with an official – the young man replied, 'We didn't break up the meeting.' Perhaps, but he certainly seemed to have been giving it a go, while also handing out mocking leaflets depicting Hailsham in a bathing costume. Alexander claimed that 'the Tory stewards became particularly violent towards us'.[23] However, a *Times* journalist at the event reported that fighting had broken out largely because of 'a group of youths whose political complexion may perhaps be judged by the refrain "M O S L E Y – Mosley!"'.

The *Daily Herald* interview also noted that 'Alexander – living "in a very small room indeed" in London's Notting Hill Gate – is learning to become a travel agent'. The young Mosley was keen to stress that 'We no longer call ourselves fascists'.[24] As for the journalist's ludicrous assertion that Alexander resembled Elvis, photographs of the time show an unsmiling young man with his dark hair brushed neatly forward over his forehead, unexceptional sideburns and no hint whatsoever of a quiff – a haircut much closer in style to that of the Austrian megalomaniac who was the special guest at his parents' 1936 wedding. Yet Presley's music was apparently seen in some quarters at the time as a malign influence on society roughly equivalent to fascism. A reader's letter to a Birmingham newspaper in 1956 calling for the council to revoke permission for Oswald Mosley's rental of the town hall for a meeting suggested that this action would be justified on the same grounds that Bill Haley's film had recently been denied a showing in the city, and concluded by asking, 'Which is the greater menace and trouble-maker, Mosley or "rock and roll"?'[25]

Cheers and Jeers

Sir Oswald Mosley became active in London during the months immediately prior to the 1958 Notting Hill riots. In March he held a large public meeting at the Porchester Hall in Paddington, just west of Notting Hill, where he was forced to deny from the platform that he had ambitions to be a dictator or that he had ever been antisemitic.[26] On May Day, when the Labour leader of St Pancras Council had the red flag flown from the top of the Town Hall on Euston Road, members of Mosley's Union Movement staged a counter-protest which dissolved into street fighting between rival factions, with multiple arrests.[27] On

4 July, Mosley's application to hold a meeting at the Seymour Hall, just north of Marble Arch, was refused by the local council,[28] and three days later *The Times* reported that traffic had been held up in Trafalgar Square the previous day when what were described as 'sightseers' followed him to his car 'after he had addressed a recruiting meeting of the Union Movement'.[29] This makes the gathering sound distinctly uncontroversial, yet a columnist from the *Chelsea News* reported that Mosley had been met with a mixture of 'cheers and jeers', as well as fascist salutes. It prompted the writer to look up Sir Oswald's listing in *Who's Who?*, noting that in Mosley's entire twenty-one-line entry there was not a single reference to the British Union of Fascists – or indeed fascism in general.[30]

Mosley was not even the only fascist to focus on Notting Hill that year. Colin Jordan was a public school-educated schoolteacher from Coventry who since his days as a student at Cambridge University had joined one far-right group after another until finally starting his own White Defence League in 1956. Inspired by his mentor, Arnold Leese (1878–1956) – who combined a distinguished career researching into the lives and behaviour of camels with a parallel existence as what the *Oxford Dictionary of National Biography* termed 'the high priest of postwar antisemitism'[31] – Jordan homed in on Notting Hill in 1958 as ripe territory for him to exploit. Within days of the riots, he and his followers were selling their six-page publication, *Black and White News*, on the streets of the district. It was designed to sow division and stir up trouble, as the *Daily Herald* commented: 'Hate-filled headlines are on every page. They say: "Whites Will be Exterminated", "Negroes Lead in Illegitimacy", "Blacks Seek White Women", "Kings of the Drug Trade", and "Blacks Milk the Assistance Board".'[32]

This gained Jordan national attention, nearly all of it hostile, but despite this he did not lose his day job teaching the young and impressionable, and two days later Alderman W. Callow, chairman of the Coventry Education Committee, issued a statement saying that while he deplored Jordan's views, 'as long as it did not interfere with his school work he was entitled to his personal opinion.'[33]

Race Riot Terror

The tensions that Mosley and Jordan were busily stoking for their own ends began to make local and then national headlines in August 1958. 'Coloured Man Tells of Teddy Boys Raid – "Gang With Sticks Wrecked Café"', said a headline in the *Hammersmith & Shepherd's Bush Gazette*.[34] The premises run by Mr Samuel Thomas in Askew Road, Shepherd's Bush, was attacked by what was described later in court as a group of roughly twenty Teddy boys on the evening of 26 July, who caused £200 of damage, and had reportedly been incited by a rumour circulating at a local dance hall that the cafe would no longer serve white people.[35]

Although the cause of the trouble was something relatively new, stories of Teds smashing up cafes had been a commonplace in local newspapers for five years by that point, and this particular attack failed to achieve national attention. However, a little under a month later, disturbances occurred – first in Nottingham, then more seriously in London's Notting Hill district – which prompted multiple uses of the term 'race riot', such as the banner headline in the *Daily Mirror* on 25 August:

200 IN RACE RIOT TERROR

Extra police yesterday patrolled a city suburb after a night in which terror came to the streets as 200 men – white and coloured – fought a running battle. The fight broke out on Saturday night in the St Ann's Well-road area of Nottingham, where about 2,000 coloured people live . . . Eight men were taken to hospital, some with stab wounds in the back and others with cuts on the head and face. Seven of them went home after treatment.[36]

Elsewhere it was reported that knives and hatchets were used, and that the crowd was dispersed by eighty policemen with the aid of dogs.[37] Observers interviewed afterward said that the street and shop windows were 'spattered with blood', with one unnamed man claiming that 'the feud started last Christmas when there was trouble between Englishmen and coloured men over a girl. There have been a lot of small fights since then.'[38] There had certainly been earlier incidents, and an eighteen-year old was given a three-year prison sentence in December on a charge of causing actual bodily harm for his part in an attack on 12 August – ten days before the St Ann's Well Road rioting – in which it was stated in court that Alphonso Walton, originally from Jamaica, had been assaulted by 'seventeen Teddy boys'.

A national outcry followed the much more widely reported events of 23 August, and the West Indian Federal Government even sent two officials from the Caribbean to investigate the causes of the rioting. A local member of the Nottinghamshire Consultative Committee for the Welfare of Coloured People claimed that the trouble had been started by the Ku Klux Klan – although how this US organisation was supposed to have stirred up trouble four thousand miles from their traditional power base he neglected to explain.[39] Meanwhile the Labour MP for North Nottingham, James Harrison, was quoted as saying that 'Britain's "ever-open door" policy of immigration was the root cause of inter-racial discontent',[40] and the Conservative MP for Nottingham Central, Colonel J. K. Cordeaux, told the press that 'there ought to be a restriction on the number of people coming into Britain from overseas'.[41] Despite such calls, the government swiftly issued an official statement ruling out any new limits on immigration – even after newspaper leader writers in various cities had come out in favour of them, mostly on the grounds of preventing resentment among the working class over the competition for jobs. For instance, only two days after the Nottingham riots, the *Manchester Evening News* declared that 'the time has surely come when Britain ought to consider limiting the flow':

> There are 412,000 people out of work in Britain, including an estimated 15,000 coloured, and it is with white–coloured relations that the immigration problem is at its sharpest. The inevitable white–coloured rivalry for work has bred resentment and prejudice on both sides, and there are unhappy possibilities of conflict.[42]

A leader in the *Coventry Evening Telegraph* put the blame on a minority of recent migrants, arguing that 'we have enough trouble with lawless people of our own without importing more from other lands, whether they happen to have white or coloured skins, and as a nation we should not be displaying intolerance if more of the unwanted were turned back'.[43] This sentiment was supported by readers in the paper's letters page who responded to the article, but it also shared common ground with the stated policies of fascists like Mosley and Jordan, who both publicly demanded compulsory repatriation.

Horror, Indignation and Disgust

The original riot in Nottingham occurred on 23 August, and was reported in the papers the following day. It may have been coincidence that in London during the early hours of 24 August, a group of nine youths decided to cold-bloodedly drive around the Notting Hill district, seeking out any West Indians they could find and viciously assaulting them with 'iron bars torn from railings, starting handles, table legs and at least one knife'[44] in a series of unprovoked attacks. These were not schoolboys, and although one of them was unemployed, the others were in regular work: a fitter, three labourers, a greengrocer, a mill hand, a printer and a plumber's mate. Most lived in Shepherd's Bush or nearby White City, one was from West Kensington, another from North Kensington and the last from Acton.[45] At their initial court appearance a week later, it was stated that 'some of the victims of these assaults were seriously hurt and were in hospital. One had what was believed to be a stab in the back.'[46]

This case, which eventually went all the way to the Old Bailey, was credited then and in the years that have followed as the spark that ignited the Notting Hill riots, which broke out five days later. Even though most of the attackers did not live in Notting Hill, they deliberately sought out that area as a place where West Indian and African immigrants might be found. In the event all nine pleaded guilty, and were each given four years in prison. Passing sentence on September 15 – only two weeks after the end of the riots – the trial judge, Mr Justice Salmon, told them:

> It was you men who started the whole of this violence in Notting Hill. You are a minute and insignificant section of the population who have brought shame on the district in which you live and have filled the whole nation with

horror, indignation and disgust. Everyone, irrespective of the colour of their skins, is entitled to walk through our streets in peace with their heads erect and free from fear.[47]

Despite such a ringing condemnation, they appealed, claiming that their actions had not triggered the riots and that the sentences were too severe, but in November the Court of Criminal Appeal upheld the original verdicts, and the presiding judge, Mr Justice Paull, had further words of condemnation:

> There is no doubt that the whole nine of them decided to go on what they themselves called a 'nigger hunting expedition' because, as one of them said, 'they had the needle because a mate of theirs had been cut by niggers.' It was clear that this was a perfectly deliberate gang affair in which these nine youths deliberately made up their minds to injure, not coloured men who had taken part in the past in any events of violence which might have occurred, but any innocent person walking in the street, provided that his colour was not the same as theirs.[48]

Suspicion, Fear, Sexual Jealousy and Economic Uncertainty

The attacks by those nine youths had initially been seen as a one-off, not linked to what happened in Nottingham. However, as September began, the four consecutive nights of ugly violence in Notting Hill made it clear that something much more wide-ranging and disturbing was taking place.

Sifting through the avalanche of commentary and reporting produced in the week following the Nottingham riot, mentions of Teddy boys are few and far between, and the gang of nine who were tried at the Old Bailey were not generally referred to as Teds in the media. Indeed, thus far Nottingham's outbreak of racial conflict in August had been often characterised by members of the public, police, politicians and journalists as stemming from concerns among the working population about competition for jobs and for housing. Yet the *Daily Express* then ran a cartoon featuring a Ted that drew an analogy between Nottingham and the situation in segregationist Southern states in America and Apartheid South Africa, who in turn used these stories as a way of trying to deflect international criticism of their own racial policies. An article in *The Times* on 29 August noted that:

> The *Johannesburg Star* gave prominence in three articles to the situation in Britain yesterday and, under the heading: 'No more the cry "Holier than thou", referred to a *Daily Express* cartoon depicting Mr Macmillan recoiling from a fight between a Nottingham 'teddy boy' and a coloured man while the smiling Governor of Arkansas [Orval Faubus, who had opposed integration of the all-white Little Rock High School in 1957] and a figure labelled 'South Africa', vaguely resembling Mr Swart [Governor General of South Africa], looked on.[49]

Consequently, even if you lived eight thousand miles away from the scene of the trouble, if anyone asked you who had caused it, the answer was apparently simple – Teddy boys. Yet again, the question arises as to what exactly was meant by the term when employed by reporters or politicians, and whether it was simply a shorthand for any thug. George Clay from *The Observer* visited Nottingham a day or so after the trouble, and while his report published on 31 August certainly refers to Teds, he steered clear of giving them all the blame and looked into a wider range of possible causes:

But some features of the incident point to its being more than just another Saturday night spree. In a number of incidents in recent weeks coloured people had been beaten up by whites. These white groups were not confined to young Teddy Boys; many were working-men in their thirties who do not normally mix with teenage hooligans. In the pubs of Nottingham this week I found the same evidence of prejudice, compounded of suspicion, fear, sexual jealousy and economic uncertainty, that I encountered in the Black Country towns when the Wolverhampton dance-hall controversy drew attention to the colour issue there.[50]

However, on the evening of the day when both these pieces were published – which was also the day that the nine youths responsible for the 24 August attacks first appeared in court – the first of a string of violent disturbances that came to be known as the Notting Hill Race Riots broke out in London, which would flare up until 5 September.

Young People Running Riot

The first recorded incident on 29 August was a confrontation near Latimer Road Tube Station between a group of white people and an inter-ethnic couple, Majbritt and Raymond Morrison. She was originally from Sweden, her husband from Jamaica. It was enough of a showdown that she was targeted the following day when the first serious rioting broke out, and the building on Bramley Road in which the couple lived alongside many black families had a petrol bomb thrown through its windows.[51] Various other incidents happened that night, with several arrests – but all this was just a prelude to the much more serious crowd violence the following day. People on both sides had armed themselves in anticipation of further trouble, and the numbers were greatly increased by onlookers, and also by troublemakers coming to the area from across the capital.

The *Daily Mirror* estimated the crowd on the night of 1 September as consisting of 'Two thousand teenagers and young children running riot'[52] while the front page of the *Newcastle Journal* the same morning proclaimed that 'About 2,000 teenagers in cars, on motor-cycles and on foot, swept into the Notting Hill and Shepherd's Bush areas of London late last night and staged a window-smashing, bottle-throwing, anti-coloured riot'.[53] This suggestion that groups of youths from all over the capital had converged on Notting Hill during the second night of trouble in an organised wave may have come from the police themselves, since it occurs in many national and local newspapers. As the *Daily Mirror* put it in the same report, 'the local youngsters thronging the area were joined at nightfall by Teddy Boy gangs from other parts of London',[54] their implication being that any teenagers involved automatically qualified as Teds. Speculating on the motives of those involved, a leader column in the *Leicester Evening Mail* implied that some, at least, were simply out looking for a fight:

> Racial animosity has been used as the excuse to spark off the vicious brawls at Notting Hill. Coloured people were the innocent victims of Teddy Boy thugs who have grasped the opportunity given them by the Nottingham riot to indulge in their favourite brand of hooliganism and hatred. It is significant that their viciousness has been directed as much against the police as coloured folk.[55]

During the following evening's disturbances, twenty-eight people were arrested, and although large crowds had once again been seen in the Notting Hill area, the police view was that most of them had just come along to watch the spectacle. By now, the rioting had almost become an open invitation to any racists within travelling distance to take to the streets, as the *Birmingham Post* made shockingly plain: 'A big crowd chanted "Down with the niggers" in Lancaster Road. One youth carried a banner with the slogan "Deport all niggers". Later, there were cries of "Down with the spades" and "Burn their houses". Police took possession of bicycle chains, knives and other weapons.'[56]

Rumours multiplied. Someone was reportedly seen waving a swastika flag, and in the disturbances on 3 September, the police spent a good deal of time searching for a van driven by someone apparently brandishing a machine-gun, although no trace could be found.[57]

Meanwhile, up in Nottingham, there had been a further outbreak of violence just as the Notting Hill riots began. 'RACE HATE CITY GOES WILD AGAIN'[58] screamed the front-page headline of *The People* – and it is not difficult to imagine how thrilled the residents of Nottingham would have been with that blanket categorisation. One week after the disturbances in St Ann's Well Road, an estimated 1,000 people were said to have 'battled with police' in the same location[59] – yet by most accounts this seems to have been purely a clash between a white crowd and officers of the law. A woman who observed the proceedings from her window told reporters, 'All the time I watched the scene I did not see a single coloured man either fighting the police or standing in the streets.'[60]

Investigations eventually concluded that this disturbance had been provoked by an ITV film crew who gathered together some local Teds to stage a mock fight in the street. The cameraman set off a magnesium flare without warning, which brought hundreds of people rushing to the scene and caused a genuine fight between the new arrivals and the large numbers of constabulary who had converged on the area under the same misapprehension.[61] As self-fulfilling prophecies go, it was very effective, and made for a misleading shock-horror headline in the next day's papers.

Bottling Out

Were Teddy boys involved in the Notting Hill riots? Unquestionably. Multiple eyewitnesses said so, both at the time and in interviews conducted over the decades that followed. In the aftermath of the trouble, when court cases inevitably followed the many arrests, four young Teds were photographed proudly walking down the street on their way to West London Police Court.[62] In advance of their initial hearing, they were happy to smile for the cameras while wearing drape jackets of varying lengths; none had velvet collars or cuffs, but there was enough of the Ted look about them that passers-by would probably have identified them as such.

There had been multiple nights of rioting in Notting Hill, with windows smashed, petrol bombs thrown, innocent people terrorised in their homes and numerous arrests. Yet the reports of the court cases that inevitably followed are sometimes curiously underwhelming given such a disturbing series of events. The newspapers had spoken of crowds in their thousands participating in the mayhem, but at one of the initial hearings in Marylebone on 3 September, the haul of weapons produced in evidence consisted of 'a foot-long iron bar, a jack-knife and two milk bottles'.[63]

Milk bottles might sound relatively innocuous, but they were one of the main weapons employed during the riots – handily available on doorsteps in the days of near-universal morning deliveries – and some were used to make petrol bombs. Many older buildings in the area had iron railings that could be uprooted or broken off to form another makeshift weapon. There was no shortage of knives in London at that time, and reports also speak of bicycle chains, hatchets and machetes being deployed by the rioters. Guns, however, seem not to have made an appearance, even though the capital had been awash with them for over a decade after large numbers had been brought home as war souvenirs. What must not be forgotten, though, is the fear in people's minds of what *might* be about to happen, the sense that your home might be set on fire at any moment by an angry mob. When the dust cleared after four days of violent clashes, there had been no deaths, but with petrol bombs being thrown through windows into living rooms or bedrooms, and from rooftops onto the attacking crowds, that was surely a matter of luck.

Tony Moore, Divisional Commander for the district in the early 1980s, provided a good account of the arrests and casualties in his 2013 book, *Policing Notting Hill: Fifty Years of Turbulence* – all the more valuable because he had access to the unpublished document produced by the Metropolitan Police in the immediate aftermath of the violence. In his opinion, what finally helped stop the nightly rioting was not only the fact that the police became more adept at bringing the situation under control, but also that after days of hot weather, on the afternoon of 3 September it began to rain, continuing heavily until the following morning:

This had the effect of keeping people in their houses and there was only one incident during the night when, in Norland Road, two black men had an altercation with two white men. However, it is interesting to note that the police report, in suggesting that 'conditions in this racial conflict had now returned to the conditions prevalent before the serious disorders commenced on 30th August', listed a further eleven incidents between 3 and 8 September. Eight involved attacks by white people on black people or their property; three involved attacks or threatened attacks by black people on white.[64]

The court proceedings at West London Magistrates' Court for Tuesday 2 September, which dealt with everyone taken into custody the previous night, provide a snapshot of who exactly was sufficiently involved to be arrested and tried. Some were charged with insulting behaviour, obstructing the police or threatening behaviour, but by far the majority were accused of possessing offensive weapons. These included hatchets, razors, butcher knives, carving knives, flick-knives, pieces of wood, a weighted leather belt and a bicycle chain.[65] We should, of course, remember that these statistics do not distinguish between weapons carried for attack and those carried for defence by residents in fear of their lives.

It was that evening of riots that prompted the *Daily Mirror* front page with the Nazi Teddy boy cartoon, when 'two thousand teenagers and young children ran riot in the Notting Hill trouble area of London'.[66] In the event, of the people that appeared in the dock, eight were aged between sixteen and nineteen, twelve were in their twenties, three in their thirties, three in their forties and one was fifty.[67] A proportion of these were black Notting Hill residents who had armed themselves following several nights of violence. Others might have been members of Mosely's Union Movement, who had a history of street violence and were looking to provoke the situation. Indeed, there is a famous photograph of two of Oswald's teenage sons, Alexander and Max, taken in Notting Hill during one of the nights of rioting, in which Max has what look to be scraped knuckles on one of his hands and a plaster across those of the other;[68] it was later claimed that the pair had dressed up as Teds in order to join in the riots. Interestingly, one resident interviewed decades later said that he heard a voice with a middle or upper-class accent in the crowd of white rioters, urging them on,[69] which would make sense if it came from a provocateur member of either the Union Movement or Jordan's White Defence League.

Europeans Only

The press photographers who asked the Mosley brothers to pose for their cameras on the streets of Notting Hill during those nights also recorded a selection of incidents, arrests and general crowd scenes. It is instructive to examine the surviving pictures – it surely would have been hard to miss a crowd of two thousand Teds in full regalia. Indeed, such a sight would have been so spectacular that most editors would have been unlikely to resist the temptation of plastering it across their front pages – but such images seem not to exist.

BBC TV made a well-researched documentary[70] in 2003 looking back at the riots – interviewing former residents from those days, both black and white, and interspersing their testimony with archive footage shot at the time. When they needed a clip of a group of threatening-looking Teds in full drapes and creepers in order to illustrate a point, they used a sequence of some 1970s Teds who would have been barely starting primary school in 1958, converted to monochrome as if to imply that it was from an earlier era. Had there been a suitable vintage Pathé newsreel clip in existence, it is a fair bet that they would have used it.

The limited number of readily available pictures taken during the nights of rioting presents a far more complex impression of events than the newspaper accounts of thousands of young people thronging the streets. In fact, the crowd sometimes looks more like a representative selection of the whole community, including small children, middle-aged women and the occasional pensioner.[71] Many, of course, had simply ventured from their homes in order to observe what was going on. Yet what was the true state of race relations in the area prior to the riots, and were any of the unremarkable-looking middle-aged and elderly people in the pictures among those who placed discriminatory adverts in the 'rooms for rent' sections of local papers? Here, for example, are several that were published just before the trouble, taken from the 29 August edition of the *Kensington Post*, which included Notting Hill in its circulation area:[72]

A SINGLE self-contained divan sitting-room. Newly decorated. Concealed electric grillers, constant hot water. Select, well-kept house. Europeans, Permanents only.

ADDISON GARDENS, W14. Well-furnished and decorated bed-sitting rooms single or double. All comforts and cooking facilities. Light and linen provided. From £3 per week. No coloured. Shepherd's Bush.

BED and breakfast £1 single, £2 double per night. Also furnished rooms with or without service at moderate terms. On all main bus routes and underground services. Very quiet. Business people only. Sorry, no coloured or Irish.

To be fair, the same pages also show that there were land-lords who specifically appealed to those who had been excluded by such adverts – although some of those might have been placed by the cynical landlords who made a killing exploiting the colour bar situation and treated West Indian renters appallingly, knowing that the latter had few options and were unlikely to take their business elsewhere:

ACCOMMODATION for coloured students. Bed-breakfast basis, inclusive service, lights, heating, hot and cold water, lounge, television, share room. Apply House-keeper, 35, Russell Road, W14.

ALL Nationalities welcome. Single divan rooms, cookers, basins.

COLOURED respectable people only please. Double room, linen, crockery supplied, share bath. 70s weekly.

WELL-FURNISHED double room with kitchenette and every convenience for married couple or students. Coloured or oriental welcome.

The divisions were there in plain sight. It was not until the introduction of the Race Relations Act in 1965 that the first attempt was made to limit racial discrimination in British law, but it was only when a subsequent act came into being three years later – a decade after the Notting Hill Riots – that it became illegal to refuse housing, employment or public services on racial or ethnic grounds. One of the first people to be prosecuted under the 1965 act was public-school fascist and would-be Notting Hill troublemaker Colin Jordan.[73] A few years earlier he had married the wealthy niece of Christian Dior in Coventry, amid much Sieg Heiling for the newsreel cameras, after which the happy couple sealed their vows by letting drops of their own blood fall onto a copy of Hitler's *Mein Kampf*. By the time of the 1968 act, they were already divorced.[74]

CONCLUSION

THIS OLD GANG OF MINE

The Titanic Sails at Dawn

After Notting Hill, it seemed as if the wind had changed. Having been headline material for half a decade, the Teds were becoming yesterday's news: the general public had seen it all before.

This cycle would repeat itself over the following decades, as the impact of each successive youth cult, initially viewed by society as a transgressive or baffling new style, was blunted by familiarity and indifference. To become a Ted in 1953 was to be a trailblazer of sorts, but by the close of that decade anyone opting for the style was following a well-trodden path. By that stage, many of the originators had moved on, and the novice ran the risk of being seen as having missed the boat.

The BBC began 1959 by broadcasting a television debate between two MPs about whether corporal punishment should be used on those of an Edwardian persuasion; it was reviewed the following day in the *Daily Herald* under the cheery headline 'Teddy Boys – Should We Beat Them?'[1] For some politicians in the wake of the Notting Hill riots, it seemed that Teds were still good for a soundbite, handy when adding flavour to a speech – although even that seemed more of a reflex reaction, born of habit. For example, in the run-up to the autumn 1959 general election, Barbara Castle, Labour MP for Blackburn and chair of the Labour Party, gave a speech to the Trades Union Congress in which she said Harold Macmillan's government had 'created a society in which the greatest rewards go not to the worker but to the gambler. They have introduced into this country the "teddy boy" economics in which it is money that breeds money rather than the value of the contribution to the production and scientific life of this country.'[2] The phrase 'Teddy boy' here is used to imply inherent criminality. By contrast, four months earlier, when addressing the nineteenth annual Co-Operative Conference in Edinburgh, Castle had referred to 'every nigger-baiting Teddy boy in Notting Hill'[3] – an expression which if uttered today would finish the career of any politician that tried to use it.

The spectre of the previous year's riots resurfaced regularly in 1959, when Oswald Mosley was actively campaigning in the area in anticipation of the general election, and the situation became more acute in the wake of the brutal racist murder in May of Kelso Cochrane, originally from Antigua, who had lived in Notting Hill since 1954. The thirty-two-year-old was stabbed on the corner of Southam Street and Golborne Road by a group of white youths,[4] and more than a thousand people attended his funeral at Kensal Green Cemetery.[5] There were fears that another wave of race riots might be on the way, but fortunately this did not come to pass. In what seems to have been a direct reference to Mosley's tactics, the Conservative MP for Croydon North East, Vice-Admiral John Hughes Hallett, expressed his opinion in June that 'gangsters' were 'responsible for outbreaks of racial violence in parts of London ... They are not Teddy boys – they are young fighting men doing the work of wild and dangerous political leaders.'[6]

Come and Wriggle

The general election in October 1959 returned prime minister Harold Macmillan's government with a greatly increased majority, and he went on television to claim that the result 'had shown the class war to be obsolete'[7] – a statement that was indicative of the optimism that would initially come to characterise the sixties, whether or not it stood up to scrutiny. Of course, with the new decade, Teddy boys did not magically disappear from public view. Quite apart from everyday sightings in cafes, youth clubs and dance halls, the long development schedules involved in film production, the staging of plays and the writing of novels meant that the Teds continued to enjoy a residual afterlife in popular culture for a number of years.

Muriel Spark's novel *The Ballad of Peckham Rye* (1960) was set in various parts of South London and featured a selection of teenage gang members, including one in a drape and drainpipes. They carry knives and razors, casually glass people in dance halls, and ask girls to dance by saying, 'Come and wriggle, Snake.'[8] Appearing at around the same time, Lynne Reid Banks's debut novel, *The L-Shaped Room* (1960), told the story of a young woman who goes to live in 'a bug-ridden room at the top of a squalid house in Fulham'.[9] One evening, she finds herself in a cafe surrounded by mocking teenagers: 'They were nearly all Teddy-boys. One of them looked me up and down and remarked with a snigger, "You can see she's got the right stuff in her."'[10] Also on sale in bookshops that year was Constantine Fitzgibbon's *When the Kissing had to Stop* (1960), a dystopian political thriller set in the near future, in which a British government opts for unilateral nuclear disarmament and civil unrest breaks out across the capital. The legacy of the Notting Hill riots was a clear inspiration: 'There were whole areas of London into which it was becoming unsafe to go, even in daylight. Knives flashed in Soho. From King's Cross to Notting Hill it was one long race-riot, and when the police attempted to intervene, they were as likely to be shot by one side as by the other.'[11]

A group of Teds in a pub in King's Cross pull out knives and fatally wound a black US serviceman, but the description of them seems to be modelled more on sixties rockers and bikers: 'At the table in the corner sat half a dozen youngish men of the type who would have been called Teddy boys ten years ago, bootlace ties, black leather windcheaters, sideburns.'[12]

None of these books used Teds as three-dimensional characters; their sole purpose was to make a brief appearance when the narrative required the threat of violence or intimidation. By contrast, in Nancy Mitford's final novel, *Don't Tell Alfred* (1960), the character who wears Teddy boy clothes receives a more rounded portrait, but this was a story written for comic effect, set in Paris in the world of upper-class diplomats; the 'Ted' in question is the wealthy dilettante son of a British aristocrat.[13] Meanwhile, the Notting Hill influence appeared once again in Laurence Payne's excellent crime novel *The Nose on My Face* (1961) in a scene when a trendy artist is visited in his studio by an inspector from Scotland Yard: 'Several of the pictures had a coarse violence about them – there was one of a negro being beaten up by a group of Teddy boys, in which the sky looked like it were raining blood.'[14]

Received impressions, second-hand sightings, blink and you miss them. Teds were still around in real life, but in popular culture a simplified caricature of them had long since taken over.

Sexually Promiscuous, Indecent, Criminal

If these works only contained passing references, the Edwardian fraternity was right at the heart of prolific crime author

John Creasey's 1961 novel, *The Toff and the Teds*. Published at a time when the Teds were rapidly being superseded by newer youth movements, it was given a misleading cover in Hodder & Stoughton's first edition, which depicted a knife-wielding delinquent with forward-combed 1960s hair and a red jacket that seemed to be based on what James Dean wore in *Rebel Without a Cause* (1955).[15] The story inside did indeed concern a group of drape-wearing teenagers and their dealings with the Honourable Richard Rollison (aka 'The Toff'), the detective who had been solving cases in Creasey's novels since 1938. Some teenage boys and girls ask him for help at the start of the novel because they are having trouble with a rival gang, the superbly named Slob Mob: 'Price appeared to be the taller of the two youths, each of whose over-long hair was combed straight back from his forehead, both of whom affected shaggy sideboards, fancy waistcoats, jackets which had been slept in, and stove-pipe trousers.'[16]

One of the Teddy girls makes an appeal to Rollison in terms which show that although the author himself was fifty-three at the time of publication, he had a far more nuanced view of such young people than others of his generation:

> We're sick and tired of being blamed for everything – well, for nearly everything. If you listened to all the pronouncements of the educationalists and the moralists you'd think that youth today was the one blot on civilisation – sexually promiscuous, indecent, criminal, out for what they can get, all that kind of tosh. And when anyone wants to take us in hand they start a club where we're supposed to do everything that our elders think we like. It so happens I don't like ping-pong, cards, physical training, jolly concert parties or sewing class, but that doesn't mean I'm a cretin or a juvenile delinquent or a natural whore.[17]

A James Dean-inspired inaccurate depiction of a supposed
Ted on the cover of Creasey's 1961 novel

This reasonable complaint was to be made by other young people in later decades, as one fashion or musical trend after another was held up for ridicule or condemnation with monotonous regularity.

I've Seen Their Type Before

On 11 September 1962, a group of former Teddy boys called the Beatles were at Abbey Road Studios having another crack at recording a song called *Love Me Do*. It was set to be their debut single, but for the initial pressing EMI opted to use a take the band had recorded the previous week.[18] Released on 5 October, it slowly climbed the charts to the lower reaches of the Top Twenty, but it wasn't until their second 45, *Please Please Me*, that they really hit the big time. Their style of music, their hair, clothes and behaviour rapidly became influential in a way that no one could have foreseen the previous December, when they attracted a crowd of just eighteen people to a gig in Aldershot.[19] On the same day that *Love Me Do* was released, the world premiere of the first James Bond film, *Dr No*, took place at the London Pavilion cinema on Piccadilly Circus, Sean Connery's suave and definitive portrayal of Ian Fleming's hero causing a sensation.[20] If you were a male British teenager that autumn, here were some ready-made role models whose appearance owed little to the Edwardian templates that had inspired young people a decade earlier.

By contrast, another British film released during those same few weeks seemed to look more to the past than the future. *The Boys* received a far more low-key premiere than the Bond film, at a cinema named La Continentale on Tottenham Court Road on 14 September.[21] If it had appeared three or four years earlier, the producers would probably have released it under the title

The Teddy Boys, since that was essentially who it depicted. A fine film, praised by reviewers for its realistic and thoughtful portrayal of four young men accused of knifing someone to death during a robbery, it nevertheless belonged to an era which was fading away rather than the 'swinging' London that was soon to take Bond and the Beatles to its heart. Although the story dealt with a crime that had taken place in January 1962, in the trial scenes the accused are referred to as Teds by witnesses and legal counsels alike.

Wilfrid Brambell plays a lavatory attendant who has a run-in with the four accused on the night of the murder, and they take offence when he calls them 'yobbos'. At the trial, the judge queries this term during his testimony:[22]

'Yobbos, what do you mean by yobbos?'
'Well, er. Yobbos is layabouts . . . I know yobbos. They're Teds. I've seen their type before.'

Another witness, played by Allan Cuthbertson, gives a similar response under cross-examination:

'What sort of boys did they seem to you? Uncouth?'
'Yes.'
'Uncivilised?'
'Yes.'
'Teddy boys?'
'Oh yes.'

The teenagers in question are dressed throughout the film in the type of short, Italian-style jackets that were fashionable that year – the kind colloquially known as a 'bumfreezer' – which is about as far away from a fingertip drape as you can get. Their trousers are narrow, but that was normal for 1962, and none of them have their hair slicked back or quiffed up. Despite that, Dudley Sutton's nicely observed character Stan Coulter still manages to convey the authentic essence of Teddy boy menace, especially when he casually removes the dirt from under his fingernails with a flick-knife during a tense stand-off with the owner of a billiard hall.

The Parade's Gone By

The shift in men's fashions can also be seen in comparing photographs of the Beatles between 1960 and 1962 with others showing how they dressed once success took hold following their first hit record. When they were still playing at the Star Club and the Kaiserkeller in Hamburg, they had been overjoyed to meet their hero Gene Vincent when he came to the port city;[23] they were pictured gathered around Vincent while dressed in the leather biker outfits they wore in imitation of his own famous stage gear. Soon, their ambitious new manager, Brian Epstein, had persuaded them to ditch the rock'n'roll leathers and clothed them in far more conventional matching outfits, with short jackets that he considered more suitable for mainstream showbusiness appearances. By 1964, fashion-conscious teenage boys were also brushing their hair forward rather than back. Quiffs and grease were out, and a shoulder-length or longer style pioneered by the likes of the Pretty Things and the Rolling Stones was something to aspire to – although this would very likely get you sent home from school. Once the change in styles began, the Edwardian look faded away quite rapidly – and not only in London, as Ted Carroll told me:

In Dublin, it started dying out in '59 when the Italian look came in, and suddenly the grease was gone, and people had short hair – it was pre-Beatles – people wore very neat tailored suits with narrow lapels and no turn-ups on them. Except, well I remember going to the Galway races, '59 or '60, and there were these travellers there, all wearing Teddy boy gear. I hadn't seen anyone wearing Teddy boy gear for about a year and a half and suddenly, here are these guys, well behind the times.[24]

In the previous decade, much had been written about the so-called 'problem' of what to do about Teddy boys and Teddy girls, but this eventually resolved itself quite naturally in the same variety of ways common to most youth movements. People got married, moved away from their previous group of teenage friends, got bored and decided to change their image, perhaps because of the demands of a new job or in order to appear 'respectable'. A proportion will have wound up in approved schools or prison – as would have been the case with any random selection of young people – but the majority blended seamlessly into the general adult population, leaving only a few old photographs in family albums to tell of their youthful appearance and habits.

In fact, anyone who had been paying attention would have noticed the Edwardian look gradually losing its dominance among teenagers for several years before the arrival of Merseybeat. In August 1960, a review in *The Times* of *The Queen's Peace*, a television play by Arthur Hailey, was scathing about its depiction of young troublemakers:

To begin with, all the teenage delinquents were too old, and so glaringly so that it became impossible to accept them at their face value. Then those louts occupying Mr Trevor Williams's beautifully observed Victorian pub were for some reason clothed in complete outfits of at least four years ago – velvet collars, chunky crêpe-soled shoes, D-A hair styles and long Teddy Boy jackets – which are now as perfectly period as knee breeches or farthingales.[25]

If even the writers at an establishment paper like *The Times* had noticed that the wind had changed, then the warning signs must have been everywhere – a change exemplified by a news item from the same paper in April 1962:

MUSEUM SEEKS TEDDY BOY COSTUME

Worthing Museum, which has a rapidly growing costume collection, wants to preserve present-day dress for the interest of generations to come, and is asking for a Teddy boy costume, 'with narrow trousers, fancy waistcoat, three-quarter jacket, Slim Jim tie and thick-soled crêpe sneakers'. The museum says the fashion has already passed, the Italian style having replaced it.[26]

Right Here on Earth

Paradoxically, for rock'n'roll-loving Teds, the 1960s provided a magnificent opportunity to see some of the finest US original artists playing live – a chance largely denied to them in the fifties owing to restrictive Musician's Union agreements that prevented most American artists from being able to tour in Britain. Gene Vincent proved so popular with UK crowds he returned multiple times throughout the decade, and he even lived in Britain for a while. Bill Haley, Johnny Burnette, Little Richard, Chuck Berry, Roy Orbison, Carl Perkins, Screamin' Jay Hawkins, Dion, Bo Diddley and the Everly Brothers all toured in the UK, and some returned regularly.[27] Extensive tours did not just cover major urban centres such as London, Manchester or Glasgow, but took in many points in between. Teds living in Grimsby in 1962 had the chance to see Jerry Lee Lewis performing at former skating rink and dance-hall-turned-cinema the Gaiety, while those of a similar mind in Nelson could watch Bill Haley and His Comets in 1964 when they played the Imperial as part of a twenty-two-date tour, and Gene Vincent brought his incendiary live show to the South Pier at Lowestoft in the same year.[28]

These tours generally sold incredibly well, regardless of what happened to be in the pop charts at the time. America seemed largely to have forgotten about many of these artists, but a hard core of British youth had not. Indeed, the worldwide rockabilly revival which began in the 1970s and gave a second career to countless neglected 1950s US musicians was built upon the sustained interest and appetite for such music in the UK.

Even in 1969 – the year of the half-million-strong hippie love-in at Woodstock – Gene Vincent once again flew in to Heathrow Airport, a decade after his first arrival, for the latest in a long line of British tours. He was met by a delegation of Teddy boys in drapes and bootlace ties who were duly photographed by the press before he was whisked away in a white Rolls Royce and escorted to London by a team of bikers. Two old 1950s ex-Teddy boy fans of his, John Lennon and George Harrison, showed up to watch his packed London show at the Speakeasy.[29]

In the early 1970s it was hardly unusual to see chart bands such as Wizzard on BBC1's weekly *Top of the Pops* wearing Teddy boy drape jackets, drainpipes and brothel creepers. By 1977, punks such as Johnny Rotten of the Sex Pistols occasionally wore such gear, as for instance did Leee Black Childers, manager of Johnny Thunders & the Heartbreakers, although this was a brave thing to do that year, risking physical violence from genuine Teds, who generally saw this as a provocative statement or even outright mockery.

However, despite the passage of years, some parents remained less than thrilled at the news that their own children might renounce 1970s fashions and music in order to become a Teddy boy. Barry was an East London teenager in 1977 who became attracted to rock'n'roll music and the Teddy boy style while still at school. The older brother of his friend Aidan was a Ted, as Barry told me: 'I remember his brother had a Triumph Bonneville, so he'd gone over more to the rocker side of things, but he was an original fifties Teddy boy, 'cause my first drape was his old drape. My parents hated the fact that I wanted to be a Teddy boy. Hated it. My father was a jazz drummer.'[30]

Just as the teenage Billy Fury had concealed his Ted gear from his parents in 1950s Liverpool, Barry did the same in mid-1970s London:

> I'd get my old school trousers, which were like flares, and I would take them in, turn them into drainpipes. I bought a pair of creepers which I had to hide. The drape I got off Aidan. Nice dark burgundy with black velvet. I used to put my flares on over the top of my drainpipes. I had a snorkel coat, with the drape turned up under that, and I'd be like 'Going out mum!' 'Yeah alright then.' I'd go round the corner, take all the gear off, roll it up, stick it in a bag and put it under the bush, and then we were off out for the night . . .'[31]

The subterfuge worked for a while, but a year or so later Barry moved on to rockabilly-style clothing: 'My mum had already found my drape anyway and destroyed that [laughs]. She put a knife through my creepers. I thought, what do I do now?' As for the public reaction Barry and his group of friends had attracted when dressed in Ted gear, it was remarkably similar to that encountered by Edwardian-styled teenagers twenty years earlier:

> We used to hang around Upton Park and around that way. We had friends who lived in blocks of flats and we'd be hanging around at the bottom of the stairs by the lift with the old tape going. Oh, people used to avoid us [laughs]. It was great. We used to jump on a bus, and we'd all pile upstairs, and the upstairs would empty, we'd have the upstairs to ourselves.[32]

Of course, by that stage, young people had the choice of a variety of subcultures, several of which had turned on each other as natural enemies to be fought when encountered – and all because of the clothing they wore.

The Oldest Bopper in Town

In a world that has long since grown used to sartorial expressions of teenage rebellion, it is hard to comprehend the impact caused by the first appearance in the early 1950s of these dandified but tough-looking figures amid the rubble and grime of post-war London. The Teddy boy image was very strong, but the simplistic and often negative view of them in the media has been largely perpetuated and uncritically recycled over the decades. Even the basic fact that the Ted style pre-dated the arrival of rock'n'roll in England by several years is little known in some quarters. By contrast, the origins of other youth groups such as mods or punks are more widely understood, having been examined over the years in painstaking detail.

For many years, the caricature of the ageing Ted rather than the original teenage version has typically been offered up for display. Think of comedian Russ Abbott clowning around as a middle-aged Teddy boy on television shows in the 1980s, or Freddie Starr wearing a red drape jacket. Paul Shane's character in the late-fifties-based BBC1 sitcom *Hi-Di-Hi* (1980–88) had a DA haircut, wore loud suits with velvet collars, sang the rock'n'roll pastiche theme tune 'Holiday Rock' and was conveniently named Ted, but he was in his forties. And in July 1992, political columnist Matthew Parris described the Conservative MP Eric Forth in the House of Commons as 'looking as out of place as a Teddy Boy dad on parents' day'.[33]

The message was clear. Teds are anachronistic, mildly ridiculous, and certainly not young. Yet even during the much-hyped 1977 punk–Ted skirmishes down the King's Road in Chelsea – during which the *London Evening Standard* sent a journalist and photographer out with a group of Teds one afternoon around the time of the Queen's Jubilee celebrations in the hope that they could capture the mayhem at first hand – many of those in the Teddy boy faction were a similar age to those they were fighting, second-generation adherents rather than fifties originals. All of which makes sense; after all, if you were one of the Londoners who adopted the style in 1953 as a sixteen-year-old, you would have been forty during that summer when the Sex Pistols were in the charts with 'God Save the Queen', and probably had better things to do on a Saturday afternoon than to go looking for a punch-up with groups of youths less than half your age.

A fine cross-section of the kind of people who were active on the UK rocking scene in the second half of the 1970s was captured on film in the 1979 photography book *The Teds* by Chris Steele-Perkins.[34] Taken at pubs like the George at Hammersmith, the Adam and Eve in Hackney, the Castle in the Old Kent Road, the Winchester at Elephant and Castle, and the Queens Hotel, Southend, the pictures recorded a selection of drape-jacketed, quiffed-up Teddy boys and Teddy girls in circle skirts or jeans, many of them either teenagers or in their early twenties. Plenty of fifties styles were on display, but this was still Britain in the decade of Monty Python, three-day weeks and *The Rocky Horror Picture Show*, rather than the era of Suez, National Service and the Goons.

Anyone adopting the Teddy boy lifestyle in the 1970s would have probably been able to find most of the required essentials, always assuming they were prepared to hunt for them; items like creepers had become a specialist taste, not generally available on the high street. That particular type of shoe was what first attracted future Sex Pistols bassist Glen Matlock to Vivienne Westwood and Malcolm McLaren's shop at 430 King's Road in the early 1970s, and he wound up getting a part-time Saturday job there. McLaren was selling Ted clothing at a time when it was an exotic choice, deliberately going against the grain on the King's Road of the flared trousers and late-hippie tie-dye orthodoxy.

In the mid-1970s, aspiring Teds might gain information from specialist publications such as *New Kommotion* and *Not Fade Away*, and buy records from places like Rock On (started by Ted Carroll in August 1971 with a stall off the Portobello Road and which went on to become a Camden Town institution), At The Hop in Fulham, Moondog's in East Ham or Vintage Records near Caledonian Road. For clothing, hand tailoring still produced the best results, and the names of trusted specialists such as Jack Geach in Harrow were circulated among those on the Ted scene. Get the details wrong, or buy something cheap and badly made, and you ran the risk of being denounced as a 'plastic', the derisive term for wannabe newcomers to the scene.

By this time, despite the BBC having finally caved to a campaign for a designated 1950s rock music show on Radio 1 following a petition and a protest march through central London by several thousand Teds on 15 May 1976,[35] the Ted subculture was operating largely under the radar, happily ignoring contemporary trends in music or fashion, as is the case to this day.

Teddy Boys Reunited

On 10 February 2018, I went to a special night at the Adam and Eve in Hackney, billed as a Rock'n'Roll Reunion – a one-off gathering of many who had frequented the pub in the 1970s when it was a Teddy boy stronghold, and most of those present seemed to have first become Teds during that decade. Similarly, a fair number of people who used to share their memories on the now inactive *Teddy Boys Reunited* website some years ago – now a private Facebook group – were those who began wearing drapes as teenagers in the 1970s. Being at the Adam and Eve that night gave me the same kind of feeling I had at the Rainbow in Finsbury Park in 1978 watching Jerry Lee Lewis;[36] in 1981 at the 3rd International Rock'n'Roll Weekend Hop at Caister, near Great Yarmouth;[37] at the Pembury Tavern in Hackney in 1982 watching the Flying Saucers;[38] or at the Lyceum Ballroom on the Strand the same year at the Buddy Holly Dance Contest when Billy Fury made a brief appearance and the floor shook as over a thousand Teds and Teddy girls jived and bopped to the sound of Howlin' Wolf's 1962 stormer 'You'll Be Mine'.[39] On the street, it might be 1978 or 2018, but inside these places it was always 1958 or thereabouts, and drainpipes and drapes would forever be an acceptable clothing choice.

These days, you can still find people who dress in Teddy boy clothing if you know where to look – in July 2023, during

MPL IN ASSOCIATION WITH MECCA LEISURE INVITE YOU TO
THE GRAND FINAL OF THE BUDDY HOLLY DANCE CONTEST

ROCK AROUND WITH BUDDY HOLLY WEEK 1982

THE BIGGEST
ROCK 'N' ROLL
PARTY
IN THE WORLD

TUESDAY 7th SEPTEMBER 1982
DOORS OPEN 8·00pm

LYCEUM
WELLINGTON STREET THE STRAND
LONDON WC2
TEL NO. 01-836 3715

ADMIT ONE. DRESS ROCK 'N' ROLL

BH 0126

RAVIN' ON THROUGH '82

BUDDY HOLLY WEEK 7th–13th SEPTEMBER 1982

A mass gathering of Teds at the Lyceum in 1982

the final edit of this book, I encountered a group of them at a record hop just north of London where the deejays played nothing but vintage fifties 78s[40] but the society that produced the 1950s originals is long gone, as are a great many of those first Teds themselves. Mostly born during the Second World War, they grew up in an era of rationing, when few houses had central heating and some still relied on outside lavatories, and many working-class people had neither a phone nor a television. Compulsory National Service awaited any teenager unable to secure an exemption, capital punishment was still the penalty for certain serious crimes and everyone was supposed to rise respectfully in the cinema at the end of a showing while 'God Save the Queen' was played.

This was the vanished world of seven decades ago. The first Teddy boys and girls sprang up in reaction to it – and were simultaneously formed by it. They will not pass this way again.

NOTES

Introduction: Don't Fear the Creeper

1 The first use of the term Teddy boy in a newspaper occurred in the front-page article 'Ronnie-the-Masher Gets 9 Months', *Daily Express*, 23 September 1953

2 Guy Cullingford, *The Whipping Boys*, London: Hammond, Hammond & Company, 1958

3 *That'll Be The Day*, 1973, directed by Claude Whatham

4 Interview with the author, 29 February 2004

5 Undated 1970s interview footage, BBC TV *Omnibus* documentary, *Halfway to Paradise*, 1998, directed by Paul Pierrot

6 Interview with the author, 10 September 2018

7 'The Teddy Boy Menace – "It's Time To HIT OUT At These Young THUGS!"', *Newcastle Evening Chronicle*, 2 June 1958

8 X-Ray Spex + Staa Marx + Wastes Of Space + Vortex DJ Jerry Floyd, Oddfellows Hall, Kingston Road, Portsmouth, 13 October 1977

9 Wayne County & the Electric Chairs + Alternative TV + Vortex DJ Jerry Floyd, Clarence Pier Ballroom, Southsea, 16 November 1977

10 Sham 69 + Staa Marx + Chaos, Clarence Pier Ballroom, Southsea, 25 November 1977

11 Ramones + Generation X + Rezillos, the Rainbow, Finsbury Park, London, 31 December 1977, recorded and later released as the double LP *It's Alive*

12 Jerry Lee Lewis + Duane Eddy, the Rainbow, Finsbury Park, London, 19 November 1978

13 The Clash + The Slits, The Locarno (Mecca Ballroom), Portsmouth, 17 December 1978

14 *Blackboard Jungle*, 1955, directed by Richard Brooks
15 'Magistrate: "Pity Police Can't Rock'n'Roll You"', *Manchester Guardian*, 12 September 1956

1: Drape Expectations

1   Frank Norman, *Banana Boy*, London: Secker & Warburg, 1969, pp. 136–7
2   Arthur Morrison, *A Child of the Jago*, London: Penguin Books, 1946, p. 105
3   Robert Westerby, *Wide Boys Never Work*, London: John Lehmann, 1948, pp. 198–9
4   Gerald Kersh, *Night and the City*, New York: Simon & Schuster, 1946, p. 357
5   Michael Hervey, *Wide Girl*, Essex: the Hampton Press, n.d. [1945], p. 12
6   John Worby, *The Other Half – The Autobiography of a Spiv*, London: JM Dent & Sons, 1937
7   'Love Among the Lice', Review of John Worby, *The Other Half – The Autobiography of a Spiv*, *The Spectator*, 15 January 1937
8   Walter Greenwood, *Only Mugs Work – A Soho Melodrama*, London: Hutchinson & Co., 1938, inside cover blurb
9   Walter Allen, 'Radio Review', *Birmingham Evening Despatch*, 15 October 1945
10 Constance Noville, 'Ex-Service Girls Think Office Work Too Tame', *Hartlepool Northern Daily Mail*, 27 February 1946
11 *Hansard 1803–2005*, Commons Sitting, Supplies and Services (Transitional Powers) Bill, 11 August 1947
12 'Trades Union Congress', *The Times*, 8 September 1959
13 Ivor Brown, 'Theatre and Life', *The Observer*, 29 August 1943
14 Ivor Brown, 'Field And Frost', *The Observer*, 13 October 1946
15 Ralph L. Finn, 'Flash Boy', *The People*, 16 December 1945
16 Robert Hewison, *In Anger – Culture in the Cold War (1945–1960)*, London: Methuen, revised edition 1988 (first published 1981), p. 22
17 John Pearson, *The Profession of Violence – The Rise and Fall of the Kray Twins' Vicious Criminal Empire*, London: Panther Books, 1977 (first published 1973), p. 30

18 Walter Musto (Art McCulloch, ed.), *The War and Uncle Walter*, London: Bantam Books, 2004 (first published 2003), p. 185

19 Harold P. Clunn, *London Marches On*, London: the Caen Press, 1947, p. 177

20 Harold P. Clunn, *London Marches On*, London: the Caen Press, 1947, p. 17

21 Henry Samuel, 'Le Corbusier Was "Militant Fascist"', *Daily Telegraph*, 16 April 2015

22 Ian Fleming, *Thrilling Cities, Part 2*, London: Pan Books, 1965 (first published 1963), pp. 24–5

23 Sally Worboyes, *East End Girl*, London: Hodder, 2007 (first published 2006), p. 3

24 'Edwardian Ball', *Picture Post*, 26 January 1946

25 'An Echo of Edwardian Elegance', *Picture Post*, 27 September 1947

26 *Hansard 1803–2005*, Commons Sitting, Consumer Goods (Shortages), 26 June 1947

27 Peter Clarke and Richard Toye, 'Cripps, Sir (Richard) Stafford (1889–1952)', *Oxford Dictionary of National Biography*, Oxford: Oxford University Press, 2004, online edition

28 'Our London Letter', *Sunderland Daily Echo and Shipping Gazette*, 7 March 1946

29 Kay Boughton, 'Edwardian Again', *Yorkshire Evening Post*, 18 December 1946

30 'Ideas and Inspirations', *Falkirk Herald*, 3 April 1946

31 'Re-Enter The Gibson Girl', *The Sketch*, 1 May 1946

32 John Paul, *Murder by Appointment*, London: Skeffington & Son Limited, 1952

33 'Fashion History Repeats Itself', *Britannia and Eve*, 1 January 1947

34 'Madame, You're Missing Something', *Britannia and Eve*, 1 February 1947

35 'Gibson Girl Clothes', *Life*, 25 August 1947

36 Marjorie Backett, 'Paris Forgets this is 1947', *Picture Post*, 27 September 1947

37 Marjorie Backett, 'Paris Forgets this is 1947', *Picture Post*, 27 September 1947

38 Joyce Mather, 'Value of Sympathetic Listening', *Yorkshire Post and Leeds Intelligencer*, 13 February 1947

39 Argus, 'Casual Comments', *Falkirk Herald*, 17 March 1948

40 'To-day's Bride', *Yorkshire Post and Leeds Intelligencer*, 31 January 1948

41 'Carrington Wedding', *Nottingham Evening Post*, 7 January 1948

42 'Frenchmen Send Poems to the Princess', *Sunday Post*, 16 May 1948

43 'Belt, Bustle and Boater', *Northern Whig*, 14 May 1949

2: Just Like Eddie

1 'Plus-Fours Again?', *Aberdeen Press and Journal*, 18 May 1948

2 Keith Colling, 'All the Rage in London, Sir', *Yorkshire Post and Leeds Intelligencer*, 11 April 1949

3 Spike Milligan, *Adolf Hitler – My Part in His Downfall*, London: Penguin Books, 1974 (first published 1971), p. 21

4 Alison Settle, 'From a Woman's Viewpoint', *The Observer*, 1 May 1949

5 'Heavy Swell . . .', *Manchester Guardian*, 3 May 1949

6 'London Letter', *Birmingham Gazette*, 2 February 1949

7 Peter Willis, 'Prince Philip – And The Secret 6', *Daily Mirror*, 15 February 1949

8 'A Generation in Revolt – Teddy Boys' West Side Story', *The Guardian*, 11 September 1962

9 Chanticleer, 'Notebook', *Daily Herald*, 23 March 1950

10 'Our London Correspondence', *Manchester Guardian*, 29 April 1950

11 'Our London Correspondence', *Manchester Guardian*, 27 April 1950

12 Harrods advert, *Tatler & Bystander*, 4 April 1951

13 Air France advert, *The Times*, 15 February 1950

14 'Hotels', *The Times*, 25 March 1950

15 'The Way Men Look', *Tatler & Bystander*, 1 August 1951

16 Clive Fisher, 'Obituary: Bunny Roger', *The Independent*, 29 April 1997

17 Eileen Ascroft, 'They Go So Well With Drainpipe Trousers', *Londonderry Sentinel*, 8 December 1951

18 'Faultlessly Dressed', *The Times*, 30 November 1951

19 'They Wear Bad-Conduct Badges', *Reveille*, 29 December 1950

20 Howard Browne, *Halo in Blood*, Harpenden: No Exit Press, 1988 (first published 1946), p. 160

21 'Savile Row', *The Economist*, 22 July 1950

22 Douglas Howell, 'Even Prince Charles Approves of Dad's New Suits', *Daily Mirror*, 6 October 1951

23 Ibid.

24 James Dowdall, 'The Dandy Comes Back to W.1.', *Picture Post*, 7 June 1952

25 'Elizabethan Fashions', British Pathé newsreel, June 1952

26 James Dowdall, 'The Dandy Comes Back to W.1.', *Picture Post*, 7 June 1952

27 Beryl Seaton, 'Class In The Kitchen', *The Spectator*, 30 March 1951

28 'He Looks Just Dandy', *Daily Mirror*, 6 June 1953

29 Ailsa Garland, 'Two Days In A Million!', *Daily Mirror*, 18 March 1953

30 Frank Entwistle, 'A Lavender Vest For The Prince', *Daily Express*, 24 April 1953

31 'Wide Boy Of Cambridge', *Daily Express*, 20 February 1953

32 Douglas Howell, 'Know Your Girl!', *Daily Mirror*, 20 April 1953

3: I'm Not a Juvenile Delinquent

1 'Perplexed', Letter to the *Portsmouth Evening News*, 1 April 1950

2 'Juvenile Delinquents', *Morning Post*, 6 November 1833

3 'Report of the Committee for Investigating the Causes of the Alarming Increase of Juvenile Delinquency in the Metropolis', *Morning Post*, 18 September 1816

4 'True Causes of the Increase of Crimes Among the Youth of the Country', *Tyne Mercury; Northumberland And Durham And Cumberland Gazette*, 20 May 1817

5 'Parliamentary Intelligence', *Public Ledger and Daily Advertiser*, 24 May 1821

6 'Bell Ringing', *Belfast Commercial Chronicle*, 9 October 1839

7 'Gossip from Truth', *Dundee Courier*, 5 January 1899

8 'Truth That Is "Ugly"', *Preston Herald*, 4 April 1914

9 'Making Cinemas Safe for Children', *Kent & Sussex Courier*, 22 May 1931

10 'Case for Juvenile Centres', *Lancashire Evening Post*, 3 January 1935

11 'Religion Put to the Test', *Hull Daily Mail*, 12 January 1938

12 'The Younger Generation – By a Judge', *Daily Herald*, 6 January 1939

13 A. E. Jones, *Juvenile Delinquency and the Law*, London: Pelican Books, 1945, p. 10

14 Ibid., p. 95

15 Ibid., p. 97

16 Christopher Logue, 'One Quick Push for Paradise', *The Guardian*, 28 August 1999

17 'Young Folk Are Liars Says Archbishop's Wife', *Daily Herald*, 1 November 1946

18 Vaughan Dryden, 'Blighties', *Blighty*, 2 October 1948

19 Clarence Rook, *The Hooligan Nights – Being the Life and Opinions of a Young and Impenitent Criminal Recounted by Himself*, London: Grant Richards, 1901 (first published 1899), p. 30

20 Ibid., p. 34

21 Robert Traini, 'London Wants 5,000 Bobbies', *Daily Herald*, 6 January 1949

22 'More Caning Will Cure It Says Youth', *Daily Herald*, 14 January 1949

23 Ibid.

24 'Conduct Code for Teen-Age Dancers', *Daily Herald*, 26 January 1949

25 'Odd Glimpses', *Dundee Courier*, 4 January 1949

26 Noel Whitcomb, 'Under the Counter', *Daily Mirror*, 1 May 1950

27 Frank Henderson, ed., *Six Years in the Prisons of England*, London: Richard Bentley, 1869, p. 76

28 Arthur Morrison, *A Child of the Jago*, London: Penguin Books, 1946, p. 11

29 Michael Gilbert, *They Never Looked Inside*, London: Hodder & Stoughton, 1953 (first published 1948), p. 9

30 '£1,100 Hold-Up at Glasgow Station', *Coventry Evening Telegraph*, 28 January 1949

31 '"Sit Down, Lady," Said 3 Toughs', *Daily Mirror*, 1 June 1949

32 'Cosh Boy', *Daily Herald*, 31 March 1950

33 'Do "Toughies" Make or Reform the Cosh Boys?', *Lincolnshire Echo*, 18 April 1950

34 'Zoot Suit Cosh Boys Find Pace Too Hot', *Sheffield Telegraph*, 27 April 1950

35 '"Spiv" Attacks Widow', *Birmingham Daily Gazette*, 10 February 1950

36 'A "Cosh Kid" Confesses', *Sunday Pictorial*, 19 March 1950

37 Ibid.

38 'Growing Crime Wave', *Leicester Daily Mercury*, 1 April 1950

39 '"Heading to Be a Cosh Boy" – Magistrate', *Hull Daily Mail*, 1 April 1950

40 *Hansard 1803–2005*, Lords Sitting, Crimes of Violence, 23 March 1950

41 'Let Boys Climb to Adventure He Says', *Daily Mirror*, 26 June 1950

42 'And a Jolly Good Time Is Had by All', *Daily Mirror*, 18 February 1950

43 Ibid.

44 A Woman Realist, 'Birch the Brute!', *Western Daily Press*, 28 March 1950

45 Eric Bradshaw, 'What Nottingham Has to Say on Flogging', *Nottingham Journal*, 23 March 1950

46 '£1,000 Robbery As They Saw "Take It from Here"', *Coventry Evening Telegraph*, 22 March 1950

47 'The Rising Generation', *Daily Herald*, 20 May 1950

48 Victor Thompson, 'The Rising Generation, Part 2 – Bop Boy', *Daily Herald*, 23 May 1950

49 Ibid.

50 Ibid.

51 'New Stage Productions', *The Times*, 12 April 1951

52 Review of *Cosh Boy* (play), *West London Observer*, 20 April 1951

53 M.D. 'A Convincing Study of Juvenile Delinquency', *Yorkshire Post and Leeds Intelligencer*, 19 June 1951

54 Review of *Cosh Boy* (play), *The Stage*, 19 April 1951

55 'Trade Show News', *Kinematograph Weekly*, 8 January 1953

56 Josh Billings, review of *Cosh Boy* (film), *Kinematograph Weekly*, 15 January 1953

57 'The Stars' New Year Resolutions', *Portsmouth Evening News*, 9 January 1953

58 Paul Holt, 'Pocket-Sized Ava', *Daily Herald*, 7 March 1952

59 Reg Whitley, 'The Girl Who Pulled Up Just In Time', *Daily Mirror*, 7 March 1952

60 Andrew Weir, review of *Cosh Boy* (film), *Yorkshire Post and Leeds Intelligencer*, 16 June 1953

61 Review of *Cosh Boy* (film), *Daily Herald*, 1 May 1953

62 Review of *Cosh Boy* (film), *Manchester Guardian*, 7 February 1953

63 C. A. Lejeune, review of *Cosh Boy* (film), *The Observer*, 8 February 1953

64 'Hull Bans "Cosh Boy"', *Kinematograph Weekly*, 12 February 1953

65 'A Blow for "Cosh Boy"', *Kinematograph Weekly*, 19 March 1953

66 'Coventry Bans Film: "Slurs Youth Clubs"', *Birmingham Daily Gazette*, 18 May 1953
67 'X Films to Be Shown Here', *Worthing Herald*, 17 April 1953
68 'Nottingham Bans Cosh Boy Film', *Nottingham Journal*, 7 May 1953
69 'The British film *Cosh Boy* . . .', *The Times*, 16 March 1953
70 '"Cosh Boy" Banned', *Daily Express*, 1 July 1953

4: Common Assault

1 For a selection of the considerable quantity of initial reports in the national and local newspapers which followed in the first weeks after the Clapham murder, see for example: 'Boy Stabbed To Death, Gang Hunted', *Daily Herald*, 3 July 1953; 'Stabbed Youth – Five to Appear in Court Today', *Manchester Guardian*, 6 July 1953; 'Clapham Murder Charge', *The Times*, 14 July 1953; 'Six Youths Charged with Murder', *Sunderland Echo*, 31 July 1953; or 'Boy Stabbed Six Times – Prosecution', *Aberdeen Evening Express*, 31 July 1953
2 'Four Youths Acquitted of Clapham Common Murder', *Manchester Guardian*, 15 September 1953
3 Ibid.
4 Ibid.
5 'Stab Case Jury Disagrees', *Daily Herald*, 22 September 1953
6 Norman Martlew, 'Coleman Was "King of the Common" to 40 Thugs', *Daily Mirror*, 23 September 1953
7 'Ronnie-the-Masher Gets 9 Months', *Daily Express*, 23 September 1953
8 Ibid.
9 Ibid.
10 'The Stooge Turns Pop', *Rock Around the World Show*, US radio broadcast, 1 May 1977
11 Ray Coleman, 'Would You Let Your Sister Go with a Rolling Stone?', *Melody Maker*, 14 March 1964
12 Maureen Cleve, 'But Would You Let Your Daughter Marry One?', *Evening Standard*, 11 May 1964
13 'The Man & the Cult', Charles Hamblett, *The Tatler*, 26 February 1966
14 'Death Sentence for Clapham Common Murderer', *Manchester Guardian*, 23 October 1953
15 'Ronnie-the-Masher Gets 9 Months', *Daily Express*, 23 September 1953

16 'London's Little Chicago – Danger on the Common', *The People*, 19 July 1953

17 Ibid.

18 Television and radio listings for 2 July, *Radio Times*, 28 June–4 July 1953

19 'Gang Boy to Die for Common Murder', *Daily Mirror*, 23 October 1953

20 Hayden Smith and Danya Bazaraa, 'Knife Crime Horror As Fatal Stabbings Rise to Highest Level Since Records Began', *Daily Mirror*, 7 February 2019

21 Lizzie Dearden, 'London Stabbings', *The Independent*, 24 April 2019

22 Mark Duell and Jack Newman, 'Lawless London's Murder Toll Soars to Its Highest Level in a Decade', *Daily Mail*, 31 December 2019

23 'Man Killed at Vigil For Knife Victim', www.bbc.co.uk, 1 April 2021

24 Kevin Rawlinson, 'Two More Stabbings Bring London to Its Worst Ever Teenage Homicide Death Toll', *The Guardian*, 31 December 2021

25 Sarah Marsh, 'Man in his Forties Stabbed to Death in South London', *The Guardian*, 29 March 2021

26 'Davies Reprieved After 91 Days', *Daily Herald*, 22 January 1954

27 Quickstep, 'Beauty in the Ballroom Is Aim for 1954', *Liverpool Echo*, 2 January 1954

28 'Ban "Creepers" From Dance Halls', *Fifeshire Advertiser*, 27 February 1954

29 Robert Traini, 'A Wife Fights Man in Train', *Daily Herald*, 24 February 1954

30 Marjorie Proops, 'Watch on Waists in Spring', *Daily Herald*, 1 February 1954

31 Hannen Swaffer, 'Gangs v. Fashion', *Daily Herald*, 27 January 1954

32 Gordon Beckles, 'One of the Silliest Synonyms', *Tatler & Bystander*, 27 January 1954

33 'The Edwardian Trend Is Now a Trace', *Tatler & Bystander*, 20 January 1954

34 Review of *The Maniac* (play), *The Stage*, 21 January 1954

35 'Root of Youth Gang Problem', *Arbroath Guide*, 23 January 1954

36 'Mother: My Son Aped "Cosh Boy"', *Yorkshire Evening Post*, 9 February 1954

37 Alan Dick, 'Boy Meets Girl – 1954', *Daily Herald*, 15 February 1954

38 'Found Dying After a Dance', *Aberdeen Evening Express*, 10 April 1954

39 '"Teddy Boy" On Stabbing Charge', *Liverpool Echo*, 28 June 1954

5: We Are the Teds

1   'The Edwardians' Honour', *Daily Mirror*, 11 May 1954
2   Disker, 'Off the Record', *Liverpool Echo*, 22 May 1954
3   Lady Sheila Child, Letter to the Editor, *Daily Express*, 12 May 1954
4   T. R. Fyvel, *The Insecure Offenders – Rebellious Youth in the Welfare State*, London: Pelican Books, 1964 (first published 1961), p. 54
5   Ibid., p. 136
6   Ibid., p. 54
7   Interview with the author, 10 September 2018
8   Julien Temple's 1986 film of the 1959 Colin MacInnes novel
9   Interview with the author, 17 May 2019
10 Ibid.
11 Ibid.
12 Ibid.
13 Bob Hind, 'Teddy Boy's Drape Is Still Looking Good', *The News, Portsmouth*, 24 January 2015
14 'Edwardian Gangs', *Manchester Guardian*, 7 May 1954
15 '480 Teddy Boys Arrested in Six Months', *Newcastle Evening Chronicle*, 6 May 1954
16 '"Edwardian Toughs" Are Now Good Little Boys', *Norwood News*, 7 May 1954
17 'District News', *Rugby Advertiser*, 14 May 1954
18 'Teddy Boys Want a Club', *The People*, 9 May 1954
19 'Six Youths Warned to Behave', *Harrow Observer & Gazette*, 20 May 1954
20 'Chairs, Bottles Used in Birmingham Gang Fight', *Birmingham Daily Gazette*, 21 May 1954
21 'Lights Out, Petting Aboard "Teddy" Train', *Daily Herald*, 24 May 1954
22 'Modern Trends in Crime', *Liverpool Echo*, 24 May 1954
23 'Analysis of "Teddy Boy" Tough', *Western Mail & South Wales News*, 18 May 1954
24 Ibid.
25 Ibid.
26 Councillor S. Curtis, letter to the *Liverpool Echo*, 27 May 1954

27   '15-Year-Old "Teddy Girl" in Southsea Brawl', *Portsmouth Evening News*, 23 June 1954

28   Ibid.

29   Ibid.

30   Edwardian's Mother, Letter to the Editor, *Liverpool Echo*, 9 June 1954

31   'Nobody'll Buy His Teddy Suit', *Daily Herald*, 22 July 1954

32   'The Plumber Who Joined the Teddy Boys', *Daily Mirror*, 20 August 1954

33   'Teddy Boy, Manchester', Letter to the Editor, *Daily Mirror*, 26 August 1954

34   'The "Teddy Boy" Orders Milk', *Northern Whig & Belfast Post*, 31 August 1954

35   'Our London Correspondence – All Dressed Up and Nowhere to Go', *Manchester Guardian*, 23 August 1954

36   John Cooper Clarke, *I Wanna Be Yours*, London: Picador, 2020, p. 98

37   T. J. Couch, Letter to the Editor, *Portsmouth Evening News*, 26 October 1954

38   June Mark, Letter to the Editor, *Newcastle Evening Chronicle*, 10 August 1954

39   Hilde Marchant, 'The Truth About the "Teddy Boys" and the Teddy Girls,' *Picture Post*, 29 May 1954

40   Ibid.

41   Ibid.

42   'Boston Teddy Boy Is Fined', *Boston Guardian* [Lincolnshire], 25 August 1954

43   'Fight in Pub and Street at Boston', *Boston Guardian* [Lincolnshire], 25 August 1954

44   'Haircuts Horrify the Head', *Daily Herald*, 9 September 1954

45   Interview with the author, 10 September 2018

46   'West Ham Sign Haley', *Daily Mirror*, 30 October 1954

6: The Beat! The Beat! The Beat!

1   Colin Escott with Martin Hawkins, *Good Rockin' Tonight – Sun Records and the Birth of Rock'n'Roll*, New York: St Martin's Press, 1991, p. 13

2   Peter Guralnick, *Last Train to Memphis – The Rise of Elvis Presley*, London: Little, Brown & Company, 1994, p. 63

3   *Billboard*, 8 April 1950

4   *Cosh Boy* (play) preview, *Daily Mirror*, 13 April 1951

5   'Best Selling Retail Rhythm & Blues Records', *Billboard*, 23 June 1951

6   'Tin Pan Alley', Pathé Pictorial newsreel number 335, 1951

7   'Well Done, Vera!', *New Musical Express*, 25 July 1952

8   'Announcing the First Record Hit Parade', *New Musical Express*, 14 November 1952

9   'Broonzy for Jackson Albert Hall Concert', *New Musical Express*, 14 November 1952

10 Steve Race, 'Opinion', *Melody Maker*, 5 May 1956

11 Laurie Henshaw, 'Rock'n'Roll Swamps '56 Music Scene', *Melody Maker*, 15 December 1956

12 'Top of the Pops', *Melody Maker*, 7 April 1956

13 Review of 'Rock the Joint' (song), *Billboard*, 26 April 1952

14 'Hank Williams', *Cash Box*, 17 January 1953

15 Review of 'How Much Is That Doggie in the Window?' (song), *Cash Box*, 17 January 1953

16 Review of 'Poon-Tang' (song), *Cash Box*, 3 January 1953

17 Harold Wentworth and Stuart Berg Flexner, *Dictionary of American Slang*, London: George G. Harrap & Co. Ltd, 1960, p. 401

18 Review of 'Crazy Man, Crazy' (song), *Cash Box*, 2 May 1953

19 'This Week's Best Buys', *Billboard*, 2 May 1953

20 Campbell Connolly & Co. advert, *New Musical Express*, 18 December 1953

21 Norman Stevens, 'It's Crazy, Man, Crazy', *New Musical Express*, 18 December 1953

22 'Ad Lib', *New Musical Express*, 18 December 1953

23 'Do You Know The Answers?', *Accordion Times & Musical Express*, 2 January 1948

24 'Decca Signs Bill Haley and Comets', *Cash Box*, 8 May 1954

25 Review of 'That's All Right' (song), *Billboard*, 7 August 1954

26 'Folk and Western Round-Up', *Cash Box*, 4 September 1954

27 Hunter Davies, *The Beatles – The Authorised Biography*, New York: Dell Books, 1968, pp. 21–2

7: Public Enemy Number One

1   Tom Jones, *Over the Top and Back*, London: Penguin Books, 2015

2   Ibid.

3   Various Authors, *Home Office – Report of the Commissioners of Prisons for the Year 1954*, London: Her Majesty's Stationery Office, 1955

4   'Now the Teddy Boys Will Be Club Boys', *Daily Herald*, 4 June 1954

5   'Wanted – Someone Not Scared of Teddy Boys'. *The People*, 9 January 1955

6   Sir Basil Henriques, 'Whither Britain's Youth?', *Belfast News-Letter*, 8 March 1955

7   'Get Writing. I'll Tell You. I Didn't Squeal First', *Crewe Chronicle*, 22 January 1955

8   '1847 Waistcoat Stolen', *Belfast News-Letter*, 22 March 1955

9   'Punish Parents for Sins of Children', *Belfast News-Letter*, 26 March 1955

10   'Teddy Talk', *Daily Express*, 19 August 1955

11   '28 Days in the Glasshouse for Refusing a Haircut', *Daily Mirror*, 28 June 1955

12   'Teddy Boy Suits Are Banned By C.O.', 11 July 1955

13   'MP Wants To See "Teddy" Parades', *Daily Express*, 6 August 1955

14   'Not the Clothes That Make the Criminal', *Manchester Guardian*, 5 September 1955

15   'The Teddy Boys Tell Macmillan "Pay Up 1s"', *Daily Express*, 16 May 1955

16   '"King Of Teddy Boys" – Five Years for Man Who Wounded Constable', *The Times*, 28 January 1956

17   'Girl 16 in Court', *Beds & Herts Pictorial*, 13 September 1955

18   'A Teddy Boy Suit That Changed His Life', *Daily Herald*, 3 November 1955

19   Ibid.

20   Charles Hamblett, 'The Many Faces of Truth', *Picture Post*, 2 April 1955

21   'Four Among the 70,000', *The People*, 15 May 1955

22   'Four Teddy Boys Heard About God', *The People*, 29 May 1955

23   Ibid.

24   'The Last Night at Wembley', *Lisburn Herald and Antrim & Down Advertiser*, 4 June 1955

25   'Britain's Juvenile Delinquency Proves to Be a Real Problem', *The Southeast Missourian*, 24 November 1955

26 Ibid.

27 *Hansard 1803–2005*, Commons Sitting, Early Day Motion – The Late Derek Bentley, 30 July 1998

28 'Less Pay For Under-21s', *The Times*, 31 December 1955

29 The Old Stager, 'A Word to Teen-age Girls', *The Sphere*, 24 December 1955

30 'Girl Who Defied 3 Policemen Is Held in Custody for Report', *Bury Free Press*, 29 July 1955

31 Ibid.

32 David Mitchell, 'What's Wrong with Teddy Girls?', *Picture Post*, 4 June 1955

33 Eve Dawoud, 'Who Were The Teddy Girls?', research project, 2006

34 Ibid.

35 Ibid.

36 Ibid.

37 Ibid.

8: On the Town

1   Onlooker, 'Pointers to the News', *Uxbridge and West Drayton Gazette*, 14 January 1949

2   'Stones Shot Through Cinema Screen', *Uxbridge and West Drayton Gazette*, 28 January 1949

3   'Damage in Penrith Cinema', *Penrith Observer*, 11 January 1949

4   'Hooliganism Is Declining in Hull Cinemas, but Vigil Still Keen', *Hull Daily Mail*, 30 March 1950

5   Ibid.

6   'Cinemas to Act Against "Teddy Boys"', *Portsmouth Evening News*, 23 October 1954

7   John Betjeman, 'Teddy Boy Technique', *The Spectator*, 18 February 1955

8   'MGM Venice Film Is Withdrawn', *Kinematograph Weekly*, 1 September 1955

9   Anthony Carthew, 'I Hope This Picture Is False', *Daily Herald*, 13 September 1955

10 Reg Whitley, 'A School Where Stilettos Flash!', *Daily Mirror*, 16 September 1955

11 Robert Greenfield, 'The Rolling Stone Interview: Keith Richards', *Rolling Stone*, 19 August 1971

12 Reg Exton, review of 'Rock Around the Clock' (song) by the Deep River Boys, *Norwood News*, 4 November 1955

13 Max Jones, 'The Spinning Disc', *Daily Herald*, 13 October 1955

14 'NME Music Charts', *New Musical Express*, 9 December 1955

15 J. B., 'Dickie Valentine', *New Musical Express*, 9 December 1955

16 Nat Hentoff, 'American Air-Mail', *New Musical Express*, 9 December 1955

17 W.M.S., '"Teddy Boys" at School', *Catholic Standard*, 4 November 1955

18 'Britain's Blackboard Jungle', *Daily Mirror*, 5 January 1956

19 '"Trouble Film" Cinemas Seek Police Aid', *Birmingham Gazette*, 27 February 1956

20 'Teddy Boys Beat Up the Rector', *Worthing Herald*, 6 April 1956

21 ITV Teddy boys interview, 25 March 1956

22 'NME Music Charts', *New Musical Express*, 20 July 1956

23 Michael Braun, 'Ssshh! It's the Beatles Talking', *Rave*, November 1964

24 'On with the Dance', *The Times*, 15 September 1956

25 'Juvenile Drama', *Liverpool Echo*, 6 July 1957

26 Peter Evans, 'Blackboard Jungle on a Wider Canvas', *Kinematograph Weekly*, 25 July 1957

27 'So Teddy Walked in . . . and OUT', *Leicester Evening Mail*, 6 September 1957

28 'Streetside Rendezvous', *Leicester Evening Mail*, 8 November 1957

29 'Duke to Attend Rank Premiere', *Kinematograph Weekly*, 16 January 1958

30 '"Rock and Roll" Ban In Blackpool', *The Times*, 7 September 1956

31 'Cinema Riot Reports "Rubbish"', *Hammersmith & Shepherd's Bush Gazette*, 31 August 1956

32 Gary Kramer, 'Rhythm & Blues Notes', *Billboard*, 13 October 1956

33 Bill Haley, 'Man with a Guitar and an Idea Who Started It All', *The People*, 14 October 1956

34 Robert Greenfield, 'The Rolling Stone Interview: Keith Richards', *Rolling Stone*, 19 August 1971

35 Interview with the author, 9 October 2018

36 'A "Night Out" – Teddy Boys Banned', *Beds & Herts Pictorial*, 14 December 1954

37 David Campbell, 'The Axe Falls On "Teddy Boy" Dancers', *Beds & Herts Pictorial*, 23 August 1955

38 '"Teddy Boys" Crash Rural Dance', *Kent & Sussex Advertiser*, 4 June 1954

39 Ibid.

40 Ibid.

41 'Alarming Scenes at Irvine Dance Hall', *Irvine Herald*, 16 July 1954

42 'The Modern Young Boy', *Kirkintilloch Herald*, 29 December 1954

43 'Teddy Boys Shut Down His Weekly Dances', *Daily Herald*, 30 November 1954

44 'Tear-Gas Floors the Dancers in a Weeping Fox-Trot', *Daily Herald*, 6 December 1954

45 'Teddy Boys Wild', *Daily Herald*, 13 December 1954

46 'Teddy Boys Tamed', *Daily Herald*, 13 December 1954

47 Tom Jones, *Over the Top and Back*, London: Penguin Books, 2015

48 Roy Day, Letter to the Editor, 'Invitation to a Dance', *Picture Post*, 11 February 1956

49 'His Suit Didn't Suit', *Sunday Pictorial*, 29 June 1958

50 Interview with the author, 25 January 2021

51 Ibid.

52 Interview with the author, 15 November 2019

53 'Rock'n'Roll Comes To Long Eaton', *Stapleford & Sandiacre News*, 1 December 1956

54 Ibid.

55 *We Are the Lambeth Boys*, 1959, directed by Karel Reisz

56 Ibid.

57 *We Were the Lambeth Boys*, 1985, directed by Rob Rohrer

58 Ibid.

59 Peter Everett, *You'll Never Be 16 Again*, London: BBC Publications, 1986, p. 27

60 Julian Symons, *The Gigantic Shadow*, London: Fontana Books, 1960 (first published 1958), p. 49

61 'Teddy Boys Frisked Ever So Gently', *Manchester Evening News*, 21 January 1958

62 Interview with the author, 25 January 2021

63 Interview with the author, 10 September 2018

64 Billy Daniels advert, *New Musical Express*, 17 December 1954

65 Assorted band concert adverts, *New Musical Express*, 17 December 1954

66 Campbell Connelly advert, *New Musical Express*, 17 December 1954

67 'NME Music Charts', *New Musical Express*, 17 December 1954

68 'Top Ten Juke Box Tunes', *Cash Box*, 18 December 1954

69 'Best Sellers in Stores', *Billboard*, 18 December 1954

70 Review of 'Alexander's Ragtime Band' (song), *Billboard*, 25 December 1954

9: We're Gonna Teach You to Rock

1 Charles Govey, 'New Bill Haley Film Even Rock'n'Rolls the Cha-Cha-Cha!', *New Musical Express*, 20 July 1956

2 Robert C. Ruark, 'Insufferable Set', *Pittsburgh Press*, 2 November 1956

3 Patrick Doncaster, 'Do We Want This Shockin' Rockin'?', *Daily Mirror*, 16 August 1956

4 Ibid.

5 Ibid.

6 Ibid.

7 Patrick Doncaster, 'Hurry! Hurry! You Cats', *Daily Mirror*, 30 January 1957

8 Patrick Doncaster, 'Popland Goes British', *Daily Mirror*, 24 January 1963

9 'How Times Have Changed!', *Midland Counties Tribune*, 7 September 1956

10 'Why All This Fuss About a Little Jiving?', *Halifax Evening Courier*, 18 August 1956

11 'Antics of the Jungle', *Reading Standard*, 21 September 1956

12 Quoted in Pete Frame, *The Restless Generation*, Rogan House, 2007, p. 192, as being from the BBC panel show *Does the Team Think?* However, Thorpe made this comment during a discussion about the banning of the film *Rock Around the Clock* in 1956, while *Does the Team Think?* did not begin broadcasting until 1957. Thorpe's discussion, alongside fellow panellists Manny Shinwell and Robert Boothby, seems to be from the episode of the *Any Questions?* radio show broadcast on 18 September 1956 in which all three participated, one month after the film's UK release when many councils issued bans.

13 Tony Miles, 'Play Me Some Silence!', *Daily Mirror*, 26 June 1956

14 'Teenagers Won't Get Jukebox', *Coleshill Chronicle*, 25 May 1957

15 Walter J. Ridley, interviewed by 'dhvinyl' for *A Personal History of the British Record Business*, 1998, https://vinylmemories.wordpress.com/2021/03/04/a-personal-history-of-the-british-records-business-94-walter-j-ridley-pt-5-and-conclusion/

16 'Presley Fever Hits Britain', *Picture Post*, 22 September 1956

17 Spencer Leigh, 'Obituary: Jeff Kruger', *The Independent*, 23 May 2014

18 'Crombie Forms Rock-and-Roll Unit', *Melody Maker*, 4 August 1956

19 'Rock and Riot Boys Don't Worry Crombie', *Melody Maker*, 8 September 1956

20 Ibid.

21 T.B., 'Crombie Rocks', *Melody Maker*, 15 September 1956

22 Ibid.

23 'Crombie Rockets Net Palladium TV', *Melody Maker*, 22 September 1956

24 Ibid.

25 'Now It's the Rock'n'Roll Sinners!', *Melody Maker*, 29 September 1956

26 'Club Haley advert', *Melody Maker*, 29 September 1956

27 'Mulligan forms Skiffle Group', *Melody Maker*, 29 September 1956

28 'Rock and Roll 1856', *Radio Times*, 9 September–15 September 1956

29 'Hamp Slants Show on Rock'n'Roll', *Melody Maker*, 6 October 1956

30 Letters – 'Spare Us This Trash, Hampton!', *Melody Maker*, 13 October 1956

31 *Mister Rock'n'Roll*, 1957, directed by Charles S. Dubin

32 'New Rockin' Horses Band Gets Rolling', *Melody Maker*, 13 October 1956

33 Bob Dawbarn, 'Rock'n'Roll Pays Off', *Melody Maker*, 8 December 1956

34 Ibid.

35 Ibid.

36 Tony Crombie, 'This Rock'n'Roll', *The People*, 7 October 1956

37 Ibid.

38 Robert Hancock, *The A&R Man*, London: Four Square Books, 1961 (first published 1958), p. 8

39 Preview of *Expresso Bongo* (play), *The Stage*, 27 March 1958

40 'British Production', *Kinematograph Weekly*, 28 May 1959

41 *Expresso Bongo* (film, 1959), directed by Val Guest

42 Ken Ferguson, 'Pop Parade', *Photoplay*, January 1957

43 '"Hottest" Bands in the Land in This Premiere Showing', *South Yorkshire Times*, 15 June 1957

44 '"Too Old for Kids' Stuff" – At 19', *Lincolnshire Echo*, 19 June 1957

45 Ian Wallis, *American Rock'n'Roll – The UK Tours 1956–72*, York: Music Mentor Books, 2003, pp. 19–22

46 'Ziggy Bows Out, Madonna Scares the Pope and Dylan Goes Electric: 50 Gigs That Changed Music', *The Guardian*, 11 February 2022

47 Ian Wallis, *American Rock'n'Roll – The UK Tours 1956–72*, York: Music Mentor Books, 2003, pp. 19–22

48 Interview with the author, 10 September 2018

49 Ibid.

50 'Crombie Quits Rock-'n'-Roll', *Melody Maker*, 3 August 1957

51 'Brighton', *The Stage*, 31 June 1958

52 Madeleine McLoughlin, 'I Was a Mug – From Here to Obscurity in 240 Days', *Sunday Pictorial*, 26 May 1957

53 Interview with the author, 29 February 2004

10: Through the Looking Glass

1 'Lost: Pure chocolate Alsatian dog', *Portsmouth Evening News*, 4 April 1953

2 Roy Ullyett cartoon – 'Steady, Now', *Daily Express*, 10 June 1954

3 Arthur Horner cartoon – 'The Teddy Boy & the Tailors', *News Chronicle*, 5 May 1954

4 'Kenton Brains Trust', *Harrow Observer*, 29 July 1954

5 'London Letter', *Birmingham Gazette*, 26 June 1954

6 Noel Whitcomb, 'Creative Peacocks', *Daily Mirror*, 26 June 1954

7 'Charivaria', *Punch*, 23 June 1954

8 Ross Shepherd, 'Jokers Wild', *The People*, 19 December 1954

9 'Dave Makes a Good Dame', *Aberdeen Evening Express*, 20 December 1954

10 Arthur Helliwell, 'Arthur Helliwell's Party!', *The People*, 26 December 1954

11 John Barber, '100 Stars with Not Much to Do', *Daily Express*, 24 June 1955

12 'A Teddy Boy – And He's at Red Circle!', *The Hotspur*, 11 December 1954

13 Ibid.

14   'Portrush Carnival', *Belfast News-Letter*, 12 August 1954

15   Arthur Helliwell, 'Teddy Cops', *The People*, 2 January 1955

16   *Hansard 1803–2005*, Lords Sitting, Broadcasting Policy, 22 May 1952

17   Stephen Taylor, *Fats Waller on the Air – The Radio Broadcasts and Discography*, Lanham, Maryland: The Scarecrow Press, 2006, p. 61

18   Clifford Davis, 'It Was Jim's Night', *Daily Mirror*, 22 November 1954

19   'Trouble in Store For *The Grove Family*?', *Daily Mirror*, 20 November 1954

20   Clifford Davis, 'Talking of Dolls!', *Daily Mirror*, 22 July 1955

21   Kenneth Baily, 'Studio Whispers', *The People*, 9 October 1955

22   'Special Enquiry – The Problem of the Teenager', *Radio Times*, 30 October–5 November 1955

23   Ibid.

24   Claire Timms, 'The Last Debutantes', bbc.co.uk, 24 September 2014

25   'Teddy Gang', *Hammersmith & Shepherd's Bush Gazette*, 3 February 1956

26   Kenneth Baily, 'They've Got Her on the Raw', *The People*, 5 February 1956

27   'A Likely Tale', *Radio Times*, 22 April–28 April 1956

28   Rowan Ayers, 'The Wharf Road Mob', *Radio Times*, 24 March–30 March 1957

29   Ibid.

30   Norman Swallow & Alan Lawson, interview with Gilchrist Calder, http://historyproject.org.uk/interview/gilchrist-gil-calder

31   Maurice Richardson, 'Death Is a Teddy Boy', *The Observer*, 31 March 1957

32   Ibid.

33   'Armchair Theatre – The Pier', *TV Times*, 6 October–12 October 1957

34   'Quatermass and the Pit', *Radio Times*, 21 December–27 December 1958

35   'Armchair Theatre – The Pier', *TV Times*, 6 October–12 October 1957

36   'TV Actor Injured', *Manchester Guardian*, 7 October 1957

37   'TV and Radio', *Daily Mirror*, 31 December 1956

38   Howard Thomas, 'The Battle for Your Favour' in Kenneth Baily, ed., *The Television Annual for 1958*, London: Odhams Press Limited, 1957, pp. 131–7

39   Ibid.

40   Ibid.

41   'Between Six and Seven', *Radio Times*, 17 February–23 February 1957

42 *All You Need Is Love: The Story of Popular Music*, London Weekend Television 17-part series, directed by Tony Palmer, 1977

43 Ibid.

44 Ian Wallis, *American Rock'n'Roll – The UK Tours 1956–72*, York: Music Mentor Books, 2003, various pages

45 Alan Lawson and Norman Swallow, 'Dennis Main Wilson: BECTU Interview Part 3 (1991)', http://www.screenonline.org.uk/audio/id/877680/index.html

11: A Drip in a Drainpipe

1   'Defiance Born of Insecurity', *Manchester Guardian*, 23 April 1959

2   Ibid.

3   V. S. Pritchett, review of *That Uncertain Feeling* by Kingsley Amis, *New Statesman*, 20 August 1955

4   Andrew James, *Kingsley Amis – Antimodels and the Audience*, Montreal & Kingston: McGill-Queen's University Press, 2013, p. 96

5   Frederick Lumley, 'The Marginal and the Mandarins', *The Spectator*, 31 May 1957

6   John Drummond, *The Teddy-Boy Mystery* (Sexton Blake Library No. 334), London: Amalgamated Press, April 1955

7   Ibid., pp. 1–2

8   James Wood, *The Shop in Loch Street*, Bath: Cedric Chivers Portway, 1974 (first published 1958), p. 58

9   Lester Wallingford, 'Exposé! – Teddy Boys vs. Gang Boys', *True Crime*, May 1956

10 Guy Cullingford, *The Whipping Boys*, London: Penguin Books, 1964 (first published 1958), p. 136

11 Elizabeth Stucley, *Teddy Boys' Picnic*, London: Anthony Blond Ltd, 1958, p. 14

12 Ibid., p. 38

13 Ibid., pp. 18–24

14 Ernest Ryman, *Teddy Boy*, London: Michael Joseph, 1958

15 Ernest Ryman, *Teddy Boy*, London: Ace Books, 1960

16 Ernest Ryman, *Teddy Boy*, London: Michael Joseph, 1958, p. 30

17 Ibid., p. 31

18   David Brett, 'Teddies, or Just Dead End Kids?', *Manchester Evening News*, 12 April 1958

19   Angus Wilson, review of *Teddy Boy* by Ernest Ryman, *The Observer*, 6 April 1958

20   John Davenport, 'Micro-Master', *The Observer*, 12 October 1957

21   Angus Wilson, *A Bit off the Map and Other Stories*, London: Secker & Warburg, 1957, pp. 8–9

22   Alan Sillitoe, *Saturday Night and Sunday Morning*, London: W. H. Allen, 1958

23   Alan Sillitoe, *Saturday Night and Sunday Morning*, London: Panther Books, 1985 (first published 1958), p. 17

24   Ibid., p. 83

25   Ibid., p. 76

26   Alan Goddard, 'The Midlander Who Is Just a Rebel', *Leicester Evening Mail*, 12 December 1958

27   Quoted on the cover of Alan Sillitoe, *Saturday Night and Sunday Morning*, London: Pan Books, 1961 (first published 1958)

28   'Eye on TV', *Halifax Daily Courier and Guardian*, 18 October 1958

29   Bill Edwards, 'Production', *Kinematograph Weekly*, 25 February 1960

30   R. B. Marriott, '"The Lily White Boys" Never Had It So Good – Or So Sad', *The Stage*, 4 February 1960

31   J. C. Trewin, 'Our Critic's First Night Journal', *Illustrated London News*, 30 January 1960

32   J. C. Trewin, 'Over and Over', *Illustrated London News*, 13 February 1960

33   Thomas Wiseman, 'Soaring – The Quiet Man of the Ginger Group', *Aberdeen Evening Express*, 30 September 1960

34   Jympson Harman, 'An Ugly Story, but Albert's All Right', *Liverpool Echo*, 29 October 1960

35   Elspeth Grant, 'Mr Finney Extorts My Respect', *Tatler & Bystander*, 9 November 1960

36   Josh Billings, review of *Saturday Night and Sunday Morning* (film), *Kinematograph Weekly*, 27 October 1960

37   Lucian Randall & Chris Welch, *Ginger Geezer – The Life of Vivian Stanshall*, London: Fourth Estate, 2002 (first published 2001), p. 15

38   Alan Sillitoe, *Saturday Night and Sunday Morning*, London: Panther Books, 1985 (first published 1958), p. 160

12: Knives in West Eleven

1   Hugh Clevely, *Public Enemy*, London: Penguin Books, 1961 (first published 1953), p. 91

2   Kevin FitzGerald, *Trouble in West Two*, London: William Heinemann Ltd, 1958, p. 188

3   Ibid., p. 252

4   Colin MacInnes, *City of Spades*, London: Penguin Books, 1985 (first published 1957), p. 98

5   Colin MacInnes, *Absolute Beginners*, London: Allison & Busby, 1980 (first published 1959), pp. 42–3

6   Bernard Kops, *Awake for Mourning*, London: MacGibbon & Key, 1958

7   '2,000 Riot – Gangs Invade "Colour" Clash Area', *Daily Mirror*, 2 September 1958

8   Vicky cartoon, *Daily Mirror*, 2 September 1958

9   Ritchie-Calder, 'Weisz, Victor [pseud. Vicky]', *Oxford Dictionary of National Biography*, Oxford: Oxford University Press, 2004, online edition

10 Robert Skidelsky, 'Mosley, Sir Oswald Ernald, sixth baronet', *Oxford Dictionary of National Biography*, Oxford: Oxford University Press, 2004, online edition

11 Ibid.

12 D. George Boyce, 'Harmsworth, Harold Sidney, first Viscount Rothermere', *Oxford Dictionary of National Biography*, Oxford: Oxford University Press, 2004, online edition

13 '84 Arrests As Thousands Stampede in London Riots', *Daily Mirror*, 5 October 1936

14 Nicholas Mosley, *Beyond the Pale – Sir Oswald Mosley, 1933–1980*, London: Secker & Warburg, 1983, p. 369

15 Kenneth Allsop, 'Will Mosley March Again?', *Picture Post*, 2 January 1954

16 Nicholas Mosley, *Beyond the Pale – Sir Oswald Mosley, 1933–1980*, London: Secker & Warburg, 1983, p. 574

17 Ibid., p. 566

18 'Labour Man's Libel Action', *The Times*, 27 March 1958

19 'Busmen Accuse Committee of Colour Bar', *Birmingham Daily Post*, 9 September 1955

20 'Student Ejected at Mosley Rally', *Birmingham Daily Post*, 29 October 1956

21 Nicholas Mosley, *Beyond the Pale – Sir Oswald Mosley, 1933–1980*, London: Secker & Warburg, 1983, p. 572

22 Henry Fielding, 'Young Mosley Follows Father', *Daily Herald*, 14 May 1958

23 Ibid.

24 Ibid.

25 'Mosley Meeting in Birmingham', *Birmingham Daily Post*, 3 October 1956

26 'I'm Not a Dictator – Mosley', *Marylebone Mercury*, 7 March 1958

27 '14 Are Held in Red Flag Clash', *Daily Mirror*, 2 May 1958

28 'Mosley Told: No Meeting at Hall', *Marylebone Mercury*, 4 July 1958

29 'Traffic Hold-Up', *The Times*, 7 July 1958

30 Watchman, 'Leader', *Chelsea News & General Advertiser*, 11 July 1958

31 David Renton, 'Jordan, (John) Colin Campbell', *Oxford Dictionary of National Biography*, Oxford: Oxford University Press, 2004, online edition

32 'Sixpennorth of Hatred', *Daily Herald*, 11 September 1958

33 'Anti-Colour Newspaper – Resolution By Trades Council', *Coventry Evening Telegraph*, 13 September 1958

34 'Gang with Sticks Wrecked Café', *Hammersmith & Shepherd's Bush Gazette*, 8 August 1958

35 'Teddy Boys Armed with Sticks Wreck Café', *Fulham Chronicle*, 29 August 1958

36 '200 in Race Riot Terror', *Daily Mirror*, 25 August 1958

37 '200 People in Nottingham Racial Clash', *Birmingham Post*, 25 August 1958

38 '200 In Race Riot Terror', *Daily Mirror*, 25 August 1958

39 'Enquiry into Racial Clash Causes', *Birmingham Daily Post*, 26 August 1958

40 'Two Moves to Stop Race Riots', *Daily Mirror*, 27 August 1958

41 Graham Cawthorne, 'Riot City MP Says "Limit Entry"', *Western Mail*, 27 August 1958

42 'Race Riots', *Manchester Evening News*, 25 August 1958

43 'Where Colour Is Concerned', *Coventry Evening Telegraph*, 27 August 1958

44 'Nine Accused of "Nigger-Hunting"', *Western Mail*, 13 September 1958

45 'Coloured Men Were Hit With Iron Bars, Court Told', *Hammersmith & Shepherd's Bush Gazette*, 29 August 1958

46 Ibid.

47 'Youths Get Four Years for "Manhunt" In Notting Hill', *Hartlepool Northern Daily Mail*, 15 September 1958

48 '"Nigger Hunt" Youths Appeal Fails', *Hammersmith & Shepherd's Bush Gazette*, 28 November 1958

49 'Britain's Racial Problems', *The Times*, 29 August 1958

50 George Clay, 'Menace Behind the Brawl', *The Observer*, 31 August 1958

51 Tony Moore, *Policing Notting Hill: Fifty Years of Turbulence*, Hook, Hampshire: Waterside Press, 2013, pp. 39 and 41

52 '2,000 Riot: Gangs Invade "Colour" Clash Area', *Daily Mirror*, 2 September 1958

53 '2,000 Teenagers in New Riots', *Newcastle Journal*, 2 September 1958

54 '2,000 Riot: Gangs Invade "Colour" Clash Area', *Daily Mirror*, 2 September 1958

55 'Job for the Public', *Leicester Evening Mail*, 2 September 1958

56 'More Racial Clashes: 28 Arrests', *Birmingham Post*, 3 September 1958

57 'A Night without Arrests', *Birmingham Post*, 4 September 1958

58 'Race Hate City Goes Wild Again', *The People*, 31 August 1958

59 Ibid.

60 Ibid.

61 Ibid.

62 Getty Images – Photo by Ron Case, 4 September 1958, 'Four men who were remanded at West London Police Court on charges relating to the Notting Hill race riots'

63 'Iron Bar, Knife and Milk Bottles Were Notting Hill Riot Weapons', *Newcastle Evening Chronicle*, 3 September 1958

64 Tony Moore, *Policing Notting Hill: Fifty Years of Turbulence*, Hook, Hampshire: Waterside Press, 2013, p. 53

65 'I Deplore This Racial Violence', *Hammersmith & Shepherd's Bush Gazette*, 5 September 1958

66 '2,000 Riot: Gangs Invade "Colour" Clash Area', *Daily Mirror*, 2
    September 1958

67 'I Deplore This Racial Violence', *Hammersmith & Shepherd's Bush
    Gazette*, 5 September 1958

68 Getty Images – Photo: Keystone / Stringer, 4 September 1958, '18-year-
    old Max Mosley and his 19-year-old brother Alex'

69 'Time Shift – Notting Hill 58', BBC TV documentary, directed by
    Amanda Reilly, 2003

70 Ibid.

71 For example: Getty Images – Photo: *Daily Express/Pictorial/Parade/*
    Hulton Archive/Getty Images, 2 September 1958, 'An unconscious
    woman is carried away from the police during the Notting Hill Race
    Riots'

72 'Accomodation', *Kensington Post*, 29 August 1958

73 David Renton, 'Jordan, (John) Colin Campbell', *Oxford Dictionary of
    National Biography*, Oxford: Oxford University Press, 2004, online
    edition

74 Ibid.

Conclusion: This Old Gang of Mine

1   Hugh Pilcher, 'Teddy Boys – Should We Beat Them?', 31 January 1959

2   'We Are Going to Win', *The Times*, 8 September 1959

3   'Co-Operative Congress Has Gloomy First Day', *The Times*, 19 May 1959

4   See 'Race-Hate Murder', *Daily Herald*, 18 May 1959 and Howard
    Johnson, 'Blonde at Window Sees Murder', *Daily Mirror*, 18 May 1959

5   'White Mourns with Black', *The People*, 7 June 1959

6   '"Paid Thugs Cause Race Riots" – MP', *Croydon Times*, 12 June 1959

7   Trevor Williams, '"My Thanks" Says Premier', *Daily Herald*, 10 October
    1959

8   Muriel Spark, *The Ballad of Peckham Rye*, London: Penguin Books, 1963
    (first published 1960), p. 58

9   Lynne Reid Banks, *The L-Shaped Room*, London: Penguin Books, 1976
    (first published 1960), back cover description

10 Ibid., p. 231

11 Constantine Fitzgibbon, *When the Kissing Had to Stop*, London: Pan
    Books, 1962 (first published 1960), p. 32

12 Ibid., p. 133

13 Nancy Mitford, *Don't Tell Alfred*, New York: Carroll & Graf, 1990 (first published 1960)

14 Laurence Payne, *The Nose on my Face*, London: Hodder and Stoughton, 1961, pp. 43–4

15 John Creasey, *The Toff and the Teds*, London: Hodder & Stoughton, 1961

16 Ibid., p. 11

17 Ibid., p. 16

18 Mark Lewisohn, *The Complete Beatles Recording Sessions*, New York: Harmony Books, 1989 (first published 1988), p. 22

19 Mark Lewisohn, *The Complete Beatles Chronicle*, New York: Harmony Books, 1992, p. 50

20 'It's Excitement – Unlimited!', *Daily Mirror*, 5 October 1962

21 Dick Richards, 'At The New Pictures', *Daily Mirror*, 14 September 1962

22 *The Boys*, directed by Sidney J. Furie, 1962

23 Mark Lewisohn, *The Complete Beatles Chronicle*, New York: Harmony Books, 1992, p. 72

24 Interview with the author, 10 September 2018

25 'Out of Date Teddy Boys', *The Times*, 12 August 1960

26 'Museum Seeks Teddy Boy Costume', *The Times*, 13 April 1962

27 Ian Wallis, *American Rock'n'Roll – The UK Tours 1956–72*, York: Music Mentor Books, 2003, various pages

28 Ibid.

29 Ibid, pp. 287–289

30 Interview with the author, 12 September 2018

31 Ibid.

32 Ibid.

33 Matthew Parris, 'Preaching to the Concerted', *The Times*, 17 July 1992

34 Chris Steele-Perkins and Richard Smith, *The Teds*, Stockport: Dewi Lewis Publishing, 2002 (first published 1979)

35 'Teddy Boys Rally to Rock Call', *Coventry Evening Telegraph*, 15 May 1976

36 Jerry Lee Lewis + Duane Eddy, the Rainbow, Finsbury Park, London, 19 November 1978

37 3rd International Rock'n'Roll Weekend Hop, Ladbrokes Caister Holiday Centre, Great Yarmouth, Norfolk, 20–22 March 1981

ACKNOWLEDGEMENTS

I'm indebted to Pete Ayrton for his initial positive response to my idea of a book about Teddy boys, and to Rebecca Gray at Profile Books for believing in it throughout the time it has taken to come to fruition.

It's been a great pleasure working with Nick Humphrey, my editor, whose advice and suggestions were first class, and I'd also like to thank Georgina Difford, Jon Petre and Robert Greer at Profile, and David Watkins and Rachel Wright.

Warm thanks as always to my literary agent and friend Caroline Montgomery at Rupert Crew for her help with this one, and also to Ricky Lee Brawn, Roger K Burton, Ted Carroll, John King, Brian Nevill, Barry Nugent, Clive Phillips, JJ Rassler, Mark Rubenstein, Caroline Stafford, Martin Stiles, Dominic Stiles, Cathi Unsworth, Paul Willetts, everyone who spoke to me off the record, and anyone I may have overlooked who offered me assistance during the writing of the book.

A raised glass to my late father and my uncles for inspiration, who in the fifties understood the importance of a sharp set of threads and a rock'n'roll haircut, and to my brother, a fellow creeper-wearer back in the day.

Above all, huge love and thanks to Katja for all her support, who read and commented on every successive draft of this book over the years, and without whom it simply would not exist.

PICTURE CREDITS

Integrated Images

All images are from the author's own collection, with the exception of:

Savile Row's Edwardian clothing revival demonstrated by a model for Pathé Pictorial and *Picture Post*, 1952 – Mirrorpix

Clapham Common murder victim John Beckley, 1953 – Mirrorpix

A teenage Ted couple dancing in Tottenham, *Picture Post*, 29 May 1954 – Getty Images

Plate Section

A variety of self-devised Ted styles captured by photographer Juliette Lasserre in 1955, the year that rock'n'roll first started properly taking hold in Britain – Juliette Lasserre/BIPs/Getty Images

Newly paroled prisoner Danny Hughes in front of a poster showing 'Forces No. 1 Pin-up' Joan Collins in the film *Cosh Boy*, May 1953 – Hulton-Deutsch Collection/CORBIS/Corbis via Getty Images

Roger Mayne's classic photograph of a group of youthful Teds in Princedale Road, North Kensington, 1956 – Roger Mayne/Roger Mayne Archive via Mary Evans Picture Library

'Call this the Devil's garb? It's smashing cloth, brother.' Teenage jivers in Bristol, April 1955 – Haywood Magee/*Picture Post*/Hulton Archive/Getty Images

Sharp-dressed teenagers at a Tottenham Dancehall, 1954 – from the *Picture Post* article, 'The Truth About the "Teddy Boys" and the Teddy Girls'. – Joseph McKeown/*Picture Post*/Hulton Archive/Getty Images

Teddy girls Rose Hendon and Mary Toovey photographed by Ken Russell in Southam Street, North Kensington, January 1955 – Ken Russell

– n.b. while this was taken as part of his sessions for the *Picture Post* assignment, it did not appear in the published article

Eileen Lewis of Bethnal Green, plus two Teddy boys duelling with toy guns – a Ken Russell photo from the 1955 *Picture Post* article, 'What's Wrong With Teddy Girls?' – Ken Russell/*Picture Post*

Marie Imiah from Glasgow in her 'Rock Around the Clock' skirt awaiting the train carrying Bill Haley and His Comets, Waterloo Station, 5 February 1957 – Staff/*Daily Mirror*/Mirrorpix

Police on the lookout for signs of trouble from the supposedly dangerous crowd queuing obediently to see *Rock Around the Clock*, Manchester, 21 September 1956– *Express* newspapers/Getty Images

Bill Haley and His Comets at the Dominion Theatre, Tottenham Court Road, on the opening day of their ground-breaking UK tour, 6 February 1957 – Harry Hammond/V&A Images/Getty Images

'When the "juke" goes wrong they start walking out. No "juke" – no business.' Teds in a London café, 13 July 1955 – Popperfoto via Getty Images/Getty Images

The Boys – novelisation of the film script by John Burke, 1962, released into a world in which Teds were already becoming yesterday's news – Author's collection

Four of the accused on their way to West London Police Court where they were remanded on charges relating to the Notting Hill race riots, 4 September 1958 – Ron Case/Keystone/Getty Images

Notting Hill race riots – scuffles with the police in Bramley Road, which resulted in several arrests that night, 31 August 1958 – Arthur Sidey/ *Daily Mirror*/Mirrorpix

INDEX

Page references in *italics* indicate images.